Cooking
1·2·3

500 fabulous three-ingredient recipes

ROZANNE GOLD

Stewart, Tabori & Chang • New York

Published in 2003 by
Stewart, Tabori & Chang
A Company of La Martinière Groupe
115 West 18th Street
New York, NY 10011

Export Sales to all countries except Canada, France,
and French-speaking Switzerland:
Thames and Hudson Ltd.
181A High Holborn
London WC1V 7QX
England

Canadian Distribution:
Canadian Manda Group
One Atlantic Avenue, Suite 105
Toronto, Ontario M6K 3E7
Canada

Library of Congress Cataloging-in-Publication Data

Gold, Rozanne.
    Cooking 1-2-3 : 500 fabulous three-ingredient recipes / Rozanne Gold.
        p. cm.
    ISBN 1-58479-286-8
    1. Quick and easy cookery. I. Title: Cooking one-to-three. II. Title.

    TX833.5.G694 2003
    641.5'55—dc21   2003050694

Design by Hotfoot Studio
Printed in Hong Kong

10 9 8 7 6 5 4 3 2 1

First Printing

contents

introduction

In cooking, like all other arts, simplicity and sincerity are the two principle elements of perfection.

Curnonsky, *Gaities et Curiosites Gastronomiques*, 1933

I've spent eight years writing books devoted to the art of simple cooking with a message that is meant to endure: just a few ingredients of uncompromising quality are all you need to create exquisite recipes. Not everyone will cook with three ingredients all the time, nor is that the goal, but this concise methodology has freed a generation of home cooks, and even professional chefs, to keep it simple.

Gastronomic trends may come and go, but when it comes to our sense of taste I have discovered that less is truly more. Overwrought dishes, chockablock with ingredients, can actually obscure flavors rather than produce the clarity we desire. A chef adds vinegar to a dish and then needs to balance it with some butter or cream. But then the dish goes limp and needs a spice, an herb, a touch of sweetness, or maybe more acidity to brighten it. Before you know it, a simple recipe elongates into a shopping list. The realization that a minimum of ingredients could maximize taste by allowing pure flavors to shine led me to develop this book's repertoire of dishes based on only three ingredients per recipe (not counting salt, pepper, or water).

For me, the 1-2-3 series has been a joyful culinary journey, full of discoveries and mishaps. Along the way, I have learned to seek out ingredients in their prime, and I've discovered the joys of using the same ingredient in myriad ways. I have become more focused and inventive in my use of new cooking techniques—like freezing olive oil to emulsify a sauce, or reducing a panoply of liquids (whether wine, stock, pan drippings, or fruit juices) to heighten flavor and add body to a dish. And I have eliminated almost all processed foods, except for a few staples that have become part of the new global pantry (see page 8). I have also learned that it is not possible to make bouillabaisse from three ingredients, and foolish to try.

Instead of streamlining complicated dishes, I *build* my recipes layer by layer. I may be inspired by an ultrafresh *tranche* of salmon, then think of two supplemental ingredients that will create harmony and amplify taste. In the parlance of the lapsed musician that I am, I think of my recipes as flavor chords, and the ingredients as notes; this way the impact of a dish is truly more than the sum of its parts. The magic lies in coaxing intense, dramatic flavors from simple combinations.

Do not misconstrue: this book delivers neither fast food nor exclusively quick-and-easy meals, and it is not an I-hate-to-cook book. Quite the contrary. "1-2-3" has been my effort to introduce to some, and amplify for others, the inherent pleasures of simple cooking.

Recipes using only three ingredients certainly are liberating. The cook can kiss the drudgery of shopping good-bye, and the meal, now freed from "ingredient overload," can be true to itself. To see an individual dish come together from a trio of raw products—or an entire dinner emerge from only nine—is nothing short of fun.

For those new to my work, *Cooking 1-2-3* brings a lighter voice to serious food through a vast array of deliciously simple recipes created by a professional chef. For old friends, I have revised and updated my favorite dishes and added hundreds of new recipes and recipe ideas.

GREAT CHEFS DO THE 1•2•3

The year was 1996 and the notion of cooking with only three ingredients was a bit startling. It was a time of gastronomic excess: food piled precariously high on plates, and waiters reciting oratorios for the day's specials. It was hip, it was daunting, and pretty soon none of us could remember what we'd eaten.

When *Recipes 1-2-3* arrived on the scene that year, there were some skeptics, but this fresh way to cook and *think* about food, focusing on restraint, technique, and quality ingredients, was a spark for a new movement in cooking. "Simple" soon became the new chic in concentric rings of culinary circles. When the famous French chef Alain Ducasse opened his much-awaited restaurant at New York's Essex House, his press release boasted of cooking with "just a few ingredients and some herbs." Laurent Gras, the chef at Peacock Alley at the Waldorf-Astoria, made headlines by cooking with only two ingredients, and Raymond Sokolov, while culture critic of the *Wall Street Journal*, threatened to do a one-ingredient cookbook. On June 17, 1997, the first three-ingredient recipe by a four-star chef, Jean-Georges Vongerichten, appeared in the *New York Times*: Sassafras Chicken (made just with chicken, wine, and sassafras root). Culinary minimalism had arrived.

ABOUT THE RECIPES

It's always been my belief that even a moderately experienced cook can taste a recipe by reading it, much in the same way that a musician hears a melody in his or her head simply by reading the score. This is *not* the case with the recipes that follow. Because the "whole is more than the sum of its parts," each of these dishes needs to be *eaten* to fully experience the reality that less is more. This is because the three specific flavors are enhanced when they're tasted together—resulting, often, in a fourth flavor; because a particular cooking technique deepens or transforms the inherent taste of a single ingredient; or because one ingredient is treated in several different ways, creating a kind of flavor reverberation. Consider tasting asparagus raw, steamed, sautéed or fried, roasted, boiled, one-by-one. Which method produces the true flavor?

Sometimes simple cooking connotes *casual* cooking. Not here. My advice is to follow these recipes carefully. Be deliberate in your actions and don't make substitutions at first, until you understand the intention and taste of the original dish. After all, changing just one ingredient alters one-third of the outcome! These recipes have been designed for harmony and balance.

Since they are the fundamentals of all cooking, salt, pepper, and water are "free" in this plan, which means they are not counted in a recipe's ingredient list. You will find them, however, in the recipe instructions as a "large pinch" or "to taste," or occasionally in specific amounts.

INGREDIENTS

Good ingredients are the essence of good cooking. And so keeping it simple has led me on an exhilarating search for the pure, untrammeled flavors of the finest ingredients—because when you cook with just three, each assumes critical importance.

Know your ingredients and treat them with respect. Inferior products will undo this book's objectives. And be willing to pay a little more for the best.

Cooking in season, then, takes on new meaning. Although we pretend to escape dependency on the seasonal cycles of nature, we delude ourselves. Raspberries shipped from Chile in sealed, gassed containers in December; broccoli harvested before a frost; tomatoes plucked green and trucked two thousand miles—all are dilute imitations of the real thing that seduce our eyes but corrupt our tastes. "If you can capture the season on the plate," goes the Japanese proverb, "then you are the master."

THE 1•2•3 PANTRY

All the recipes in this book are made with fresh, natural, nutrient-rich ingredients. Some also call for a selection of top-quality jarred or prepared foods, all products that make up a professional chef's larder.

With respect to salt, I generally use table salt but mention kosher salt and fine or coarse sea salt when specificity matters. Freshly ground pepper means black or white peppercorns, just milled from a pepper mill. When coarse pepper is required, use the flat side of a large knife or cleaver to crush the peppercorns, and then with a sharp blade, chop the crushed peppercorns evenly. Buy cracked or butcher-ground black pepper in supermarkets if you must, but you'll sacrifice the heady fragrance.

Water is essential in boiling and steaming, of course, but is even more valuable when used to deglaze pots and pans, to extract every bit of residual flavor. The great French chef, Bernard l'Oiseau, built an entire cuisine using water as a dominant ingredient. I use tap water for cooking, but you may use filtered or bottled water if your environment dictates.

I always use unsalted butter as I prefer its taste and can always add salt, if needed. I use extra-large eggs because my mother does. It's as simple as that.

My new global pantry includes several flavored oils, including garlic and lemon olive oil (or you can follow my recipes to make these yourself); dark Asian sesame oil; roasted peanut oil; walnut oil; and two kinds of olive oil, extra-virgin and pure, the latter for cooking. Experiment with several brands, then stick to what pleases your palate.

Since I love acidity in my dishes, I use balsamic vinegar, raspberry vinegar, various wine vinegars, and apple cider vinegar. In some cases, good old distilled white vinegar does the trick. And don't be afraid to use freshly squeezed lemon or lime juice in place of vinegar to brighten the taste.

In my pantry, you will also find hoisin sauce, all kinds of mustards, wasabi powder, tandoori paste, sun-dried tomatoes in oil, pomegranate molasses from Lebanon, a tin of leatherwood honey from Australia (its flavor and aroma are extraordinary), mysteriously smoky paprika from Spain, and several types of dried mushrooms.

In my freezer, there is always prepared pesto, puff pastry, a bottle of vodka, super-premium chocolate, and my ice cream canister, ready for a party.

So here is a list of my staples, which you should consider having on hand at all times, too:

> Salt—table salt, kosher salt, fine and coarse sea salt
> Peppercorns—whole black peppercorns, whole white peppercorns
> Garlic olive oil—purchased or homemade (page 228)
> Lemon olive oil—purchased or homemade (page 228)
> Tahina (sesame paste)
> Dark Asian sesame oil
> Roasted peanut oil
> Sun-dried tomatoes in oil
> Pesto—buy refrigerated then freeze if you want
> Hoisin sauce
> Black olive paste—purchased or homemade (page 234)
> Rolled anchovies with capers
> Pomegranate molasses
> Za'atar (a spice mixture of hyssop, sumac, and sesame seeds)
> Wasabi powder
> Puff pastry, frozen
> Cinnamon-sugar—purchased or homemade (page 242)
> Vanilla-sugar—purchased or homemade (page 242)

ENTERTAINING 1 • 2 • 3

As the "Entertaining Made Easy" columnist for *Bon Appétit*, I address the needs of readers who love to entertain, but yearn to do it simply and with great style. Limiting the number of ingredients in a menu is one liberating way to focus on the many other aspects of party-giving. Consider the immediate satisfaction of streamlined shopping for weekday guests, or the virtues of creating a dinner party or holiday meal by joyfully going through the express lane at the supermarket.

The five hundred recipes for food and drink that follow provide the three-ingredient building blocks for successful entertaining. If you're not a great cook, choose recipes or menus that feel familiar, and focus your creative energies on some other facet of entertaining such as the décor, flowers, or tabletop design. Or, if you like to improvise, simply insert a new 1-2-3 recipe, or two, into your own party repertoire.

The thirty-one menus (pages 325–328) will help you entertain with the greatest possible ease, providing the promise of abundance without the burden. My 1-2-3 recipes are all meant to increase the pleasure—and frequency—of entertaining at home.

WINES 1 • 2 • 3

Curnonsky, the Prince of Gastronomes (so dubbed in 1927) said "Cuisine is when things taste like themselves," and spoke of maximizing the inherent essence of ingredients—the *droit en goût*—with unadulterated flavors.

If the art of simple cooking is about ensuring that ingredients "taste like themselves," then the same should be true of wine. America imports wines from more places than any other country. So, for better or worse, many big wine-producing regions have begun making wines to satisfy our collective palate, rather than focusing on the characteristics that make each wine distinctive in the first place. Sadly, the real (and to some, romantic) sense of place, or *terroir*, often eludes us.

But the good news is that most wine, from everywhere, has improved in quality. Finding wines that "taste like themselves" is a wonderful, risk-free adventure that can cost you little but immeasurably enhances your gastronomic pleasure.

A good wine merchant is useful here though not essential. The world's awash in surplus grapes, so wines don't have to cost a lot. You'll find many interesting options piled in bins and boxes at the front of your favorite wine shop. When entertaining, you ought to try at least two or three varieties at the same meal, without fear. This experimentation is guaranteed to spark conversation and good cheer. To start, look for:

> Malbec from Chile or Argentina
> Minervois from Languedoc-Roussillon (France)
> Riesling from Alsace (France)
> Sauvignon Blanc from New Zealand and South Africa
> Tempranillo from Spain
> Chenin Blanc from the Loire region (France)
> Gruner Veltliner from Austria (a personal favorite)
> Nero d'Avola from Sicily
> Vinho Verde from Portugal
> Syrah from California
> Beaujolais from France

When matching food and wine, I consider three components—the flavor, texture, and weight of the food and the wine. Often a wine can emphasize desirable flavors in a particular recipe—for example, the soft herbal notes in a merlot can bring out the rosemary essence of a lamb dish. Conversely, specific dishes can enhance desirable qualities in the wine. Fleshy black olives can intensify the earthiness of a cabernet or Bordeaux.

Breaking the traditional rules of food and wine pairing can add another level of interest to a dish, for example, salmon. A lightish pinot noir (red) pairs beautifully with Salmon Osso Buco (page 119), whereas a dry Gewürztraminer (white) is a winner with Seared Salmon with Cornichon Vinaigrette (page 118). The preparation of the primary ingredients gives the predominant cue.

Sometimes the same dish can taste great with a white and a red—but for different reasons. Compare the Roasted Peppers with Feta and Honey (page 307) with sauvignon blanc and with, unexpectedly, cabernet sauvignon.

You will find wine suggestions to go with the menus, which begin on page 325. I encourage you to keep a notebook of the food and wine matches you have enjoyed for future reference.

DARE TO BE SIMPLE

The French have a saying that "*l'exces est tout un default*" (excess is always a fault). As early as 1654, Nicholas de Bonnefons, a valet in the court of Louis XIV (a regime in which excess was considered a virtue), wrote a book entitled *Les Delices de la Campagne*, in which he advocated, above all, simplicity: "Let a cabbage soup be entirely cabbage…and may what I say about soup be a law applied to everything that is eaten."

At the turn of the twentieth century, the renowned Auguste Escoffier, "king of chefs and chef of kings," daringly proclaimed "*faites simple*" (keep it simple). "Two of the most valuable words he ever wrote," said the English food writer Elizabeth David, years later, and I agree.

The novelist Colette, famous for her simple Chicken *à la Cendre* (in ashes), denounced the indiscriminate excess of ingredients, a trend that characterized Gallic cooking in the 1920s. She said, "It seems that we are a long way removed from the discreet combinations of flavors, thought out at length, that were once the basis of French gourmandise."

Sometime in the late 1950s, our own James Beard, father of American cuisine and a master of simplicity, stated "Natural foods without embellishment taste wonderfully if they are well cooked." In the 1970s, nouvelle cuisine turned the culinary world on its axis by advocating a simpler and more natural approach to cooking and the presentation of food. Decades later, Boston's visionary chef, Lidia Shire, boldly said, "Some of the best dishes in the world have no more than three ingredients."

Today many chefs are delving further into the depths of simplicity and ingredient-driven cuisine; some are focusing on technique or technology, while others aren't even *cooking* their food any more; instead they serve much of their menu raw. (Perhaps they should no longer be called cooks!)

Given where we are in the culinary galaxy, and in our lives, keeping it simple seems to be a most sensible approach to cooking. It's as easy as 1-2-3.

acknowledgments

This book is dedicated to my father, Bernard (Bill) Gold who taught me the pleasures of giving. My father was a football star (first Sugar Bowl touchdown, 1943; Washington Redskins draftee), war hero (a recipient of the Distinguished Flying Cross and Air Medal), and the world's best salesman. His special gift was making those around him feel important. You were proud to be his friend. You felt important because you were. My father loved the interconnectedness among people, and he rewarded everyone with food. Extravagant dinners, huge tins of Middle Eastern pastries, the best chocolate truffles came your way, all the time, and for no particular reason.

He loved simple food cooked to perfection. He also adored candy, ice cream, cheesecake, and White Castle burgers. He discovered hot new restaurants before the critics did and became a patron of some of New York's best. He understood, at his core, the pleasure that food—and it's sharing—could bring. I was hooked at an early age.

On Sundays, while watching football on our big TV, my father typically grilled knockwursts and made tuna fish sandwiches with finely minced onion and relish. (I loved that wooden bowl and the *mezzaluna* he always used for chopping). Some Saturdays he would boil up half-a-dozen lobsters to snack on throughout the day. Dad was also famous for his griddled doughnuts. He would find the biggest glazed yeast doughnuts and fry them in a skillet with a pat of butter, pressing down hard, then flipping them like pancakes.

In the old days, one of my father's favored spots was the Rainbow Room atop Rockefeller Center. It was our family's "special occasion" place. You can imagine his delight when our company came to own and operate the restaurant, from 1987 to 2000. Later in life, the Jolly Fisherman on Long Island became his second home.

Our last meal together was at Peter Luger's in Great Neck, New York, February 11, 2003.

Much love goes to my beautiful mother, Marion Gold, my brother Leon and sister-in-law Gail, my son, Jeremy Whiteman, and to my husband, Michael Whiteman, who has guided me through life in my adult years, tending my wounds, stimulating my mind, and touching my gladdened heart.

To my extraordinary friends: Amy Berkowitz, Steve North, Arthur Schwartz, Bob Harned, Dale Glasser Bellisfield, Ben and Phyllis Feder, Ann Berman Feld, Dr. Judy Nelson, Suzie Segal, Francesco de'Rogati, Rona Jaffe, Marc Summers, Susy Davidson, Diana Carulli Dunlap, Barbara Cohen, Ann Stewart, Robin Zucker, Phyllis Glazer, Erica Marcus, Lari Robling, Fern Berman, Marcy Blum, Lila Gault, Eddie Schoenfeld, Sally-Jo O'Brien, and Audrey Appleby.

To my colleagues: Leslie Stoker, President and Publisher of Stewart, Tabori & Chang, Jack Lamplough, Galen Smith, and Sarah Scheffel at STC, Neil Rosini (my lawyer), Helen Rothstein Kimmel (nutritionist for all my 1-2-3 books), Kate Merker (sous-chef extraordinaire), Katie O'Kennedy, Kristine Kidd, and Barbara Fairchild (my bosses at *Bon Appétit*), and Dennis Sweeney (Joseph Baum & Michael Whiteman Co.).

To the chefs who respect simplicity and value the beauty of restraint,

To the many readers who made the 1-2-3 series possible,

To the waiters and waitresses, captains and busboys, who took good care of my father,

Thank you.

vegetables

In season, nature gives us permission to keep it simple. And so this chapter begins my treasury of three-ingredient recipes with more than thirty fresh vegetables cooked in a variety of ways that maximize their flavor and retain their inherent goodness. (For cold vegetables and salads, see pages 86–101.) The idea to start with vegetables reflects my adoration for them all—I've never encountered one I didn't enjoy—and is a subtle nudge for everyone to include more vegetables in their diet.

Organized alphabetically, vegetables A to Z demonstrates that there are myriad, and often instantaneous, ways to create delicious vegetable dishes with a minimum of effort. My wish is that you'll be seduced by the finest-looking and best-smelling produce available—whether at the supermarket, farm stand, or specialty grocer—and then run home as fast as possible to prepare it, capturing the current season on your plate.

Beginning the chapter are ineffably smooth vegetable purees. Once the hallmark of nouvelle cuisine, they remain a simple way to add luxury to any meal. Even better, they come in a rainbow of colors and can be made in advance. You can enliven any simple main course with one, two, or even three of these purees.

Many of these superfresh vegetable recipes offer such high flavor profiles and assertive textures that, in combination, they become meals in themselves, and meatless ones at that.

We have witnessed a gradual greening of America over the last quarter-century, and recently, the quality and variety of vegetables have improved and expanded exponentially. A new age of produce has truly arrived. The movement to replant heirloom varieties, the growth of organic farms, better distribution systems, the rise of sustainable agriculture with its characteristic respect for the seasons, the market's continued enthusiasm for the new and the exotic, the passion of local farmers for hand selecting and "small-batch cultivation," and their devotion to flavor and good nutrition will provide us all with many new and gratifying choices in the years ahead.

"Eat all the colors" is one of the nutrition community's mantras for optimal health. Nowhere is this more bountifully expressed than in the following ninety recipes and as many recipe ideas . . . and these only begin to scratch the surface of this beneficent earth. You may be surprised to find yourself turning to this chapter every day.

ALABASTER (TURNIP AND POTATO)

2½ pounds white turnips
2½ pounds large red-skinned potatoes
8 tablespoons unsalted butter

Scrub turnips and potatoes, but do not peel. Place in a large heavy pot with a cover and add salted water to cover. Bring to a boil, then lower heat to medium. Cover and cook for 40 minutes, or until vegetables are very soft. Drain in a colander. Peel turnips and potatoes under cool running water.

In a large bowl, mash both vegetables well with a potato masher. Add butter, a little bit at a time. Add salt and white pepper to taste, then whip with a wire whisk until smooth and fluffy. Serve immediately or reheat over low heat.

Serves 6 or more

ACORN SQUASH AND CARROT PUREE

Fat-free and slightly sweet.

3 large acorn squash, about 1½ pounds each
2½ pounds carrots
⅔ cup apple butter

Preheat oven to 325°F. Cut each squash in half and remove seeds and membranes. Cut off rind with a small sharp knife. Cut squash into 1-inch cubes.

Peel carrots and cut into 1-inch pieces. Mix squash and carrots with ⅓ cup apple butter, ½ teaspoon salt, and freshly ground black pepper. Place mixture on a rimmed baking sheet large enough to accommodate vegetables in one layer. Add ¼ cup water and cover with aluminum foil.

Bake for 1 hour. Remove foil. Add ½ cup water and bake 20 minutes longer. Transfer vegetables to bowl of a food processor and process in several batches until very smooth. Transfer to a large saucepan and add remaining apple butter and salt and pepper to taste. Reheat gently.

Serves 8

ROASTED BEET PUREE WITH ALLSPICE

The beets are slow-roasted to intensify their flavor. As an optional garnish, you can sauté some of the beet greens in additional oil, or fry julienned beets in oil until crispy.

2½ pounds beets
¼ cup peanut oil
2 teaspoons allspice berries

Preheat oven to 400°F. Trim beets, but do not peel. Wash well. Rub beets with a little peanut oil and place in a heavy pie tin. Add ¼ cup water and bake for 2 hours until very soft.

When beets are cool enough to handle, peel with a small sharp knife. Cut into large chunks and place in bowl of a food processor. Add remaining peanut oil and process until smooth. Transfer puree to a large saucepan. Add salt and pepper to taste. Smash allspice berries with the flat edge of a chefs' knife to coarsely crush. Finely chop allspice and sprinkle over hot puree.

Serves 6

BROCCOLI-GINGER PUREE

5-inch piece fresh ginger
1½ large heads broccoli, about 2 pounds
6 tablespoons heavy cream, plus more if necessary

Peel ginger with a small sharp knife. Grate ginger on the large holes of a box grater. Place grated ginger in a paper towel and squeeze juice into a small cup. You should have about 2 tablespoons juice. Set aside.

Bring a large pot of salted water to a boil. Cut stems from broccoli. Peel stems and cut into small pieces. Cut remaining broccoli into small florets. Add stems to boiling water and cook for 5 minutes. Add florets and cook 8 minutes longer, or until broccoli is tender but still bright green.

Thoroughly drain broccoli in a colander and place in bowl of a food processor. Process until broccoli is in small pieces. With the machine on, add ginger juice and cream. Process until very smooth. Add salt and freshly ground black pepper to taste. When ready to serve, heat in saucepan, adding more cream or water if too thick.

Serves 6

BUTTERNUT SQUASH AND ORANGE PUREE

2 medium butternut squash, about 3½ pounds total
3 large oranges or blood oranges
4 tablespoons unsalted butter

Preheat oven to 400°F. Cut squash in half lengthwise, then cut each piece in half crosswise. Remove seeds and membranes. Place in a rimmed baking sheet, cut side down, and add ½ cup water. Bake for 1 hour, turning squash over after 40 minutes. Squash should be slightly caramelized.

Meanwhile, cut 2 oranges in half and squeeze to get ½ cup juice. Grate rind of remaining orange and set zest aside. Cut away pith and rind from this orange and cut in between the membranes to release segments. Dice the segments.

Remove squash from oven. Using a spoon, remove flesh from skin. Place flesh in bowl of a food processor and process with butter and enough orange juice to make a thick puree. Season with salt and freshly ground black pepper. Serve hot with diced oranges on top.

Serves 6

SPINACH AND CELERY PUREE

1 pound (½ large bunch) celery, with leaves
12 ounces fresh curly spinach leaves
3 tablespoons unsalted butter, chilled

Wash celery well. Remove leaves and set aside. Cut celery into 1-inch pieces. Wash spinach well and remove thick stems. Set aside. Place celery in a medium pot with water to cover. Cook for 15 to 18 minutes over medium heat, or until celery is soft. Add spinach and cook over high heat for 2 minutes, stirring constantly, until wilted.

Drain vegetables in a colander. Pat dry. Place in bowl of a food processor and puree until very smooth. Mixture will be bright green. Add butter, cut into small pieces, and salt and freshly ground black pepper to taste. Serve hot, garnished with reserved celery leaves.

Serves 6

SWEET POTATO-CIDER PUREE

Sweet, sassy, and velvety. It's fat-free, too, and sure to become a holiday favorite.

3 pounds sweet potatoes
6 cups apple cider
5-inch piece fresh ginger

Scrub potatoes, but do not peel. Place in a large pot with a cover. Add salted water to cover. Bring to a boil, then lower heat to medium. Cover and cook for 45 minutes, or until potatoes are soft.

Meanwhile, put cider in a large nonreactive saucepan and bring to a boil. Lower heat to medium and continue to cook for about 30 minutes, until reduced to 1½ cups.

Peel ginger and mince to yield ⅓ cup. Set aside.

When potatoes are soft, drain in a colander and peel under cool running water. Cut potatoes into chunks and place in bowl of a food processor. Add reduced cider and minced ginger and process until very smooth and velvety. Season with salt and just a little black pepper. Serve hot.

Serves 6

ULTIMATE POTATO PUREE

This special technique allows you to make pureed potatoes in a food processor with irresistibly creamy results.

1½ pounds medium Yukon gold potatoes
1½ cups half-and-half
5 tablespoons unsalted butter, at room temperature

Scrub potatoes but do not peel. Place in a medium pot with a cover. Add salted water to cover. Bring to a rapid boil, then lower heat to medium. Cover pot and cook for 25 minutes, or until potatoes are soft. Drain in a colander and peel under cool running water. Cut potatoes in chunks and place in bowl of a food processor.

Quickly bring half-and-half to a boil in a saucepan and pour over potatoes. Process until potatoes are smooth. Add butter and process until very smooth. Add salt and white pepper to taste. Reheat gently before serving.

Serves 4

VEGETABLES A TO Z

The following recipes and recipe ideas were designed to highlight the freshness and integrity of more than thirty vegetables. They're replete with interesting techniques for slow-cooking, steaming, and high-temperature roasting.

OVEN-ROASTED ASPARAGUS WITH FRIED CAPERS

Ruth Reichl, editor-in-chief of Gourmet *magazine, thinks this is the best dish I've ever created. An intense dose of heat keeps these spears green and snappy. Crispy fried capers add a startling accent.*

> 2 pounds medium-thick asparagus
> ¼ cup extra-virgin olive oil
> ¼ cup large capers in brine, drained

Preheat oven to 500°F.

Remove the woody bottoms of asparagus, then trim stalks to equal length. Drizzle 2 tablespoons olive oil on a rimmed baking sheet. Place asparagus on the pan and roll them in the oil. Sprinkle lightly with salt. Roast for 8 minutes, shaking the pan several times during roasting. Transfer to a warm platter.

Meanwhile, in a small skillet, heat remaining oil. Fry capers over high heat for 1 minute. Pour over asparagus. Pass the pepper mill.

Serves 4

ASIAGO-CRUSTED ASPARAGUS WITH POACHED EGGS

Serve this as a generous side dish, a terrific first course, or for brunch.

> 2 pounds medium-thick asparagus
> 3 ounces Asiago cheese, freshly grated, about 1 cup
> 4 extra-large eggs

Preheat broiler.

Remove the woody bottoms of asparagus, then trim stalks to equal length. Using a light touch, peel asparagus with a vegetable peeler. Bring a large pot of salted water to a boil. Add asparagus and cook, uncovered, over medium heat for 7 to 8 minutes, or until just tender but still bright green. Drain and refresh under cold running water. Pat dry.

Place asparagus on an ovenproof platter. Set aside ¼ cup cheese and sprinkle remaining cheese over asparagus. Place under broiler for about 1 minute, until cheese turns golden and a little crisp.

Meanwhile, fill a large nonstick skillet with 1 inch salted water. Bring water to a boil, lower heat to medium-high, then gently crack eggs into water. Cook for about 5 minutes, until yolks begin to set, but are still runny.

Using a slotted spoon, place eggs on warm asparagus and sprinkle with remaining cheese, kosher salt, and lots of coarsely cracked black pepper. Serve immediately.

Serves 4

POACHED ASPARAGUS WITH WASABI BUTTER

Celebrate spring by serving this alongside grilled fish or chicken, poached eggs, a thick rare steak . . . you get the idea.

    5 tablespoons unsalted butter, at room temperature
    1 tablespoon wasabi powder
    2 pounds thick asparagus

Cut butter into pieces and place in the bowl of an electric mixer. Mix wasabi with ½ tablespoon water to make a paste. Add paste to butter with a pinch of salt and mix until wasabi is incorporated. Scrape mixture into a small bowl. Refrigerate until cold.

Remove the woody bottoms of asparagus, then trim stalks to equal length. Using a light touch, peel stalks with a vegetable peeler. Fill a medium skillet with several inches of salted water. Bring to a boil. Add asparagus and cook for about 10 minutes, until stalks are easily pierced with the tip of a sharp knife. They should still be bright green. Drain well and place on a warm platter.

Using a small spoon, scrape curls of wasabi butter onto hot asparagus. Sprinkle with salt and coarsely ground black pepper. Serve immediately.

Serves 4 or more

STIR-FRIED ASPARAGUS

    1½ pounds medium-thin asparagus
    3 tablespoons dark Asian sesame oil
    4 tablespoons balsamic vinegar

Remove the woody bottoms of asparagus, then trim stalks to equal length. Using a vegetable peeler, peel bottom two-thirds of asparagus. Cut each stalk on the bias into 2-inch pieces.

Heat sesame oil in a wok or large nonstick skillet. Add asparagus and stir-fry, tossing constantly, until asparagus begins to caramelize, about 8 minutes. Add 3 tablespoons vinegar and cook several minutes longer, until asparagus is tender but still a little crunchy. Toss with coarse sea salt and lots of coarsely ground black pepper, and sprinkle with remaining vinegar.

Serves 4

ASPARAGUS WITH WHITE WINE ZABAGLIONE

This elegant and unexpected vegetable preparation was inspired by a trip to the Veneto region of Italy. Zabaglione—traditionally made with sweet wine and served as a dessert sauce or custard—is equally celebratory made with an off-dry wine and served over vegetables such as boiled asparagus, roasted beets, steamed broccoli, and grilled zucchini.

1¾ pounds medium-thick asparagus
4 large egg yolks
½ cup off-dry Riesling

Remove woody bottoms of asparagus, then trim stalks to equal length. Bring a large pot of salted water to a boil and add asparagus. Cook for about 8 minutes, until just tender.

Meanwhile, place egg yolks, wine, and a large pinch of salt and freshly ground black pepper in a heavy metal bowl over a pot of simmering water. Using a wire whisk, whip mixture for about 8 minutes, until very thick but light and foamy. (It should resemble mayonnaise or whipped heavy cream).

Working quickly, drain asparagus and transfer to a warm platter. Spoon hot zabaglione over asparagus. Serve immediately, passing the pepper mill.

Serves 4

MORE 1·2·3 ASPARAGUS IDEAS

- Dip hot poached or steamed asparagus spears into the runny yolk of a soft-boiled egg in an eggcup. Sprinkle with truffle oil and coarse sea salt.

- Spoon dark Asian sesame oil over warm asparagus and sprinkle with toasted sesame seeds.

- Wrap bundles of hot steamed asparagus with paper-thin slices of prosciutto. Pour melted Camembert cheese over the bundles.

- Sauté asparagus in garlic olive oil (page 228) until caramelized. Top with shards of provolone or aged Gouda cheese.

- Asparagus, Netherlands Style: Pour salted butter that has been clarified over a stack of poached asparagus and dust with lots of freshly grated nutmeg.

- Top sautéed asparagus with leftover tomato sauce and mozzarella cheese. Bake until bubbly.

For more asparagus recipes, see pages 80, 91, 111, 192, 217, 221, and 314.

BABY BEETS WITH ROQUEFORT AND HAZELNUT OIL

This can be served as a sexy first course or side dish.

2 pounds baby beets (or the smallest beets you can find)
4 ounces Roquefort cheese
5 tablespoons hazelnut oil

Cut greens from beets, leaving 1 inch of the stem. Save tops for another use. Peel beets with a vegetable peeler. Bring a large pot of salted water to a boil. Add beets and cook for 20 minutes, or until tender when pierced with the tip of a sharp knife.

Drain in a colander. Cut beets in half if small, into wedges if larger.

Place beets on a warm platter. Crumble cheese and scatter evenly on beets. Drizzle with hazelnut oil. Dust with freshly ground black pepper. Serve immediately.

Serves 4

RUBY BEETS AND GREENS WITH GARLIC OIL AND LEMON

2 large bunches beets with greens attached
⅓ cup garlic olive oil (page 228)
1 large lemon

Preheat oven to 400°F.

Remove beet stems and greens and reserve them. Discard roots. Trim and scrub the beets but do not peel them. Place them in a shallow casserole with ½ inch water and bake for 1½ hours, until tender when pierced with a knife. Add a little more water during baking, if necessary. Let cool for 10 minutes and peel. Cut beets into 1½ by ¼-inch batons.

Place beets in a bowl and toss with 1 tablespoon garlic oil. Grate rind of 1 lemon and add zest to beets. Squeeze lemon to get 3 tablespoons lemon juice. Add 1 tablespoon lemon juice, reserving the rest. Sprinkle with salt and keep warm.

Bring a large pot of salted water to a boil. Wash beet greens well and break them into large pieces. Add greens to boiling water and cook for 5 minutes or longer, until tender.

Drain well and toss with remaining garlic oil, 2 tablespoons lemon juice, and salt and freshly ground pepper to taste. Serve on a warm platter, scattered with cooked beet batons.

Serves 4

BEETS *AL FORNO* WITH GORGONZOLA AND BALSAMIC SYRUP

Serve this oven-baked dish instead of a salad after the main course.

    6 very large beets, about 4½ pounds
    1 cup balsamic vinegar
    4 ounces creamy Gorgonzola cheese

Preheat oven to 400°F.

Scrub beets but do not peel them. Lay out 2 large pieces of aluminum foil and place 3 beets on each. Loosely wrap foil around beets, making a balloon shape. Fold and seal tightly on top and place both packets on a rimmed baking sheet. Bake for 1 hour and 45 minutes, or until tender. Remove from oven but keep sealed in foil packets.

Meanwhile, place vinegar in a nonreactive saucepan and bring to a boil. Lower heat and simmer until vinegar is reduced to ½ cup. Keep warm.

Cut foil and quickly peel beets, using a small sharp knife. Cut beets into wedges and place on a warm platter. Drizzle reduced vinegar onto beets and sprinkle with cracked black pepper. Cut cheese into thin slices and place on top of beets.

Serves 4

WARM ROASTED BEETS AND CRISPY GREENS WITH VINEGAR BUTTER

    10 to 12 medium beets with greens attached, about 4 pounds
    4 tablespoons unsalted butter
    2 tablespoons tarragon, raspberry, or champagne vinegar

Preheat oven to 300°F.

Remove beet stems and greens and reserve them. Wash beets, scrubbing thoroughly. Remove any roots. Place in oven directly on the rack and roast for 2 hours, or until tender when pierced with a sharp knife.

Wash beet greens and remove leaves. Discard stems. Dry leaves thoroughly, then finely chop. Place on a rimmed baking sheet and bake for 25 to 30 minutes, or until crisp. Turn once or twice during baking. Remove from oven and sprinkle with salt.

Meanwhile, melt butter in a small saucepan. Add 1 tablespoon vinegar and cook over high heat for 1 minute. Keep warm.

When beets are tender, remove from oven. Peel and cut beets into ½-inch chunks. Place in a bowl. Add vinegar butter and toss with salt and freshly ground black pepper to taste. Top with crispy greens and toss again with remaining vinegar.

Serves 6

MORE 1•2•3 BEET IDEAS

- Toss wedges of freshly boiled beets with orange butter made from orange zest, juice, and unsalted butter. Add coarsely ground black pepper.

- Grate raw beets on the large holes of a box grater and toss with a little flour. Press into flat pancakes and fry in olive oil until crispy. Sprinkle with salt.

- Sauté beet greens with sun-dried tomatoes packed in olive oil, sliced fresh garlic, and some water. Cook, covered, until tender.

- Peel baby beets, leaving some of the stem and greens. Place in a packet of aluminum foil, adding sprigs of fresh rosemary, lemon-scented olive oil, and kosher salt. Wrap tightly and bake for 45 minutes.

For more beet recipes, see pages 70, 232, and 298.

STEAMED BROCCOLI WITH STIR-FRIED PECANS

This is the best way imaginable to get anyone to eat broccoli.

1 large head broccoli
½ cup coarsely chopped pecans
3 tablespoons Chinese oyster sauce

Cut broccoli into large florets, leaving 1½ inches of the stem attached. Discard the remaining stems or save for another use. (You will have about 1 pound florets.) Place broccoli in a steamer basket and steam over boiling water for 10 to 12 minutes, until soft but still bright green.

Meanwhile, toast pecans in a small nonstick skillet until they become dark brown. Be careful not to let them burn.

In a large bowl, toss hot broccoli with toasted pecans and oyster sauce. Season with salt and freshly ground black pepper. Serve immediately.

Serves 4

ROASTED BROCCOLI AND GRAPE TOMATOES

Roasting vegetables at a very high temperature intensifies their flavor and natural sugars. It's a great way to feed a crowd while keeping your cool.

1 very large head broccoli, or 2 smaller ones
60 grape tomatoes
¼ cup extra-virgin olive oil, plus more for drizzling

Preheat oven to 450°F.

Remove broccoli florets and cut into medium pieces. Peel stalks of broccoli, then cut stalks into ½-inch pieces. Place broccoli pieces in a large bowl and add tomatoes that have been washed and dried thoroughly. Toss with olive oil and add salt and freshly ground black pepper.

Place vegetable mixture on a large rimmed baking sheet or shallow roasting pan in 1 layer. Roast for 18 minutes, shaking the pan twice during baking so the vegetables don't stick. Remove from oven and sprinkle with salt. Transfer to a warm platter and drizzle with a little extra olive oil. Serve immediately.

Serves 6

BROCCOLI SMOTHERED IN WINE AND OLIVE OIL

This time you want your broccoli slightly soft and yielding, not al dente. Use the best olive oil you can afford.

> 1 very large head broccoli, or 2 smaller ones
> 1 cup Chardonnay
> 3 tablespoons extra-virgin olive oil

Remove florets from broccoli and separate into large pieces. Peel stems with a vegetable peeler, and then slice them into ⅓-inch-thick rounds.

Bring a medium pot of salted water to a boil. Add florets and sliced stems and boil for 10 minutes. Drain in a colander, saving ½ cup cooking liquid. Return cooked broccoli to the pot with reserved cooking liquid, wine, 2 tablespoons olive oil, ½ teaspoon kosher salt, and ¼ teaspoon whole black peppercorns. Bring to a boil. Cover pot and lower heat. Simmer for 20 to 22 minutes, until broccoli is tender.

Remove broccoli with a slotted spoon and transfer to a shallow bowl or platter. Cook liquid over high heat until it's reduced to ½ cup. Pour over hot broccoli. Drizzle with remaining olive oil and sprinkle with kosher salt. Serve immediately.

Serves 4

MORE 1·2·3 BROCCOLI IDEAS

- Blanch broccoli florets, then sauté them in unsalted butter with lots of finely chopped shallots until soft. Sprinkle with coarse sea salt and freshly ground black pepper.

- Steam large heads of broccoli and serve them under a blanket of cheddar cheese sauce made by grating sharp cheddar into a little hot cream, or wine, or beer and stirring until smooth.

- Mix hot broccoli florets with oil-cured black olives and lemon-scented olive oil (page 228). Add salt and pepper to taste.

For more broccoli recipes, see pages 18, 72, and 191.

CHOPPED BROCCOLI RABE WITH ROASTED RED ONIONS

4 very large red onions, about 2 pounds total
3 tablespoons unsalted butter
2 large bunches broccoli rabe, about 1 pound each

Preheat oven to 375°F. Peel 1 onion and cut it into very small dice. You will have approximately 1½ cups. Set aside.

Cut remaining unpeeled onions in half through the equator. Spread 1 tablespoon butter on the bottom of a rimmed baking sheet large enough to hold onion halves in one layer. Place onions in pan, cut side down. Roast for 30 minutes. Press onions with a spatula to release any juices, and carefully turn them over. Roast 30 minutes longer.

Meanwhile, trim ½ inch from stems of broccoli rabe and discard. Wash broccoli rabe thoroughly but do not dry. Cut stems into ¼-inch pieces and leafy parts into ½-inch pieces. In a large pot, melt remaining butter. Add diced onion and cook over medium heat for 5 minutes, until onion is soft but not brown.

Add broccoli rabe, 1 teaspoon salt, and ¼ cup water. Turn heat to high and cook for 10 minutes, stirring frequently. Reduce heat to medium, cover, and cook for 10 minutes, or until tender. Uncover and cook 1 minute longer to let any moisture evaporate. Add freshly ground black pepper. Transfer to a warm platter and surround with hot roasted onion halves.

Serves 6

BROCCOLI RABE WITH HOT PEPPER FLAKES

Bitter, salty, and hot. I love this atop simple grilled fish.

1 large bunch broccoli rabe, about 1 pound
3 tablespoons garlic olive oil (page 228)
¼ teaspoon or more crushed red pepper flakes, or
  1 small dried hot red pepper

Trim broccoli rabe and wash well, removing any tough stems. Bring a large pot of salted water to a boil. Add broccoli rabe and bring to a boil again. Boil for 5 minutes and drain.

In a large skillet, heat garlic oil and red pepper flakes or the dried pepper, crumbled. Add blanched broccoli rabe and toss well with oil. Cover the pan and cook over low heat for 10 to 15 minutes, until tender. Stir several times during cooking. Add kosher salt to taste.

Serves 2 or 3

- Boil broccoli rabe in salted water until tender. Drain and briefly sauté with coarsely chopped anchovies with some of their oil. Scatter toasted pine nuts on top.

- Toss freshly cooked broccoli rabe with chicken stock that has been reduced by half and a handful of white raisins. Add freshly ground black pepper.

BRUSSELS SPROUTS WITH TANGERINE BEURRE NOISETTE

Beurre noisette is simply butter that is browned until it has a nutty aroma and taste. It partners beautifully with the sweet acidity of tangerines.

> 3 tangerines
> 1 pound small-as-possible Brussels sprouts
> 3 tablespoons unsalted butter

Grate rind of tangerines to get 1 teaspoon zest. Set aside.

Peel 2 tangerines and trim off as much pith as possible. Cut into segments along the membranes.

Bring a large pot of salted water to a boil. Wash and trim Brussels sprouts, removing any bruised outer leaves. Boil for 8 minutes and drain.

In a large nonstick skillet, melt 1 tablespoon butter. Add Brussels sprouts, tangerine segments, and zest. Cook over medium heat for 5 minutes. Cut remaining tangerine in half and squeeze juice from one half into pan. Cook over high heat for 1 minute, adding salt and freshly ground black pepper. Keep warm.

In a small nonstick skillet, melt remaining butter and cook over medium heat until butter is browned and smells faintly nutty. Be careful not to burn. Squeeze in juice of remaining tangerine half. Cook for 30 seconds and pour over cooked Brussels sprouts. Serve immediately.

Serves 4

BRUSSELS SPROUTS WITH SUN-DRIED CRANBERRIES

A perfect dish for the holidays, the Brussels sprouts can be parboiled early in the day and sautéed right before serving. Chopped sun-dried cherries would be cheery, too.

> 1¼ to 1½ pounds medium Brussels sprouts
> 1 cup unsweetened dried cranberries
> 6 tablespoons unsalted butter

Bring a large pot of salted water to a boil. Wash and trim Brussels sprouts and remove any bruised outer leaves. Add Brussels sprouts and boil for 10 minutes. Transfer to a colander, rinse under cold running water, and drain. Dry on paper towels, then cut sprouts in half through the stem end.

Meanwhile, place cranberries in a small bowl and add boiling water to cover. Let sit for 15 minutes. Drain and pat dry.

Melt butter in a very large skillet. Add Brussels sprouts and cranberries and cook over medium-high heat for about 10 minutes, until Brussels sprouts are tender but still green with some golden patches. Add salt and freshly ground black pepper to taste. Serve immediately.

Serves 6

MORE 1•2•3 BRUSSEL SPROUTS IDEAS

- Toss boiled Brussels sprouts with a syrupy reduction of orange juice and balsamic vinegar for a vibrant, fat-free side dish.
- Sauté blanched halved Brussels sprouts in salted butter and toss with freshly roasted chestnuts and coarsely ground black pepper.
- Cook small Brussels sprouts in tomato juice until tender. Remove sprouts and continue to cook juice until syrupy. Pour over Brussels sprouts and scatter freshly grated Parmesan on top.
- Make a Brussels sprouts puree. Boil sprouts in salted water until tender. Process them with butter, toasted caraway seeds, and some cooking liquid.

BRAISED CABBAGE IN RIESLING

Humble cabbage, first soaked, then simmered long and slow, is exalted by its slightly floral bath and buttery finish.

    1 large green cabbage, about 3 pounds
    3 cups dry Riesling
    6 tablespoons unsalted butter, melted

Wash cabbage and remove very dark outer leaves. Cut cabbage in half and remove core. Cut cabbage into ½-inch-thick slices. Soak in cold water mixed with 1 tablespoon kosher salt for 1 hour. Drain well. Put cabbage in a heavy, medium pot with a cover. Add wine and cover pot. Simmer over low heat for 1½ hours.

With a slotted spoon, transfer cabbage to a large nonreactive bowl. Mix with melted butter and lots of freshly ground black pepper. Quickly reduce cooking liquid until it's syrupy and lightly browned. Pour over cabbage. Add salt to taste. Reheat before serving.

Serves 8

RED CABBAGE WITH VINEGAR AND WILDFLOWER HONEY

Anything acidic will "fix" the color of red cabbage—in this case apple cider or sherry vinegar. I've also used raspberry vinegar with great success.

1 medium red cabbage, about 2½ pounds
½ cup apple cider or sherry vinegar
6 tablespoons wildflower honey, or other aromatic honey

Wash cabbage and remove any dark outer leaves. Cut cabbage in half and remove core.

Using a sharp knife, shred cabbage into ⅛-inch slices. Place cabbage in a large nonreactive pot with a cover. Add vinegar, 3 tablespoons honey, 3 cups water, 1 teaspoon whole black peppercorns, and 2 teaspoons kosher salt. Bring to a boil. Lower heat to medium and cover pot. Cook for 2 hours, stirring occasionally. Remove cover and cook 30 minutes more.

Drain cabbage in a colander, saving all the cooking liquid. Return liquid to pot and add remaining honey. Cook over high heat until reduced to a thick syrup, about ¾ cup. Return cabbage to pot and mix well with syrup. Adjust seasonings, adding more salt or vinegar. Cook 5 minutes more. Reheat before serving.

Serves 6

SAVOY CABBAGE WITH BACON AND CUMIN

1 large Savoy cabbage, about 3 pounds
2 tablespoons cumin seeds
6 ounces thick-sliced bacon

Wash cabbage and remove very dark outer leaves. Cut cabbage in half through the stem end and slice paper-thin across the width. Toast cumin seeds in a small, heavy, dry skillet until fragrant.

Cut bacon into 1-inch pieces and place it in a very large nonstick skillet or a pot large enough to hold all the cabbage. Cook bacon over medium heat until fat is rendered and bacon begins to crisp. Add cabbage and cook 10 minutes more, until cabbage begins to wilt. Add ½ cup water, coarsely ground black pepper, and more salt, if needed. Cook until water evaporates and cabbage is tender, about 8 minutes longer. Sprinkle with the toasted cumin seeds. Serve hot.

Serves 4

MORE 1·2·3 CABBAGE IDEAS

- Cook shredded Napa cabbage with diced pancetta until wilted and lightly caramelized. Splash with champagne vinegar.

- Finely chop red or green cabbage and smother it in unsalted butter and gin. Cover and cook until very soft, adding water if necessary. Add kosher salt and freshly ground black pepper.

- Parboil wedges of red cabbage for 15 minutes. Drain under cold water and slice. Line casserole with bacon strips and top with cabbage. Cover with chicken stock and top with more bacon slices. Cover and simmer for 1 hour, until cabbage is soft and liquid is absorbed.

For more cabbage recipes, see pages 101, 163, and 194.

CONFIT OF CARROTS AND LEMON

Steaming carrots and lemons slowly in a mixture of oil and water makes for very tender carrots and edible lemon slices. You may substitute bunches of fresh baby carrots, or cut larger carrots into whatever shape you choose.

1½ pounds medium carrots
2 medium thin-skinned lemons
3½ tablespoons extra-virgin olive oil

Peel carrots and slice them on the bias into long ovals, ¼-inch thick.

Place carrots in a 4-quart pot with a cover. Cut 1 lemon in half and squeeze juice into pot. Finely slice remaining lemon and add to pot. Add oil, ⅓ cup water, ½ teaspoon kosher salt, and ½ teaspoon black peppercorns. Bring to a boil. Cover pot, lower heat, and simmer for 35 to 40 minutes. Do not lift lid—shake pot back and forth several times during cooking instead.

Uncover and stir. Add kosher salt and pepper to taste.

Serves 4

JULIENNED CARROTS WITH PARMESAN

Inspired by a recipe from cooking teacher Giuliano Hazan, this is a wonderful accompaniment to roast veal and poultry, or a great addition to a vegetarian meal.

1½ pounds carrots
4 tablespoons unsalted butter
½ cup freshly grated Parmesan cheese, preferably Parmigiano-Reggiano

Peel carrots. Cut into sticks approximately 1½ inches long by ¼ inch thick.

Slice butter into a large nonstick skillet. Put carrots in skillet in no more than 2 layers. Place skillet over medium-high heat. When butter has melted, toss carrots with butter and add salt and freshly ground black pepper. Add ¼ cup water. Cook, uncovered, allowing the liquid to evaporate completely before adding more water, about ¼ cup at a time, until carrots are tender, about 25 minutes. Stir frequently during cooking.

Turn heat to high and brown the carrots, about 2 minutes. Sprinkle with cheese and transfer to a warm platter.

Serves 4 or more

SLOW-COOKED BABY CARROTS WITH SWEET GARLIC

With this technique, copious amounts of garlic give up their bite, becoming sweet and yielding.

1½ pounds peeled baby carrots
12 small cloves garlic
¼ cup extra-virgin olive oil

Place carrots in 1 layer in a large nonstick skillet or shallow flameproof casserole with a cover.

Cut garlic cloves in half and add to carrots. Add olive oil and just enough water to cover carrots. Add ½ teaspoon salt. Bring to a boil. Reduce heat to low and place cover askew. Simmer for 50 minutes or longer, until carrots are tender.

With a slotted spoon, transfer carrots and garlic to a bowl. Reduce pan juices over high heat until thick and syrupy. Toss with carrots, adding salt and freshly ground black pepper to taste.

Serves 4 or more

GLAZED CARROTS

In the French classic carrots Vichy, the carrots do not get brown. Here, though, a touch of caramelization gives them an extra dimension. For another inspiring variation, substitute one-quarter cup sweet Marsala for the sugar and cook until a glaze forms.

6 large thick carrots, about 1¼ pounds
3 tablespoons sugar
3½ tablespoons unsalted butter

Peel carrots and cut into ¹⁄₁₆-inch-thick rounds. Place in a large bowl and toss with sugar. Add a liberal sprinkling of salt. Melt butter in a large nonstick skillet and add seasoned carrots. Cook over medium-high heat, turning often, until the carrots are soft and even a bit blackened around the edges, 12 to 15 minutes. Add salt and freshly ground black pepper.

Serves 4

MORE 1·2·3 CARROT IDEAS

- Make a carrot puree: Boil chunks of carrots until soft. Puree in a food processor with hot melted chicken fat. Add kosher salt and black pepper. Reheat and sprinkle with fresh thyme leaves.

- Make carrots al forno: Peel whole carrots and parboil for 10 minutes. Place in a casserole with chicken stock just to cover. Dot with butter and bake for about 30 minutes, or until tender.

- Sauté julienned carrots in garlic olive oil (page 228) until just tender. Deglaze pan with dry vermouth, adding salt and pepper to taste.

- Peel and shred 1 pound carrots. Melt 1 stick butter with zest and juice of a large navel orange. Add shredded carrots and sauté over high heat until carrots are tender and juices are reduced.

For more carrot recipes, see pages 17 and 77.

NIGELLA'S CAULIFLOWER NUGGETS

Nigella Lawson, the fabulous British cookbook author, tastemaker, and TV star, loves simplicity as much as I do. Her cauliflower nuggets use only two ingredients; I added the third.

1 large head cauliflower, about 2¾ pounds
2 to 3 tablespoons extra-virgin olive oil
¼ cup ground cumin

Preheat oven to 425°F.

Remove core from cauliflower. Break head into small florets, about ¾-inch wide. Place in a large bowl and toss with olive oil. Sprinkle with salt and pepper to taste and toss with cumin. Place n a rimmed baking sheet and roast for 30 minutes, or until soft and caramelized, turning once during cooking. Sprinkle with salt and pepper. Serve hot or at room temperature.

Serves 4

SAUTÉED CAULIFLOWER WITH GARLICKY BREADCRUMBS

1 very large head cauliflower, or 2 small heads
7 tablespoons garlic olive oil (page 228)
4 ounces day-old crusty baguette

Remove core from cauliflower. Break up head into small florets. Boil florets in salted water for 15 minutes, until soft. Drain well in a colander.

In a large skillet, heat 4 tablespoons garlic oil. Add cauliflower and cook over high heat until cauliflower browns and starts to look fried. Sprinkle with salt and pepper.

Meanwhile, heat remaining garlic oil in a small nonstick skillet. Crumble bread to yield 1 heaping cup. Add to hot oil, stirring constantly until golden and crisp. Add salt and sprinkle breadcrumbs over hot cauliflower. Serve immediately.

Serves 6

CAULIFLOWER-APPENZELLER CASSEROLE

This unexpected trio of ingredients makes an extraordinarily appealing, and pungent, side dish. Use Appenzeller cheese imported from Switzerland for best results, although Gruyère may be substituted.

1 very large head cauliflower, or 2 small heads
1¼ cups (12-ounce can) good-quality crushed tomatoes
6 ounces Appenzeller cheese

Preheat oven to 375°F.

Bring a large pot of salted water to a boil. Remove core from cauliflower and cut head into large pieces. Cook over medium heat for 15 to 20 minutes, or until tender but not too soft. Drain well in a colander. Pat dry. In 2 batches, process cooked cauliflower in a food processor until it's fairly smooth, with some small pieces. (You do not want to liquefy the cauliflower.) Stir in 1 cup tomatoes and season with salt and freshly ground black pepper.

Cut rind off cheese. Remove a 2-ounce chunk and set aside. Cut remaining cheese into small cubes and stir into cauliflower. Put mixture in a shallow baking dish. Spread evenly with remaining tomatoes. Grate reserved cheese on the large holes of a box grater and scatter on top. Bake for 15 minutes, or until hot and bubbly.

Serves 6

MORE 1·2·3 CAULIFLOWER IDEAS

- Steam large florets of cauliflower until tender. Melt unsalted butter and add several crushed anchovies. Heat until anchovies "melt." Pour over cauliflower with cracked black pepper.

- Boil large cauliflower florets until tender. Heat ¾ cup heavy cream in a small saucepan, whisking furiously until warm. Stir in ¾ cup grated Pecorino Romano cheese and simmer, whisking, for 2 minutes, or until thick and smooth. Pour over cauliflower and briefly place under a broiler to brown.

- Toss medium cauliflower florets with extra-virgin olive oil and tandoori paste. Roast at 425°F for 30 minutes, or until soft, shaking pan often. Drizzle with more oil.

- Boil cauliflower nuggets in salted water until just tender. Drain and toss with finely chopped nuts sautéed in unsalted butter.

  For one more cauliflower recipe, see page 71.

CORN OFF THE COB

Even with no fat added, this flavor triology tastes strangely, wonderfully buttery.

5 large ears yellow corn
1 large red bell pepper
1 small bunch fresh thyme

Remove husks and silk from corn. Using a sharp knife, cut corn kernels from cobs, cutting very close to cobs. You should have 4½ to 5 cups corn. Set aside in a large nonstick skillet.

Remove core and seeds from bell pepper and cut peppers into fine julienned strips about 2½ inches long by ⅛ inch wide. Add to skillet along with ½ cup water. Bring to a boil, immediately lower heat to medium, and cook until corn is tender, about 5 minutes. Stir frequently, adding a little more water if needed.

Remove enough leaves from thyme to yield 1½ tablespoons. Add to corn along with salt and freshly ground black pepper. Cook 1 minute longer, or until almost all cooking liquid has evaporated. Serve immediately, garnished with tiny sprigs of thyme.

Serves 4

FIRECRACKER CORN

   8 tablespoons unsalted butter
   1½ canned chipotle chili peppers in adobo sauce
   12 large ears yellow or white corn, or a combination

Cut butter into pieces and place in bowl of an electric mixer. Finely chop peppers to yield 1½ tablespoons chopped peppers. Add peppers and 1 teaspoon adobo sauce (reserve the rest of the adobo sauce) to butter with a large pinch of salt. Add to butter with a large pinch of salt. Mix until incorporated; do not overprocess.

Pack chipolte butter into a 5-ounce ramekin, smoothing top with a knife. Drizzle a little reserved adobo sauce to glaze. Refrigerate until ready to use.

Bring a large pot of salted water to a boil. Remove husks and silk from corn. Add corn to water and cook for 5 minutes. Or cook, husk and all, on an outdoor grill. Serve hot with cold chipotle butter and small bowls of kosher salt.

Serves 12

GOLDEN CORN WITH SAFFRON BUTTER

An "a-maizing" combo of great taste and brilliant color.

   4 tablespoons unsalted butter
   ¼ teaspoon packed saffron threads
   6 large ears sweet corn

Melt butter in a small nonstick skillet. Add saffron, a pinch of salt, and freshly ground white pepper, and heat for 1 minute over medium heat. Let sit for 1 hour to allow saffron to infuse butter.

Remove husks and silk from corn. Bring a large pot of lightly salted water to a boil. Add corn and boil until tender, about 5 minutes. Remove from water and pat dry.

Heat saffron butter and, using a pastry brush, brush it on corn to coat. Place corn under a broiler, as far away from the heat source as possible. Broil briefly on all sides until a dark golden color. Remove from broiler and brush again with saffron butter. Serve immediately.

Serves 6

MORE 1·2·3 CORN IDEAS

- Make creamed corn by cooking 2 cups corn kernels, freshly cut from the cob, in 1 cup heavy cream for 10 minutes. Remove corn with slotted spoon and reduce cream until thick. Return corn to pan. Add salt, pepper, and a bit of minced fresh rosemary.

- Serve hot steamed corn on the cob with wide bowls of freshly grated Parmigiano-Reggiano and butter. "Roll buttered corn in the cheese between bites," recommends author James Peterson.

- Make chef Michel Nischan's "marshmallow" corn: Remove silk from corn and replace husks. Cut in half. Soak in milk warmed with sugar for 2 hours. Grill until tender.

For more corn recipes, see pages 75 and 124.

BRAISED ENDIVE WITH BAY LEAVES

Elegant, torpedo-shaped endives are marinated, then slowly transformed into a very silky, aromatic side dish. Delicious hot, at room temperature, or chilled. I like to use fresh bay leaves, which are now available in many supermarkets, but good-quality dried bay leaves can be substituted.

6 medium-large Belgian endives
1/2 cup extra-virgin olive oil
12 fresh bay leaves or dried California bay leaves, plus more for garnish

Wash endives and remove any dark outer leaves. Place endives in a shallow baking dish with a cover. Pour olive oil over endives. Place bay leaves under, in between, and on top of endives. Cover and marinate for several hours at room temperature.

Preheat oven to 275°F.

Sprinkle endives lightly with salt. Cover and bake for 1½ hours, shaking the baking dish several times. Serve immediately, or reheat briefly at 475°F before serving. Add salt and freshly ground black pepper to taste. Decorate with more bay leaves.

Serves 6

BELGIAN ENDIVE AND BLUE CHEESE GRATIN

A splendid sidekick to grilled steaks, or by itself with a glass of wine and crusty bread.

8 large Belgian endives, about 2½ pounds
6 ounces Danish blue cheese
¾ cup heavy cream

Preheat oven to 350°F.

Wash endives and trim bottoms with a sharp knife. Drop into a medium-large pot of salted boiling water. Bring to a boil again, lower heat, and simmer for 10 minutes.

Drain and cool in a colander, squeezing gently to remove excess moisture. Place endives in a heavy shallow casserole large enough to hold them in one layer. Sprinkle with freshly ground black pepper. Crumble cheese onto endives and pour cream over top. Bake for 30 minutes, or until tender. Place under a broiler for 1 minute, until lightly browned. Let cool for 5 minutes, then serve with cream sauce spooned over the top.

Serves 8

MORE 1•2•3 ENDIVE IDEAS

- Wrap 2 slices of bacon around each endive and secure with toothpicks. Place in a shallow casserole with ¼ cup water. Bake for 40 minutes at 400°F. Add 2 tablespoons balsamic vinegar and bake 10 minutes longer. Splash with additional vinegar.

- To grill endives, cut heads in half lengthwise and soak in cold water for 10 minutes. Toss with extra-virgin olive oil and grill, turning often, for 10 minutes. Sprinkle with fresh herbs (rosemary, basil, or mint), more olive oil, and kosher salt.

- Place halved endives in a casserole with chicken stock to cover. Dot with butter and bake about 40 minutes, until caramelized. Dust with freshly ground white pepper.

For one more endive recipe, see page 94.

BRAISED FENNEL WITH SUN-DRIED TOMATOES AND LEMON

2 large fennel bulbs, fronds attached
½ cup packed sun-dried tomatoes in oil
2 lemons

Remove any brown spots from fennel. Cut bulbs and 3 inches of stalks into ½-inch pieces. (Reserve the extra fronds.) Coarsely chop sun-dried tomatoes, reserving their oil.

Heat 3 tablespoons tomato oil in a large heavy saucepan with a cover. Add fennel and sauté over high heat for 5 minutes, until it begins to soften. Add chopped sun-dried tomatoes and ½ cup water. Cook over high heat for 1 minute and cover. Reduce heat to medium and cook 20 minutes longer, until fennel is very tender and caramelized. It will look slightly translucent.

Grate zest of 1 lemon and squeeze lemon to get 2 tablespoons juice. Add 2 teaspoons zest (reserve the rest) and the lemon juice to fennel, stir, and cook, uncovered, for 1 to 2 minutes. Add salt and freshly ground black pepper to taste.

Transfer to a bowl. Sprinkle with additional lemon zest and finely chopped fennel fronds. Add paper-thin slices of remaining lemon. Serve immediately.

Serves 4

PARMESAN-ROASTED FENNEL

Slow-baking these pale green bulbs brings out their natural sugars. The aniselike flavor marries well with the sweet nutty taste of real Parmigiano-Reggiano.

> 3 medium-large fennel bulbs
> ¼ cup extra-virgin olive oil
> ¾ cup freshly grated Parmigiano-Reggiano

Preheat oven to 400°F.

Trim fronds and stalks from fennel bulbs and set aside. Remove any dark spots from fennel. Cut bulbs in half lengthwise through the root end.

Place bulbs, cut side up, in a shallow baking dish. Rub salt and freshly ground black pepper into cut sides. Drizzle each half with ½ tablespoon olive oil and bake for 25 minutes. Turn the bulbs, adding a little more oil if necessary. Lower heat to 350°F and bake 20 minutes longer.

Turn fennel over so cut sides are up. Sprinkle each half with about 2 tablespoons grated cheese and bake 5 minutes longer. Finely chop some of the reserved fennel fronds and sprinkle over the roasted fennel.

Serves 6

MORE 1·2·3 FENNEL IDEAS

- Cut fennel through the root end into thick slices. Boil until just tender. Layer in a casserole with tomato sauce and slices of smoked mozzarella. Bake at 400°F for 10 minutes, or until bubbly.

- Sauté slivers of fennel and red onion in olive oil until caramelized. Sprinkle with fennel fronds, kosher salt, and freshly ground black pepper.

- Add small cubes of boiled fennel to hot cooked white beans. Toss with cubes of Gorgonzola cheese and chopped fennel fronds.

  For more fennel recipes, see pages 76 and 97.

SIMPLE GREEN BEANS

1 pound young green beans
¼ cup extra-virgin olive oil
2 tablespoons red wine vinegar

Wash beans and trim ends. Using a small sharp knife, cut beans in half lengthwise to make long, thin pieces.

Bring a medium pot of salted water to a boil. Cook beans for 3 to 4 minutes, or until tender but still bright green. Drain immediately. Whisk together olive oil and vinegar. Toss with warm beans. Add kosher salt and freshly ground black pepper to taste.

Serves 4

HARICOTS VERTS À LA CRÈME

Haricots verts are a variety of green bean. They are thinner, dark green, and more flavorful than the common ones—and worth the extra price.

1¾ pounds haricots verts
⅓ cup minced shallots
1 cup heavy cream

Wash beans, trim ends, and set aside. Place shallots and cream in a small saucepan. Add a pinch of salt and freshly ground white pepper. Bring to a boil. Immediately lower heat and simmer for 20 minutes, or until cream thickens and reduces to ¾ cup.

Meanwhile, bring a pot of salted water to a boil. Cook beans until just tender, about 10 minutes. Drain beans in a colander and return to pot. Spoon cream sauce over beans and reheat gently. Add salt and white pepper to taste.

Serves 6

BLASTED GREEN BEANS WITH OIL-CURED OLIVES

In this hip method, the beans get slightly browned and the olives intensify in flavor.

1 pound slender green beans
3 tablespoons garlic olive oil (page 228)
½ cup pitted oil-cured black olives

Preheat oven to 500°F.

Wash beans, trim ends and remove strings. Place beans on a rimmed baking sheet. Drizzle with 2 tablespoons garlic oil and toss to coat. Sprinkle with salt and pepper. Bake for 6 minutes. Add olives, shaking pan to turn beans and incorporate olives. Bake 5 to 6 minutes longer. Beans will be slightly wrinkled and brown in patches. Transfer to a warm platter. Toss with remaining garlic oil.

Serves 4

GREEN BEANS AND POTATOES IN PESTO

¾ pound green beans
1¼ pounds Yukon gold or red potatoes
6 tablespoons good-quality prepared pesto

Wash beans and trim ends. Cut beans in half crosswise. Set aside.

Bring a medium pot of salted water to a boil. Peel potatoes and cut into 1-inch chunks. Add potatoes to boiling water. Cook over high heat until just tender, 13 to 14 minutes.

Add bean pieces and cook another 5 minutes, or until tender and bright green. Drain potatoes and beans in a colander, saving 2 tablespoons cooking liquid. Loosen pesto with this liquid. Shake off excess water from vegetables and place in a bowl. Toss with pesto, adding salt and freshly ground black pepper to taste.

Serves 4

MORE 1·2·3 GREEN BEAN IDEAS

- Steam trimmed green beans in a steamer basket. Toss with roasted garlic butter, made by roasting a whole head of garlic and squeezing pulp into ¼ cup unsalted whipped butter.

- Boil green beans for 2 minutes, drain, and pat dry. Toss with seasoned flour and fry in grapeseed oil. Sprinkle with salt.

- Drain canned water chestnuts and sauté in unsalted butter until golden. Add blanched green beans and cook until tender. Toss with a little more butter, salt, and pepper.

- Split green beans in half lengthwise and sauté in lemon-scented olive oil (page 228). Add crushed macadamia nuts and cook until nuts are toasted. Add salt and pepper to taste.

For one more green bean recipe, see page 64.

WILTED KALE AND BACON

This method is suitable for other leafy green vegetables, including mustard greens, collards, and chard—all nutritional powerhouses.

1 large bunch kale
9 slices hickory-smoked bacon
6 tablespoons distilled white vinegar

Remove stems from kale. Wash leaves well and chop coarsely. You should have about 12 cups packed leaves.

Cut bacon into 1-inch pieces and place in a large heavy pot. Cook bacon slowly over low heat until it just begins to crisp and its fat is rendered. Add kale and turn up heat. Add vinegar and ¼ cup water. Cook for 4 minutes over high heat, stirring constantly, until kale is wilted and tender, adding a little more water if needed. Add salt, freshly ground black pepper, and another splash of vinegar if desired.

Serves 4

MORE 1•2•3 KALE IDEAS

- Sauté finely chopped kale in lots of garlic olive oil (page 228), and finish with capers and a little caper brine. Add freshly ground black pepper.
- Boil shredded kale and finely diced scallions until just soft. Drain and add to a hot pan with sautéed chopped chorizo. Cook until tender.

- Reduce 1 cup heavy cream to ½ cup. Cook ¾ pound kale leaves in salted boiling water until tender. Squeeze out excess water and chop. Heat with cream and grated lime zest.

POACHED LEEKS WITH ROASTED GARLIC AND BRIE FONDUE

This impossibly rich dish is improbably low in calories.

1 large head garlic
8 medium leeks, about 2 pounds
6 ounces ripe double-cream Brie cheese, well chilled

Preheat oven to 400°F.

Wrap garlic in a large piece of aluminum foil to make a pouch, and seal top tightly. Place in a pie tin and roast for 1 hour. Remove from oven, open foil packet, and let cool.

Trim leeks, leaving only 2 to 3 inches of dark green tops. Remove roots. Split leeks in half lengthwise, stopping 2 inches from the root end, to keep them intact. Wash thoroughly between leaves.

Place leeks in a large skillet with a cover. Arrange them in 1 layer and cover leeks with 2 inches water. Add 1 tablespoon kosher salt and bring to a boil. Lower heat to medium and cover skillet. Cook for 20 minutes, or until tender.

Meanwhile, remove rind from cheese. Cut cheese into small pieces and place in a small saucepan. Add 3 tablespoons poaching liquid from leeks. Cut cooked garlic in half through the diameter and squeeze the garlic pulp into saucepan. Add freshly ground white pepper and heat, stirring constantly, until cheese melts.

Remove leeks from water and drain well. Pour melted cheese over leeks and serve hot.

Serves 4

- Roast slender leeks in a bath of garlic olive oil (page 228) and water until tender. Sauté diced fresh tomato in additional garlic oil until soft. Season with kosher salt and pepper, and pour over leeks.

- Cut leeks into 2-inch lengths and cook in butter in a covered pan for 5 minutes. Add enough dry white wine to cover leeks, replace cover, and cook until soft. Remove leeks and reduce pan juices until golden, whisking in a little more butter to thicken. Add salt and pepper to taste.

- Make high-temperature leeks: Trim leeks and cut into thirds. Roll in extra-virgin olive and sprinkle with kosher salt. Roast at 425°F for 25 minutes, until golden. Add a few drops of lemon juice.

For more leek recipes, see pages 77, 108, 138, 148, 174, and 214.

MUSHROOMS IN SHERRY-PEPPER CREAM

This is just the sort of thing you want next to your steak, under your roasted chicken, or on your piece of toast.

8 ounces cremini or shiitake mushrooms
6 tablespoons or more heavy cream
3 tablespoons or more dry sherry, preferably fino

Wipe mushrooms with a damp cloth. Cut mushrooms in half if large. In a medium nonstick skillet, cook heavy cream over high heat until it starts to thicken and bubble. Add 2 tablespoons sherry and the mushrooms.

Stirring constantly, cook mushrooms over medium heat until they begin to soften, about 3 minutes. Add remaining sherry, salt, and lots of coarsely ground black pepper. Cook 1 to 2 minutes longer, until mushrooms give up some of their liquid. You may adjust the sauce by adding a little more cream or sherry, if necessary. Serve hot.

Serves 4

ROASTED SHIITAKES WITH GARLIC OIL AND WINE

12 ounces large shiitake mushrooms
3 tablespoons garlic olive oil (page 228), plus more for drizzling
⅓ cup dry white wine

Preheat oven to 350°F.

Line a rimmed baking sheet with a sheet of aluminum foil large enough to hold the mushrooms in a single layer. Sprinkle the pan with garlic oil and wine. Place mushrooms, stem side up, on the pan and sprinkle with kosher salt and freshly ground black pepper. Bake for 20 minutes. Turn mushrooms over and bake 10 minutes longer. Remove from oven and slice mushrooms thickly on the bias. Serve with pan juices and drizzle with a little more garlic oil.

Serves 4

MORE 1·2·3 MUSHROOM IDEAS

- Spread rosemary branches on a rimmed baking sheet. Distribute shiitake or portobello mushrooms on top. Drizzle with olive oil and kosher salt. Bake at 500°F for 10 minutes, or until soft.

- Sauté fresh morel or chanterelle mushrooms in unsalted butter with snippets of fresh tarragon. Season with salt and pepper.

- Stuff large portobello mushroom caps with chopped spinach mixed with pesto or prepared creamed spinach mixed with Pernod. Bake at 400°F for 15 minutes, or until bubbly.

- Cut a large rectangle of aluminum foil or parchment paper. On one half of foil, arrange 1 pound wild mushrooms (such as porcini and chanterelles). Add fresh lemon juice and extra-virgin olive oil, and season with salt and pepper. Fold foil in half and tightly crimp edges to seal. Roast at 350°F for 30 minutes.

For one more mushroom recipe, see page 317.

GIANT ONIONS *BALSAMICO*

3 very large yellow onions
4 tablespoons extra-virgin olive oil
3 tablespoons balsamic vinegar

Preheat oven to 425°F.

Peel onions and cut them in half through their equators. Put onions, cut sides down, in a heavy shallow flameproof casserole (preferably metal) or on a rimmed baking sheet. Pour 2 tablespoons olive oil over the onions. Add a sprinkling of kosher salt and freshly ground black pepper.

Bake for 20 minutes; cut side of onions will be blackened. Turn over and flatten with a spatula. Bake 15 minutes longer. Turn again, flatten with a spatula, and bake 20 minutes more.

Remove onions from casserole when soft and caramelized. Add remaining olive oil and vinegar to the pan. Cook over high heat for 1 minute and pour over onions.

Serves 6

ROASTED PEARL ONIONS, SHERRY VINEGAR GLAZE

Boiling the onions briefly makes peeling them a snap. Sherry vinegar and honey add alluring sweet and sour notes. A perfect foil for any fatty meat, especially pork.

1¼ pounds (about 60) white pearl onions
1 cup sherry vinegar, preferably Spanish
3 tablespoons honey

Preheat oven to 350°F.

Bring a medium pot of water to a boil. Add unpeeled onions and boil for 3 minutes. Rinse onions in a colander under cold running water. Trim root ends using a small sharp knife, then peel.

In a small bowl, mix together vinegar, honey, 2 tablespoons water, and a large pinch of kosher salt and freshly ground black pepper. Place onions in a shallow casserole large enough to hold them in one layer. Pour vinegar-honey mixture over onions. Roast until tender, about 1 hour and 20 minutes, shaking pan often during cooking so that onions are evenly glazed.

Most of the liquid will evaporate, leaving the onions a dark golden brown. If too much liquid remains, use a slotted spoon to transfer onions to a warm platter and reduce liquid to ¼ cup. Pour glaze over hot roasted onions.

Serves 4

WARM ONION GRATIN

4 medium-large yellow onions
⅓ cup heavy cream
4 ounces Gruyère cheese

Preheat oven to 450°F.

Add 1 tablespoon salt to a 9 by 11-inch shallow flameproof casserole of water. Bring to a boil. Peel onions and cut each horizontally into 3 thick slices. Add onions to boiling water and lower heat to medium. Cook until tender, about 10 minutes, keeping onions in their original shape, as slices will begin to separate. Drain onions thoroughly.

Pour cream over onions and sprinkle lightly with salt and freshly ground black pepper.

Grate cheese on the large holes of a box grater and sprinkle it over onions. Bake for 8 minutes, then place under a broiler for 30 seconds until cheese is melted and golden.

Serves 4

MORE 1·2·3 ONION IDEAS

- Peel 6 large onions and place them in a shallow flameproof casserole. Drizzle with olive oil and brown over high heat for 3 minutes. Add 1 cup wine, or dry Marsala, and ½ cup water. Bake at 300°F for 2 hours.

- Cut large onions in half and bake until soft. Scoop out centers and chop them. Sauté in butter with chopped spinach until cooked. Fill onion shells with mixture. Dot with more butter and broil, to brown tops.

- When cipollini are available (small, flattish Italian onions), peel 1½ pounds and mix with ¼ cup extra-virgin olive oil. Place in pan with 1 tablespoon tomato paste diluted in ½ cup boiling water. Cover and cook over medium-low heat for 45 minutes, or until tender.

For more onion recipes, see pages 27, 60, 74, 107, 120, 125, 142, 145, 162, 172, 236, and 237.

LIME-GLAZED PARSNIPS

Once you make this lovely dish, I assure you that parsnips will become a family favorite.

1½ pounds medium parsnips
2 limes
3 tablespoons extra-virgin olive oil

Peel parsnips and cut into sticks about 3 inches by ½ inch. Place in a 4-quart nonreactive saucepan.

Grate zest of 1 lime. Cut lime in half and squeeze juice. Add lime zest and juice to parsnips. Add olive oil, ⅓ cup water, ½ teaspoon salt, and ½ teaspoon whole black peppercorns. Bring to a boil. Cover saucepan and lower heat to maintain a simmer. Cook for 40 minutes. Do not lift lid; shake pot back and forth several times during cooking instead.

Uncover and stir. Add salt and freshly ground black pepper to taste. Garnish with remaining lime, cut into wedges.

Serves 4

FRENCH PARSNIPS

6 medium parsnips, about 1¼ pounds
2½ tablespoons unsalted butter
1 tablespoon sugar

Peel parsnips and cut on a slight bias into very thin slices.

Place parsnips in a medium saucepan. Add butter, cut into small pieces, sugar, ¾ cup water, and a large pinch of salt and freshly ground white pepper. Bring to a boil and stir. Cover pan, lower heat to medium, and cook, stirring often, until all the water has been absorbed and parsnips are tender, about 15 minutes. If liquid remains, uncover and cook over high heat until its absorbed.

Serves 4

MORE 1•2•3 PARSNIP IDEAS

- Peel parsnips and cut into pieces that look like french fries. Toss with olive oil, melted butter, and salt. Roast at 400°F for about 20 minutes, turning often, until tender and golden brown.

- Peel parsnips and slice into thick ovals on the bias. Boil for 10 minutes. Pat dry and sauté in butter with lots of finely chopped shallots and coarsely ground black pepper.

- Peel parsnips and cut into 1-inch pieces. Boil until soft. Puree in a food processor with hot cream and bits of cold butter. Add salt and freshly ground white pepper.

For one more parsnip recipe, see page 80.

SWEET PEAS AND SMOKY GRITS

Small fresh peas in season are always preferred, but you can substitute frozen petit pois, thawed.

    1 cup fresh shelled peas, about 1 pound before shelling
    8 ounces smoked cheddar cheese
    1 cup old-fashioned grits

Preheat oven to 350°F.

Bring a small pot of salted water to a boil. Add peas and cook until almost tender. (Cooking time will depend on size and age of peas.) Drain well.

Grate cheese on the large holes of a box grater and set aside.

In a heavy medium saucepan, bring 5 cups water and 1 teaspoon salt to a boil. Slowly add grits, lower heat to medium, stir, and cover. Cook for 10 minutes, stirring often so that no lumps form. Remove cover, and add peas and all but 1 cup cheese. Add salt and freshely ground black pepper to taste. Cook uncovered 10 minutes longer, stirring often, until grits get thick.

Pour mixture into a shallow 9 by 11-inch casserole sprayed with nonstick cooking spray. Top with remaining cheese and bake for 15 minutes, or until bubbly.

Serves 6

SAUTÉED PEAS AND PANCETTA

    3 cups fresh shelled peas, about 3 pounds before shelling
    2 tablespoons garlic olive oil (page 228)
    3 ounces pancetta

Bring a medium pot of salted water to a boil. Add peas and cook until almost tender but still bright green. (Cooking time will depend on size and age of peas). Drain thoroughly.

In a medium nonstick skillet, put garlic oil and pancetta that has been diced into small pieces. Heat until pancetta begins to crisp. Add peas and cook over medium-high heat until tender.

Serves 4

MORE 1·2·3 PEA IDEAS

- Cook shelled peas in boiling salted water until tender. Toss with unsalted butter and freshly chopped spearmint, or with lemon-scented olive oil (page 228) and chopped dill.

- Place blanched peas and lots of sliced leeks in a shallow pan with a little water, unsalted butter, kosher salt, and black pepper. Cook until tender.

- Put small green peas in a pan with heavy cream and a little water. Cook until tender and toss with freshly snipped basil, salt, and pepper.

For one more pea recipe, see page 121.

PEPPER CONFIT WITH SHERRY VINEGAR

Here confit *means slow-cooked in a covered pan in oil and vinegar—half braising, half steaming— until the peppers become incredibly sweet and tender. It's a simple technique that works well with many vegetables.*

4 very large bell peppers (red, yellow, orange, or a combination)
¼ cup extra-virgin olive oil
2 tablespoons sherry vinegar, preferably Spanish, plus more for serving

Wash peppers and dry them. Cut each pepper into 8 large wedges, removing core and any seeds. Place peppers, olive oil, vinegar, and ½ teaspoon whole black peppercorns in a heavy medium pot with a cover.

Bring to a boil. Cover pot and reduce heat to low. Simmer for 45 minutes without lifting cover, as the steam helps soften the peppers. Shake pot back and forth several times during cooking.

Transfer peppers and juices to a warm platter. Add salt to taste and sprinkle with additional vinegar. Serve warm, at room temperature, or chilled.

Serves 4

ROASTED YELLOW PEPPERS, CAPER-RAISIN EMULSION

A puree of capers and golden raisins was made famous by chef Jean-Georges Vongerichten. Although it tastes strange on its own, he pairs it brilliantly with scallops; I think this simplified version with roasted yellow peppers is special .

6 large yellow bell peppers
½ scant large capers in brine, drained
¾ cup golden raisins

Preheat broiler.

Wash peppers and dry them. Rinse capers and drain.

Place whole peppers on a baking sheet and broil for several minutes on all sides, until blackened completely. Transfer peppers to a paper bag, close tightly, and steam for 5 to 10 minutes.

Pour 1 cup boiling water over raisins. Let sit for 5 minutes. Drain well. Put in a blender or food processor with capers. Process until smooth, adding ¼ cup soaking water. Add freshly ground black pepper. Continue to process until very smooth.

Remove peppers from bag and scrape off all the blackened skin. Do not rinse peppers. Put them on a plate to collect any sweet juices. Cut each into quarters, lengthwise, removing the core, seeds, and any coarse membranes.

Place warm peppers and any juices on a platter and sprinkle very lightly with salt. Dot caper-raisin mixture over peppers. Serve slightly warm or at room temperature.

Serves 6

SAUTÉED PEPPERS WITH ZA'ATAR

Za'atar, a spice mixture from the Middle East, adds great complexity to big sweet squares of red, yellow, and orange bell peppers softened in butter. This dish is a wonderful accompaniment to grilled fish, roast chicken, or leg of lamb.

    4 very large bell peppers, in assorted colors
    3 tablespoons unsalted butter
    2 tablespoons za'atar

Wash peppers and dry them. Cut peppers in half and remove the core, seeds, and any coarse membranes. Cut pepper halves into 1-inch squares.

Put 2½ tablespoons butter in a very large nonstick skillet. Heat butter and add peppers. Cook over medium-high heat, stirring often, for 10 minutes. Add kosher salt and freshly ground black pepper to taste and continue to cook for 5 minutes, or until peppers are browned and soft. Add za'atar and continue to cook for 2 to 3 minutes. Add several tablespoons of water, and cook until most of the liquid has evaporated. Add remaining butter and stir until melted. Taste again for seasonings, adding salt, pepper, or more za'atar to taste.

Serves 4

MORE 1·2·3 PEPPER IDEAS

- Put pepper halves, cut side down, on a rimmed baking sheet with olive oil and kosher salt. Roast at 375°F for 50 minutes. Drizzle with green or black olive tapenade that has been thinned with some water or juices from the roasted peppers.

- Toss strips of roasted peppers with chili oil, and mix with chunks of hot boiled potatoes.

- Make warm pickled peppers: Cut 6 red peppers into thick strips. Boil in 2 cups white vinegar and 1 cup sugar for 5 minutes. Drain. Add salt and pepper.

  For more pepper recipes, see pages 92, 99, 113, 140, and 307.

VERY LEMONY MASHED POTATOES

    3 pounds large baking and boiling potatoes, combined
    3 large lemons
    6 tablespoons unsalted butter

Peel potatoes. Cut into eighths and place in a large pot with a cover. Add enough cold water to just cover potatoes. Add 2 teaspoons salt. Bring to a rapid boil. Lower heat to medium, cover, and cook for 20 to 25 minutes until potatoes are soft but not falling apart.

Meanwhile, grate rind of 1 to 2 lemons to get 2 teaspoons zest. Cut lemons in half and squeeze to get ⅔ cup juice. Place juice in a small nonstick skillet and cook over medium-high heat until reduced to ½ cup. Set aside.

When potatoes are done, drain in a colander, saving 1 cup cooking liquid. Put potatoes in a large bowl, and using a potato masher, mash until smooth, slowly adding reserved cooking liquid. Add lemon zest and reduced lemon juice. Cut butter into small pieces and add to potatoes, continuing to mash until creamy. Add salt and freshly ground white pepper to taste. Reheat potatoes gently.

Serves 6

GARLIC-MASHED YUKON GOLDS

2 pounds Yukon gold potatoes
12 large cloves garlic, peeled
¼ cup extra-virgin olive oil

Peel potatoes. Put potatoes and 10 cloves garlic in a large saucepan. Add cold water to cover potatoes. Add 1 teaspoon kosher salt and bring to a boil. Lower heat to medium-high and cover, with the lid askew. Cook until tender, about 35 minutes.

Meanwhile, heat 1 tablespoon olive oil in a small skillet. Slice remaining garlic paper-thin and add to skillet. Cook over low heat until very soft but not brown, about 5 minutes. Set aside.

When potatoes are tender, drain in a colander, reserving 1¼ cups cooking liquid. Push potatoes and garlic through a ricer, or place in a large bowl and, using a potato masher, mash thoroughly. Add remaining olive oil and cooked sliced garlic in its oil, and, mixing constantly, gradually add enough cooking liquid to make potatoes smooth and creamy. Add salt and freshly ground white pepper to taste. Reheat gently until hot.

Serves 4

GRATIN DAUPHINOISE

A gratin is the golden, epicurean crust that forms on the surface of savory baked or broiled dishes. Pungent Gruyère makes a genial topping that acts as a protective layer, preventing the potatoes from drying out.

2½ pounds Yukon gold or all-purpose potatoes
3 cups half-and-half
2 cups shredded Gruyère cheese, about 6 ounces

Preheat oven to 350°F.

Peel potatoes. Slice potatoes very thin with a sharp knife and put them in a medium pot with half-and-half, 2 teaspoons salt, and freshly ground white pepper. Stir well and simmer the potatoes for 15 minutes, or until they are just beginning to soften.

Transfer potatoes and half-and-half mixture to a shallow medium casserole. The liquid should come just to the tops of the potatoes. Cover evenly with the shredded cheese. Bake for 35 to 40 minutes, or until potatoes are tender and cheese is golden brown.

Serves 6 or more

POTATO GALETTE WITH TRUFFLE OIL

2 medium-large Yukon gold potatoes, about ¾ pound
1½ tablespoons unsalted butter, at room temperature
1 teaspoon white truffle oil

Peel potatoes and slice into paper-thin rounds using a thin-bladed knife or a mandoline.

Spread 1 tablespoon of butter over the bottom and halfway up sides of an 8-inch nonstick skillet with a cover. Place 1 potato slice in center of pan and, in a tight overlapping pattern, make concentric circles of potatoes in two thin layers. Sprinkle lightly with salt and freshly ground pepper. Dot with remaining butter.

Cook over high heat for 3 minutes. Press firmly with a spatula. Reduce heat to low. Cover pan and cook for 5 minutes. Turn potatoes over. Cover pan and cook for 5 minutes on other side. Uncover pan and cook over medium-high heat for 10 minutes, turning several times so that each side of the galette turns golden and crispy. Total cooking time should be about 18 minutes. When potatoes are cooked through, sprinkle with truffle oil. Cut in half and serve immediately.

Serves 2

PAN-FRIED SAGE POTATOES

4 large red-skinned new potatoes, about 1½ pounds
3 tablespoons extra-virgin olive oil, plus ¼ cup for frying sage leaves
2 bunches fresh sage

Peel potatoes and cut each into 4 long wedges, then cut each wedge into thin ⅛-inch-thick triangular slices.

In a very large nonstick skillet with a cover, heat 3 tablespoons olive oil. Add potatoes and cook over high heat for 5 minutes, stirring often. Turn potatoes over, and cook on other side for 5 minutes. Potatoes will begin to crisp and turn golden brown.

Cover pan, lower heat, and cook 5 minutes longer. Julienne enough sage to get 3 tablespoons, reserving the rest of the leaves. Uncover pan and add sage. Stir well, add salt and freshly ground black pepper to taste, and cook another 5 minutes. Total cooking time should be about 20 minutes.

Meanwhile, in a small nonstick skillet, heat ¼ cup olive oil over high heat. When oil is very hot, add 8 to 12 whole sage leaves. Sage will crisp in 30 seconds. Remove sage from oil.

Transfer potatoes to a warm platter and garnish with fried sage leaves.

Serves 4

DOUBLE-BAKED CHEESE POTATOES

Serve these to your favorite couch potatoes. One potato is a side dish; two are dinner, if you add a salad.

12 ounces Cotswold cheese (a cheddar cheese from England
   flavored with onions and chives)
4 large baking potatoes, 12 ounces each
1½ cups milk

Preheat oven to 425°F.

Grate cheese on the large holes of a box grater. Set aside. Wash potatoes well. Dry thoroughly and put directly on oven rack. Bake for 55 to 60 minutes, until potatoes are tender when pierced with a fork. Remove potatoes from oven.

With a sharp knife, cut potatoes in half lengthwise. Scoop out potato flesh with a fork, being careful not to break potato shell, and place in a bowl. Heat milk in a small saucepan. Add hot milk and all but 1 cup grated cheese to potatoes. Using a potato masher, mash potatoes until creamy and smooth. Add salt and freshly ground black pepper. Fill potato shells with mixture, mounding on top. Sprinkle evenly with reserved cheese.

Place potato halves in a shallow baking dish. Return to oven and bake for 8 minutes. Put under broiler for 1 minute, or until cheese is lightly browned.

Serves 8

WASABI-WHIPPED POTATOES

Also called Japanese horseradish, wasabi can most easily be found in powdered form. It is a very modern and pungent addition to spuds.

2 pounds Yukon gold potatoes
2 tablespoons wasabi powder
8 tablespoons unsalted butter

Wash potatoes, scrubbing them well. Place unpeeled potatoes in a large pot of boiling salted water. Cover pot. Lower heat and cook for 35 to 40 minutes, or until potatoes are very tender. Drain in a colander, saving ¼ cup cooking liquid.

Peel potatoes quickly and place in a large bowl. Mash with a potato masher until smooth and creamy. In a small cup, dissolve wasabi powder in ¼ cup cold water. Stir until smooth. Add to mashed potatoes.

Cut butter into small pieces and add to potatoes. Using a wire whisk or electric beater, whip potatoes until thick and creamy, adding a little reserved cooking liquid. Add salt and freshly ground black pepper to taste and serve hot.

Serves 4

SHREDDED POTATO PANCAKES

This recipe yields two large potato pancakes that are then cut into wedges. The secret to the creamy filling and crispy exterior is parboiling the potatoes, then grating them on a box grater. I serve these large latkes on Hanukkah; they absorb less oil than the smaller ones.

2 pounds large boiling potatoes
3 tablespoons coarsely grated onion
¼ cup olive oil

Wash potatoes, but do not peel them. Bring a large pot of salted water to a boil and add potatoes, making sure they are covered by the water. Cook for about 15 minutes; potatoes should still be a bit firm. Rinse under cold water. Cool potatoes and peel with a sharp knife. On the large holes of a box grater, shred potatoes lengthwise into a bowl. Stir in onion, 1 teaspoon kosher salt, and freshly ground white pepper.

Heat 1 tablespoon olive oil in a 10-inch nonstick skillet over moderate heat until hot but not smoking, then add half the potatoes, spreading with a spatula to form an even cake. Cook until underside is golden brown, about 12 minutes.

Invert a large plate over skillet and invert pancake onto plate. Add 1 tablespoon olive oil to skillet and slide latke back into skillet. Cook until underside is golden brown, about 10 minutes. Slide pancake onto plate and keep warm in a 200°F oven. Repeat process, to make a second pancake. Sprinkle with salt and cut into wedges.

Serves 6

MORE 1·2·3 POTATO IDEAS

- Peel medium potatoes and cut 5 or 6 parallel slits about two-thirds of the way through the width. Insert small sprigs of thyme in slits and drizzle garlic olive oil (page 228) over top. Bake about 45 minutes at 400°F until tender.

- Wash large baking potatoes and cut lengthwise into 12 wedges. Toss with olive oil and put on a rimmed baking sheet. Bake at 400°F for 40 minutes. Sprinkle with salt and sweet or smoked paprika.

- Boil all-purpose potatoes until tender, then chill well. Cut into large chunks and sauté with caraway seeds in grapeseed oil until golden and crispy.

- Scrub small all-purpose potatoes. Toss with olive oil and kosher salt and bake in a casserole on a bed of fresh bay leaves, covered, for 1 hour. Cut potatoes in half and drizzle with more olive oil.

- Coat chunks of Yukon gold potatoes with a paste made from finely chopped fresh rosemary, garlic olive oil (page 228), and kosher salt. Bake for 45 minutes, or until tender.

- Cut waxy potatoes into small cubes. Cover with light cream mixed with grated onion and cook until soft. Add salt and freshly ground white pepper.

- Peel large potatoes. Using a melon baller, scoop balls from potatoes. Cook in boiling salted water for 10 minutes. Drain well. Fry in 1 inch peanut oil until crispy. Sprinkle with finely chopped parsley and salt.

- Fill hot baked potatoes with Roquefort cream made from pureeing cottage cheese with crumbled Roquefort cheese.

For more potato recipes, see pages 17, 19, 40, 73, 77, 81, and 100.

RUTABAGA MASH WITH GLAZED SHALLOTS

I adore rutabagas, a fleshy root vegetable also known as Swedes. They are covered with a thin layer of wax to help preserve them.

2 large rutabagas, about 4 pounds total
12 medium shallots
4 tablespoons unsalted butter

Using a small sharp knife, peel rutabagas. Cut them into quarters with a large knife. Place in a large pot with salted water to cover. Bring to a boil. Lower heat and cook for 40 minutes, or until very soft.

Meanwhile, bring a medium saucepan of water to a boil. Add unpeeled shallots and boil for 5 minutes. Drain in a colander and peel. Heat 3 tablespoons butter in a large nonstick skillet and add shallots. Cook over low heat for 25 to 30 minutes, until shallots are soft, golden, and caramelized. Do not let them get too brown. Add salt and freshly ground black pepper to taste. Keep warm.

Thoroughly drain rutabagas in a colander. Cut into large chunks and, using a potato masher, mash well with remaining butter. Or you can process briefly in a food processor with the butter; the mixture should be rather smooth but still contain some small pieces. Fold in half the shallots and add salt and freshly ground black pepper to taste. Place in a bowl and top with remaining shallots. Serve immediately or reheat gently before serving.

Serves 6

MORE 1•2•3 RUTABAGA IDEAS

- Peel rutabagas and cut into wedges. Toss with olive oil and salt and roast at 400°F for 50 minutes. Sprinkle with crumbled freshly cooked bacon.

- Peel rutabagas and cut into small cubes. Cook in half-and-half just until soft. Top with freshly grated Parmigiano-Reggiano and bake at 400°F for 10 minutes, or until bubbly.

- Cut rutabagas into thin strips and sauté in butter until soft and golden. Sprinkle with fresh thyme leaves and coarsely ground black pepper.

- Peel rutabagas and cut into "French Fries." Toss with vegetable oil and bake at 425°F for 40 minutes, turning often. Sprinkle with malt vinegar and salt.

For one more rutabaga recipe, see page 78.

SNOW PEAS AND BABY CORN

This is an excellent way to add color, crunch, and flavor to almost any simple grilled dish. Roasted peanut oil, available in many supermarkets and health food stores, is less intensely flavored than dark Asian sesame oil but it's far more complex than plain peanut oil.

1½ pounds fresh snow peas
15-ounce can whole sweet baby corn
2 tablespoons roasted peanut oil

Wash snow peas under cold water. Pat dry. Trim ends using a sharp knife and remove strings.

Place corn in a colander and rinse well under cold water. Pat dry. Using a small sharp knife, cut larger corns in half lengthwise.

In a pot fitted with a steamer basket, bring a few inches of water to a boil. Place snow peas and corn in steamer basket. Cover and steam for 8 minutes. Snow peas should be tender but still bright green. Transfer snow peas and corn to a bowl or platter. Add roasted peanut oil and toss with salt and coarsely ground black pepper.

Serves 4

MORE 1·2·3 SNOW PEA IDEAS

- Trim snow peas. Cook lots of chopped shallots in butter until soft. Add snow peas and cook until tender. Season with salt and pepper.

- Julienne snow peas and cook in salted water until just tender. Toss with lemon-scented olive oil (page 228) and sprinkle with toasted sesame seeds.

For one more snow pea recipe, see page 64.

SAUTÉED SPINACH WITH BURNT ALMONDS

2 pounds curly spinach
½ cup sliced almonds with skins
3 tablespoons garlic olive oil (page 228)

Remove any tough stems from spinach and discard. Wash leaves carefully in a colander. Drain but do not pat dry.

In a small nonstick skillet, cook almonds over medium heat, shaking pan back and forth until they begin to darken. Add a large pinch of salt and set aside.

In a large wok or very large nonstick skillet, heat garlic oil. Add spinach with water still clinging to leaves and toss over medium-high heat until it wilts and softens. Do not overcook, as you want spinach to stay bright green. Add salt and freshly ground black pepper to taste. Transfer to a warm platter and scatter toasted almonds on top.

Serves 4

LEMON-KISSED WILTED SPINACH

¼ cup extra-virgin olive oil
2 medium lemons
2 pounds curly spinach

Put olive oil in a small bowl. Grate rind of 1 lemon to get 2 teaspoons zest. Squeeze lemon to get 3 tablespoons lemon juice. Stir zest and juice into oil.

Wash spinach well, discarding any tough stems. Bring 1 inch of salted water to a boil in a large pot. Add spinach, toss, and cook until just wilted. Drain off any liquid. Toss with lemon oil. Add salt and freshly ground black pepper to taste. Remove skin and pith of remaining lemon and slice thinly. Garnish spinach with lemon slices.

Serves 4

"CREAMED" SPINACH

There is no cream at all in this very creamy spinach. Pureed cottage cheese and a bit of butter add the mouthfeel and flavor we all love. Frozen spinach works especially well in this rendition.

2 10-ounce packages frozen leaf spinach
1¼ cups low-fat cottage cheese
2½ tablespoons unsalted butter

In a large saucepan with a cover, bring ½ cup water plus ½ teaspoon salt to a boil. Add frozen spinach and bring to a boil again. Cover and reduce heat to medium-high. Cook for 10 minutes, stirring several times. Drain thoroughly in a colander, making sure to shake out all the water.

Place hot spinach in bowl of a food processor. Add cottage cheese and all but 1 teaspoon butter. Process until very, very smooth. Return to saucepan. Add salt and freshly ground white pepper to taste. Heat gently and transfer to a warm bowl. Place remaining butter on top.

Serves 4

ULTRARICH CREAMED SPINACH

This suave recipe uses cream liberally. Its interesting technique is adapted from Eberhard Muller, one of New York City's great chefs.

2 pounds baby spinach
¾ cup heavy cream
3 large garlic cloves, peeled and smashed

Wash spinach and dry very well. Remove stems.

Put cream and garlic in a small saucepan and bring to a boil. Whisking constantly with a wire whisk, boil for 30 seconds. Transfer cream and garlic mixure to a small bowl. Set aside to steep while you prepare spinach.

Bring a large pot of salted water to a boil. Add spinach and boil for 2 minutes. Drain well and squeeze dry with your hands to remove all moisture. Put dried spinach in bowl of a food processor. Process until a smooth, thick, pastelike puree results.

Transfer spinach to a medium saucepan. Remove garlic from cream and discard. Add cream to spinach and cook over low heat, stirring, until cream is incorporated into spinach and mixture is hot. Add salt and freshly ground black pepper to taste.

Serves 4

MORE 1·2·3 SPINACH IDEAS

- Cook spinach in a hot wok with a little dark Asian sesame oil and grated fresh ginger. Stir until wilted.
- Cut large spinach leaves into long strips (julienne) and cook in butter. Garnish with chopped boiled egg and kosher salt.

- Sauté spinach with chopped anchovies and a little anchovy oil. Add toasted pine nuts or plumped raisins.

  For more spinach recipes, see pages 19 and 95.

SUGAR SNAPS WITH DICED BACON AND RADISHES

The red and white of meticulously cut radishes mimic the tiny crisped cubes of bacon.

> 1 pound sugar snap peas
> 1 large bunch medium to large red radishes, about 4 ounces
> 4-ounce piece of slab bacon

Wash snap peas and dry. Trim ends and remove strings. Set aside.

Wash radishes and dry; remove leaves. Trim ends. Carefully cut radishes into ¼-inch cubes. Set aside.

Cut bacon into ¼-inch cubes to resemble size of radish pieces. Place bacon in a large nonstick skillet. Cook over medium heat until fat is rendered and bacon is cooked, about 5 minutes.

Meanwhile, bring a large pot of salted water to a boil. Add snap peas and diced radishes. Cook for 3 to 4 minutes, until sugar snaps are tender but not soft. Drain in a colander. Pat dry with paper towels.

Immediately add snap peas and radishes to pan with bacon. Heat gently, adding salt and freshly ground black pepper to taste. Serve hot.

Serves 4

SUGAR SNAPS IN CITRUS BUTTER

1¼ pounds sugar snap peas
1 large orange, blood orange, or tangerine
3 tablespoons cold unsalted butter, chilled

Wash snap peas and dry. Trim ends and remove strings. Bring a large pot of salted water to a boil. Add sugar snaps and cook for 3 minutes, or until tender but not too soft. Their color should remain a brilliant green.

Meanwhile, grate rind of orange to get 1 tablespoon zest. Cut orange in half and squeeze to get ⅓ cup juice.

When sugar snaps are done, drain well in a colander and put them back in pot. Add orange zest, orange juice, and the cold butter cut into small pieces. Heat slowly for 1 to 2 minutes, whisking constantly until sauce emulsifies and snap peas are hot. Add salt and freshly ground black pepper to taste.

Serves 4

MORE 1•2•3 SUGAR SNAP IDEAS

- Toss hot cooked sugar snaps with sesame oil and scatter black sesame seeds on top.
- Sauté sugar snaps with strips of julienned bell peppers in unsalted butter until tender. Add salt and pepper to taste.

- Cook blanched sugar snaps in a little sauce made from reduced cream and a touch of honey mustard until tender.

DRY-CURRY SWEET POTATOES

This is a recipe from my sister-in-law, Gail, who is a great cook and a great host.

1½ pounds medium-large sweet potatoes
2 tablespoons good-quality curry powder
2 tablespoons olive oil

Preheat oven to 375°F.

Peel sweet potatoes. Cut into 1-inch chunks and place them in a shallow medium casserole. Sprinkle with curry powder and 1 teaspoon salt, then drizzle with olive oil. Toss well.

Bake for 45 minutes, turning potatoes once or twice so they brown evenly and don't stick. Serve immediately.

Serves 4

ROASTED SWEET POTATOES AND SHIITAKES

3 or 4 large sweet potatoes, approximately 2½ pounds
8 ounces shiitake mushrooms
3 tablespoons or more olive oil, garlic oil, or lemon oil (page 228)

Preheat oven to 400°F.

Peel sweet potatoes. Cut into ¾-inch cubes and set aside.

Trim bottom half of shiitake stems and discard, leaving caps and upper half of stems attached. Wipe mushrooms clean with a damp cloth.

Place sweet potatoes and shiitakes on a rimmed baking sheet. Toss with 2 tablespoons oil and 2 tablespoons water. Sprinkle lightly with salt. Bake for 1 hour, turning several times with a spatula. Sweet potatoes should be tender and lightly browned. Add a little water or more olive oil during baking if sweet potatoes begin to stick.

Transfer sweet potatoes and shiitakes to a warm platter. Or, if serving later, leave on baking sheet and reheat in a 475°F oven for 5 or 6 minutes. Drizzle with remaining olive oil and season with salt and freshly ground black pepper.

Serves 6

SWEET POTATO-CHEDDAR GRATIN

This looks a lot like a big birthday cake. It is even better when reheated the second day.

4 very large sweet potatoes, about 3½ pounds
12 ounces sharp white cheddar cheese
1 cup sour cream

Preheat oven to 350°F.

Bring a large pot of salted water to a boil. Add unpeeled sweet potatoes and boil for 15 to 20 minutes, until you can pierce them easily with a fork. Do not let them get too soft. Drain in a colander under cold running water and peel. Cut into ⅓-inch-thick slices and pat them dry with paper towels.

Grate cheese on the large holes of a box grater (you should get about 4 cups). Set aside. Line bottom of a 9-inch springform pan with a round of waxed paper or aluminum foil. Sprinkle ½ cup cheese on bottom. Add a layer of sweet potato slices, overlapping slightly, until bottom is covered. Spread ⅓ cup sour cream over potatoes. Sprinkle with salt and freshly ground white pepper, and cover with a third of the remaining cheese. Repeat process twice, ending with a layer of cheese. Press down on mixture with a spatula.

Place springform pan on a baking sheet. Bake for 40 minutes, until golden brown. Press down with a spatula once or twice during baking. Let rest for 10 minutes before serving. Much of the liquid will be reabsorbed. Loosen edges of gratin with a knife. Remove from pan and cut into wedges.

Serves 8 or more

MORE 1·2·3 SWEET POTATO IDEAS

- Slow-roast sweet potatoes at 250°F for 3 hours. Split them open. Top with salted whipped butter, maple syrup, and cracked black pepper.

- Mash cooked sweet potatoes with pineapple juice that has been reduced by half and a little hot bacon fat. Scatter with crisp crumbled bacon.

- Blanch julienned strips of sweet potatoes, then stir-fry them in roasted peanut oil with chopped scallions.

- Using a melon baller, scoop out balls from large sweet potatoes. Bake at 375°F in a foil pouch with bits of unsalted butter, fresh thyme, salt, and pepper for about 45 minutes, or until tender.

For more sweet potato recipes, see pages 19, 78, and 320.

ALMOND-CRUSTED BAKED TOMATOES

6 medium-large ripe tomatoes
½ cup sliced almonds with skins
¾ cup freshly grated Parmigiano-Reggiano

Preheat oven to 425°F.

Wash tomatoes and dry thoroughly. Cut stem ends off tomatoes and scoop out ½ inch tomato flesh. Salt insides of tomatoes and turn them upside down on paper towels to drain.

Place almonds in a small nonstick skillet and toast over medium heat, tossing occasionally, until golden. Let cool for 5 minutes. Place cooled almonds in bowl of a food processor and process until finely ground. Add cheese and freshly ground black pepper, and pulse to combine.

Fill tomato cavities with almond-cheese mixture, mounding it on top. Place tomatoes on a rimmed baking sheet with a few tablespoons water. Bake for 10 to 15 minutes, or until tomatoes are soft and stuffing is crusty on top.

Serves 6

FRIED RED TOMATOES

This couldn't be easier: the moisture from thick slices of tomatoes eliminates the need for egg or milk to make the cornmeal stick. Needless to say, green tomatoes may be substituted.

4 firm ripe medium tomatoes
1 cup stone-ground yellow cornmeal
Corn oil for frying

Wash tomatoes and dry thoroughly. Slice off top and bottom ends of tomatoes. Cut each tomato into 3 thick slices.

Place cornmeal on a flat plate. Dredge both sides of each tomato slice in cornmeal. Make sure tops and bottoms of slices are thickly coated; edges will not get coated.

Heat ¼ inch corn oil in a large nonstick skillet, then add tomatoes in 1 layer. Cook over medium heat for 2 minutes on each side, until tomatoes are crisp and golden brown. Do not overcook; you want tomato slices to retain their shape.

Sprinkle generously with salt and freshly ground black pepper. Serve immediately.

Serves 4

SHORT-STACK TOMATOES AND ONIONS

If desired, you may use an herb-scented or flavored olive oil (basil, hot pepper, or rosemary).

4 medium-large ripe tomatoes, about 1½ pounds
2 large red onions
¼ cup extra-virgin olive oil, plus more for drizzling

Preheat oven to 400°F.

Wash tomatoes and dry thoroughly. Using a sharp knife, cut a ¼-inch slice off top and bottom of each tomato. Slice each tomato into 3 thick slices. Reassemble each of them to look like a whole tomato.

Peel onions and slice into 8 ¼-inch slices and 4 thinner slices. Layer thicker onion slices in between tomato slices, ending with a thin slice of onion on top of each tomato stack. Drizzle 1 tablespoon olive oil over each stack and sprinkle with salt and freshly ground black pepper. Place a short skewer in center of each stack to help hold them together.

Carefully place in a rimmed baking sheet and bake for 1¼ hours. Baste with pan juices twice during baking, making sure tomatoes hold their shape. Remove from oven and let rest for 15 minutes. The bottoms of the tomatoes will be soft, so transfer carefully with a spatula to serving plates. Spoon pan juices over tomatoes and serve. Drizzle with additional olive oil, if desired.

Serves 4

SLOW-ROASTED PLUM TOMATOES

You may also use a variety of small heirloom tomatoes. Delicious in a salad, or on a sandwich, atop grilled fish, or as a vegetable accompaniment.

> 12 large plum tomatoes
> ¼ cup extra-virgin olive oil, plus more for drizzling
> 4 large garlic cloves

Preheat oven to 250°F.

Wash tomatoes and dry thoroughly. Cut in half lengthwise. Line a rimmed baking sheet with parchment paper. Place tomatoes, cut side up, in a single layer.

Place olive oil in a small skillet and add garlic that has been finely chopped. Cook garlic for 1 minute, being careful not to let it brown. Drizzle oil and garlic over tomatoes. Bake for 2½ to 3 hours. The tomatoes should retain their shape. Drizzle with a little more oil, if desired, and sprinkle with salt and freshly ground black pepper.

Makes 24 pieces

MORE 1•2•3 TOMATO IDEAS

- Mix toasted breadcrumbs with a bit of pesto and pack onto halved tomatoes. Bake until soft, then broil for 30 seconds.

- Cut a selection of heirloom tomatoes in half. Place on a bed of fresh thyme or rosemary and drizzle with olive oil. Bake at 275°F for 3 hours, turning once. Add kosher salt.

- Cut plum tomatoes in half and discard insides. Place a fresh basil leaf in tomato shell and fill with a large chunk of fresh mozzarella. Bake at 450°F for 10 minutes, or until bubbly.

For more tomato recipes, see pages 25, 71, 74, 78, 90, 93, 98, 170, 205, and 235.

TURNIP AND HAVARTI TORTE

Similar in structure to the Sweet Potato–Cheddar Gratin (page 58), this torte has a more mysterious nature. If you're lucky enough to have turnip leaves attached to your turnips, you can simply steam them, then toss with a little more butter and serve alongside the torte.

> 2½ to 3 pounds very large white turnips
> 3 tablespoons unsalted butter
> 1 pound caraway Havarti cheese, sliced very thin

Trim turnips and wash well. Place them, unpeeled, in a large pot of salted water. Bring to a boil and cook for 30 minutes over high heat, or until just tender but not very soft. Drain, cool, peel, and cut into ¼-inch thick slices. Pat slices dry with paper towels.

Preheat oven to 375°F.

Spread butter on bottom and sides of a 9-inch springform pan. Arrange a layer of cheese slices on bottom of pan using one quarter of the cheese. Add a layer of turnip slices (overlapping slightly) and sprinkle very lightly with salt and freshly ground black pepper. Repeat procedure twice, beginning and ending with a layer of cheese.

Place springform pan on a baking sheet. Bake for 40 minutes. The cheese should be golden brown. Let cool slightly before serving. Remove from pan and cut into wedges. Can be made a day ahead and reheated.

Serves 8 or more

ROSEMARY-ROASTED TURNIPS

6 medium turnips, about 2 pounds total
1 small bunch fresh rosemary
3 or more tablespoons extra-virgin olive oil

Preheat oven to 375°F.

Peel turnips and cut each into 6 or 8 wedges. Set aside. Finely chop enough rosemary needles to get 3 heaping tablespoons. Reserve the rest. Using a mortar and pestle or a blender, make a paste of the rosemary, 3 tablespoons olive oil, and 1½ teaspoons kosher salt.

Place rosemary mixture in a large bowl and add turnips. Toss to coat, adding a little more olive oil if necessary. Season with a grinding of black pepper. Place seasoned turnips in a shallow roasting pan or on a rimmed baking sheet. Bake for 40 to 45 minutes, or until tender, frequently turning so that both sides get browned.

Remove from oven and transfer to a warm platter. Sprinkle with additional finely chopped rosemary.

Serves 4

MORE 1·2·3 TURNIP IDEAS

- Boil turnip greens in a pot of salted water for 2 minutes and add small peeled turnips. Cook for 10 minutes, or until tender. Sauté in olive oil and sprinkle with toasted pecans.

- Cook small peeled turnips in chicken stock until they're tender and most of stock has evaporated to create a glaze. Set turnips aside, add a little white wine or sherry, and cook sauce until syrupy. Pour over turnips.

- Mash hot boiled turnips with lots of diced red onions that have been caramelized in butter until deeply browned.

For more turnip recipes, see pages 17 and 73.

WATERCRESS SAUTÉ WITH GARLIC CHIPS

This is easily adapted to a variety of leafy greens. It's delicious made with mesclun.

4 large bunches watercress
4 large cloves garlic
3 tablespoons extra-virgin olive oil

Wash watercress and dry thoroughly. Cut away most of the stems and discard.

Peel garlic cloves and cut lengthwise into very thin slices.

Heat olive oil in a large nonstick skillet until very hot. Add sliced garlic and remove pan immediately from heat. The garlic will get crispy and brown, but removing pan from stovetop will prevent garlic from burning. Add watercress to pan. Cook over high heat for 1 minute, stirring constantly with a wooden spoon until watercress just begins to wilt. Sprinkle with salt and serve immediately.

Serves 4

MORE 1•2•3 WATERCRESS IDEAS

• Chop watercress leaves and boil for 1 minute. Mash with steamy boiled potatoes and lots of butter to make whipped potatoes with lots of flavor. Add salt and pepper, of course.

• Stir-fry some watercress in a little dark Asian sesame oil and soy sauce.

For more watercress recipes, see pages 91 and 126.

SLOW-COOKED ZUCCHINI WITH THYME

6 small zucchini, about 1½ pounds total
¼ cup extra-virgin olive oil
1 large bunch fresh thyme

Wash zucchini well and pat dry with paper towels. Cut into ¼-inch-thick rounds.

Put 2 tablespoons olive oil in each of 2 large nonstick skillets. Place zucchini in pans in 1 layer. Cook slowly over low heat on 1 side for 10 minutes until zucchini are golden. Carefully turn over and cook for 10 minutes on the other side.

To each pan, add ¼ cup boiling water and a large pinch of salt. Simmer slowly for 5 to 10 minutes, or until all the water has evaporated and zucchini are soft but still hold their shape. Transfer zucchini to a platter.

Add 3 tablespoons thyme leaves to one of the pans, along with the oil remaining in the other pan. Fry thyme leaves for 1 minute, until they begin to crisp. Scatter over zucchini and garnish with sprigs of fresh thyme. Add freshly ground black pepper.

Serves 4

SHREDDED ZUCCHINI WITH BASIL

It is unusual to shred zucchini, but the result is a clean, herbal taste and unexpected texture. Also nice with a combination of yellow and green squash.

3 medium zucchini, about 1 pound
1 bunch fresh basil
1 tablespoon unsalted butter

Wash zucchini and dry well. Grate on the large holes of a box grater. Let sit in a colander to drain.

Meanwhile, wash basil and dry. Chop enough to pack ⅓ cup, reserving the rest. Place drained zucchini in a bowl with chopped basil and a large pinch of salt and freshly ground black pepper.

In a large nonstick skillet, melt butter. Add zucchini mixture. Cook over medium heat for 10 minutes, stirring often, until zucchini is soft and golden. Garnish with small basil leaves.

Serves 2

SPRING VEGETABLES À LA VAPEUR

The zucchini is used as one member of the vegetable trilogy and also is pureed into a delectable jade-green sauce. This is fat-free and very satisfying.

3 medium zucchini, about 1 pound
¾ pound fresh snow peas
¾ pound fresh green beans

Wash zucchini and dry. Cut 2 zucchini into ⅓-inch cubes. (The best way to do this is to cut the zucchini lengthwise into 3 slices, then cut each of these slices into 3 lengthwise pieces, then cut crosswise into small cubes.) Set aside.

Cut remaining zucchini into 1-inch pieces and place these in a small saucepan. Add water just to cover and ¼ teaspoon salt. Bring to a boil. Lower heat and cook for 15 minutes, until zucchini is very soft. Using a slotted spoon, transfer cooked zucchini to bowl of a food processor, reserving some of the cooking water. Process until very smooth and creamy, adding enough cooking water to make a thick sauce. You should get about ⅔ cup puree. Set aside.

Trim snow peas, removing strings. Trim ends of green beans and cut in half lengthwise.

Bring a large pot of water fitted with a steamer basket to a boil. Place snow peas and green beans in basket. Place reserved zucchini cubes on top. Cover and steam for 7 minutes.

Lightly salt vegetables and transfer to a platter. Heat zucchini sauce, adding salt and freshly ground black pepper to taste, and pour over vegetables.

Serves 6

FRIED ZUCCHINI AND LEMON SALAD

This is one of my favorite inventions—especially the fried lemon part. Hot, warm, or room temperature, it adds syncopated bursts of flavor to almost any main course.

4 or 5 medium zucchini, about 1½ pounds
⅓ cup or more extra-virgin olive oil
2 thin-skinned lemons

Wash zucchini and pat dry. Cut on the bias, into about ⅓-inch-thick slices. Pour ¼ inch olive oil into a medium nonstick skillet. Fry small batches of zucchini in hot shallow oil, turning once, until each side is dark golden brown. Drain on paper towels and set aside in a bowl.

Slice lemons very thin, about ⅛-inch. Add them to the hot oil and fry, turning once, for about 2 minutes. The lemons should brown and the oil thicken into a delicious sauce. Add cooked lemons and a little of the oil from pan to zucchini. (If oil gets too dark, do not add it to the zucchini. Add a drizzle of uncooked olive oil and a squeeze of lemon juice instead.) Sprinkle with salt and freshly ground black pepper.

Serves 4

MORE 1•2•3 ZUCCHINI IDEAS

- Cut small zucchini into ½-inch-thick rounds. Cook with canned crushed tomatoes in puree and a handful of pitted oil-cured olives. Cook until zucchini is tender.

- Cut zucchini in half lengthwise. Drizzle with olive oil and salt, and roast until tender. Sprinkle heavily with freshly grated Pecorino Romano cheese and a little more oil. Broil briefly.

- Cut zucchini on the bias into ¼-inch-thick ovals. Cook in lemon olive oil until soft. Add crumbled feta cheese and cracked pepper.

- Cut zucchini in half across the width and then across the length. Marinate in a mixture of fresh lime juice, grated lime zest, and peanut oil. Grill on both sides until zucchini is soft with dark brown patches.

- Slice zucchini into very thin rounds. Dredge with flour. Heat grapeseed oil to 360°F. Fry until golden brown. Sprinkle with salt.

- Steam thin strips of zucchini until just tender. Toss with pesto and a little lemon juice and zest.

For more zucchini recipes, see pages 70, 119, and 195.

soups and simple breads

Soup is gastronomy's kindest course.

It wafts hospitality and resurrects long-lost memories; it mitigates colds and uplifts spirits; it stimulates or satisfies appetites, depending upon the body's needs; and it resonates with affection. Soups also can be an exercise in culinary balance—attention-getting, but not so aggressive as to dull the taste buds or fill you up. The following soups come in a rainbow of colors and textures, and all are suave and refined. They are all generally meant to begin a meal.

Despite hundreds of years of culinary tradition, I've found that using water rather than stock can enhance the elemental flavors of soup's pristine ingredients—primarily fresh vegetables, but also chicken and shellfish. These tastes are augmented by an herb, a cooking technique, or the secondary use of a particular ingredient. For example, my creamy broccoli soup (which uses no cream) benefits from fragrant basil in two ways: the basil flavors the cooking liquid—water—and it becomes the basis of a compound butter that floats atop the soup. My corn soup uses the fresh kernels but also gets its flavor from extracting corn "milk" from the cobs. In Shrimp and White

Beans *en Brodo*, shrimp shells impart their salty essence and make a complex background for whole shrimp and beans, all bound with a bit of pesto.

My simple soups exaggerate the essence of their components by slow-roasting or long, gentle simmering. Sometimes the third ingredient is the surprise—whether it's dark Asian sesame oil to integrate the unexpected flavors of tomato and cantaloupe or a bit of scotch to add a sweet and smoky note to a creamy parsnip soup.

Soup speaks to the seasons, and so I offer several options meant to be served icy cold, and a slew of hot soups, potages, and bisques, featuring flavors that are released by warmth.

Many of these soups can be made in advance. In fact, in some cases, they benefit from time, which allows their flavors to coalesce and their textures to deepen.

If you double the portions and add a simple bread, even refined soups can become meals in themselves. Of course, you can buy a crusty baguette, a wholesome loaf of whole grain bread, or even add a favorite cracker; but it's a generous host who creates homemade breads that fill the kitchen with enticing aromas. You'll find ten examples herein.

ZUCCHINI BISQUE WITH SNOW CRAB

Threads of rosy-tipped snow crabmeat look pretty atop this jade green soup, but you may want to splurge on jumbo lump crabmeat. This also is delicious hot.

> 1½ pounds medium zucchini
> 1 small bunch fresh dill
> ½ pound snow crabmeat

Wash zucchini thoroughly. Trim ends and cut zucchini into ½-inch-thick slices. Place in a large saucepan.

Wash dill and chop finely to yield ¼ cup, reserving remaining sprigs. Add to pot with half the crabmeat and any accumulated juices. Add 1¼ cups water and 1 teaspoon kosher salt. Water will not completely cover zucchini.

Bring to a rapid boil. Lower heat to medium and cover pan. Cook for 20 minutes, or until zucchini is very soft. Let cool for 5 minutes. Transfer contents to a blender. Process for several minutes until very smooth. Mixture should thicken and become foamy. Add salt and freshly ground black pepper to taste and refrigerate, covered, for several hours or until very cold.

Serve soup in chilled soup bowls with a mound of remaining crabmeat in center of each serving. Garnish with reserved fresh dill sprigs.

Serves 4

ROASTED BEET-ORANGE SOUP WITH CRÈME FRAÎCHE

Roasting beets intensifies their sweet flavor.

> 1 pound large beets, weighed without greens
> 4 medium oranges
> 8 ounces crème fraîche, about 1 cup

Preheat oven to 400°F.

Peel beets with a vegetable peeler. Loosely wrap beets in an aluminum foil pouch and tightly seal at the top. Place in a pie tin or on a rimmed baking sheet and bake for 1½ hours, or until a knife easily pierces beets.

Grate rind of enough oranges to yield 1½ tablespoons zest. Cut oranges in half and squeeze to get 1 cup juice. Set aside.

Remove beets from oven. Carefully open package to allow steam to escape. Cut beets into large chunks and place in bowl of a food processor. If there is any cooking liquid from beets in foil package, add that as well. Process, gradually adding all of the orange juice, then ½ cup crème fraîche. Continue processing until very, very smooth. This may take a few minutes.

Transfer soup to a bowl. Add 1 tablespoon reserved zest. Season with salt and freshly ground black pepper to taste, and add more orange juice or crème fraîche to balance flavors. Cover and chill soup for several hours, or until very cold.

Serve in chilled soup cups or bowls. Top with a dollop of crème fraîche. Add remaining zest or a tiny slice of orange and coarsely ground black pepper.

Serves 4

CAULIFLOWER VICHYSSOISE WITH CHIVES

This is the most suave cold soup imaginable. In late spring, you can get chives with their flowers attached for a lovely garnish.

> 2½ pounds cauliflower, 1 very large head or 2 small
> 2 bunches fresh chives, with chive flowers if available
> 1 cup light cream, plus more for thinning

Trim base of cauliflower, removing stems and any dark spots. Break into small florets.

Place in a medium pot with a cover. Add 5 cups water and ½ teaspoon salt. (Water may not cover cauliflower.) Cut enough chives into ½-inch lengths to get a scant ½ cup and add to pot with cauliflower. Reserve the rest of the chives.

Bring the soup to a boil, then lower heat. Cover pot and cook for 25 minutes, or until cauliflower is very soft. Transfer vegetables and cooking water to bowl of a food processor. (You will need to work in two batches.) Process until ultra-smooth, gradually adding light cream. Transfer to a bowl. Add salt and freshly ground white pepper to taste. Let cool. Cover and refrigerate for several hours or until very cold.

When ready to serve, taste soup, adjusting salt and pepper, and adding a little more cream if soup is too thick. Ladle into chilled bowls. Finely mince remaining chives and sprinkle liberally on top. Break apart chive flowers, if you have them, and scatter a few petals on top.

Serves 6

ICED TOMATO-CANTALOUPE SOUP

If you can't find very ripe, dark red cherry tomatoes and a very sweet cantaloupe, make this soup another day. Eat a cherry tomato and then pop a piece of melon in your mouth; you'll know immediately. Both purees are poured into the bowl at the same time, swirling their vibrant colors together.

> 2 pints very ripe, dark red cherry tomatoes
> 1½-pound very sweet cantaloupe
> 4 teaspoons dark Asian sesame oil

Remove stems from tomatoes. Wash tomatoes and dry well. Place them in a blender with ¼ cup water and a large pinch of kosher salt. Process on high until very, very smooth.

Add salt and freshly ground black pepper to taste, and pour into a small pitcher or large measuring glass with a spout. Cover and refrigerate until very cold.

Remove rind and seeds from melon. Cut melon into small chunks to get 1 pound. Place in a blender with ¼ cup water and process on high until very, very smooth. Transfer to another small pitcher or large measuring glass with a spout. Cover and refrigerate until very cold, 2 to 3 hours.

When ready to serve, pour both soups into chilled soup bowl at the same time. The colors will meet in the center and swirl around a bit. (Or you can pour the soups ahead of time and keep them in the refrigerator until very cold.) Just before serving, drizzle each portion with ½ to 1 teaspoon sesame oil.

Serves 4

CUCUMBER-YOGURT FRAPPE

This is equally refreshing made with spearmint instead of cilantro.

> 1½ pounds cucumbers
> 1 bunch fresh cilantro
> 2 cups plain yogurt

Peel cucumbers. Cut in half lengthwise and use a small spoon to scoop out seeds. Cut cucumbers into ½-inch chunks. Finely chop cilantro.

Working in two batches, put cucumbers, all but ¼ cup yogurt, and 6 tablespoons cilantro in a blender. Process until very, very smooth. Add kosher salt and freshly ground black pepper to taste.

Cover and refrigerate for several hours; the colder the better. The soup will thicken a bit. Serve with a dollop of remaining yogurt and garnish with chopped cilantro and coarsely ground black pepper.

Serves 4

HOT SOUPS

BROCCOLI SOUP WITH SWEET BASIL BUTTER

Basil is used in two ways for this voluptuous soup: as a flavoring agent for the broth, and in a stylish compound butter that floats on top.

> 1 large head broccoli, about 1½ pounds
> 1 large bunch fresh basil
> 4 tablespoons unsalted butter, chilled

Peel broccoli stalks with a vegetable peeler, removing all the tough exterior. Cut off woody bottoms and discard. Cut stalks and florets into ½-inch pieces. Place in a medium pot with a cover.

Wash basil and pat dry. Remove leaves, reserving the smallest ones for garnish. Add ½ cup tightly packed basil leaves to broccoli. Cover with 5 cups cold water and ½ teaspoon salt. Bring to a boil. Lower heat to medium, cover pot, and cook for 20 minutes, or until tender.

Meanwhile, place butter and ¼ cup tightly packed basil leaves in bowl of food processor. Add a large pinch of salt and process until just combined. Place basil butter on a piece of wax paper and roll to make a log, about ½ inch in diameter. Refrigerate until firm.

When broccoli is tender, transfer to a blender using a slotted spoon. Reserve 2 cups of the cooking water and add the rest to the broccoli. Blend until very smooth, about 2 minutes, adding 2 tablespoons of the basil butter in small bits as you process. (You may need to do this in several batches.) When puree is very smooth, return it to pot. Add salt and freshly ground black pepper to taste. Add some additional cooking water if soup is too thick.

Heat gently. Ladle hot soup into soup cups or bowls. Place a thin slice of basil butter on top and garnish with small basil leaves.

Serves 6

TURNIP AND POTATO SOUP WITH PANCETTA CROUTONS

  4 medium-large white turnips, about 1½ pounds
  2 large waxy white potatoes, about ¾ pound
  6-ounce piece pancetta

Peel turnips and potatoes. Cut into large pieces and put in a large saucepan. Add 4 cups cold water, or enough to just cover vegetables. Add a 2-ounce piece of pancetta and 1 teaspoon salt. Bring to a boil. Lower heat to medium and cook, with cover askew, for 40 minutes, until potatoes and turnips are very soft. Remove pancetta and set aside.

Place vegetables and cooking water in bowl of a food processor. (You may need to do this in 2 batches.) Process until very smooth and return to saucepan. Set aside.

Cut cooked pancetta and remaining raw pancetta into ¼-inch cubes. Place in a small nonstick skillet and cook slowly over low heat until pancetta is crisp and fat is rendered, about 15 minutes.

Add 2 tablespoons pancetta drippings (or more to taste) to soup. Reheat gently, adding salt and freshly ground black pepper to taste. Ladle into soup bowls and garnish with crisped pancetta.

Serves 4 or more

ROASTED TOMATO AND ONION SOUP

The intensity of flavor comes from slow-roasting the vegetables for three hours.

> 4 large ripe tomatoes, about 2 pounds
> 8 medium onions, about 2 pounds
> 3 tablespoons extra-virgin olive oil, plus more for drizzling

Preheat oven to 250°F.

Bring a medium pot of water to a boil. Make a small *x* in bottom of each tomato using a small sharp knife. Plunge tomatoes in water for 1 minute. Drain in a colander and peel. Cut tomatoes in half and place, cut side down, on a large rimmed baking sheet.

Place whole unpeeled onions on baking sheet. Drizzle 1 tablespoon olive oil over tomatoes and onions, using your hands to coat them well. Sprinkle tomatoes with salt.

Roast for 3 hours.

Remove from oven and slip onions from skins. Place tomatoes and 6 peeled onions in bowl of a food processor. Process until very smooth. Add ½ to ⅔ cup water and 2 tablespoons olive oil and process again.

Transfer soup to a large saucepan and bring to a boil. Add salt and freshly ground black pepper to taste. Ladle hot soup into soup bowls. Peel and cut remaining roasted onions in half lengthwise and place 1 half in center of each serving. Drizzle with more olive oil.

Serves 4

BRIE AND PEAR SOUP

> 3 large ripe pears, preferably red-skinned
> 2 cups chicken broth
> 8 ounces double-cream Brie cheese

Cut pears in half and reserve 1 piece. Peel the rest of the pears and cut them into thick slices, removing the seeds. Put broth and pear slices in a large saucepan and simmer for 15 minutes, or until pears are very soft.

Transfer pears and broth to a food processor and process until very, very smooth.

Return soup to pot and simmer.

Trim rind from Brie and cut cheese into small pieces. Slowly add cheese to soup, stirring with a wooden spoon until cheese melts and soup is smooth and creamy. Add salt and freshly ground white pepper to taste. Garnish with slivers of remaining pear half.

Serves 4

FRESH CORN SOUP WITH SCALLION BUTTER

6 large ears yellow corn
2 large bunches scallions
5 tablespoons unsalted butter, softened

Using a sharp knife, cut corn kernels from cob; you should have about 5 cups.

Cut white parts from scallions and finely chop them to get ⅔ cup. Set aside. Finely chop enough of the green parts to get 2 tablespoons. Reserve remaining scallion greens.

Place 3 tablespoons butter on a cutting board. Work green part of scallions into butter. Place on waxed paper and roll into a small log, about 1 inch in diameter. Refrigerate until firm.

Meanwhile, melt remaining butter in a medium pot with a cover. Do not let brown. Add ⅔ cup chopped scallions and ½ cup water. Cover and simmer for 10 minutes. Add corn, 5 cups water, 2 teaspoons salt, and ¼ teaspoon freshly ground white pepper. Bring to a boil, lower heat, and simmer, covered, for 10 minutes, or until corn is tender.

Transfer contents in small batches to a blender or food processor. Puree for several minutes, until very smooth. Strain through a coarse-mesh sieve, pressing hard on the solids. Discard solids.

Reheat soup and add salt and white pepper to taste. Ladle soup into bowls and top with a thin slice of scallion butter. Chop remaining scallion greens and scatter on soup.

Serves 4

SHRIMP AND WHITE BEANS *EN BRODO*

This has all the virtues of a chunky chowder without any cream. It also has the allure of a great shrimp dish, with the intoxicating fragrance of basil.

1 heaping cup small white beans, about 6 ounces
¾ cup good-quality prepared pesto
1½ pounds uncooked medium shrimp, shell on

Soak beans for 12 hours or overnight in water to cover. Drain beans and put in a small pot with a cover. Add water to cover by 1 inch. Add 3 tablespoons pesto and bring to a boil. Cover pot and lower heat. Simmer beans for about 1 hour and 15 minutes, or until just tender.

Meanwhile, remove shells and tails from shrimp. Set aside shrimp and put shells and tails in a large saucepan with 6 cups water and ¾ teaspoon salt. Bring to a boil, then lower heat and simmer for 25 minutes. Strain shrimp broth through a fine-mesh sieve into a clean pot. Discard shells.

Add raw shrimp and remaining pesto to strained broth. Cook over low heat for 3 minutes, or until shrimp just become opaque. Add salt and freshly ground black pepper to taste.

Drain beans and add to soup. Reheat soup before serving and ladle into bowls.

Serves 6

SWEET GARLIC-FENNEL BISQUE

As rich and satisfying as oyster bisque, but perfect for vegetarians.

    3 large heads garlic, about 4 ounces
    2 cups heavy cream
    2 large fennel bulbs, about 1 pound each

Peel garlic and place in a medium pot with a cover. Add cream and bring just to a boil. Lower heat, cover, and simmer for 40 minutes, or until garlic is very soft.

Meanwhile, remove fronds from fennel, wrap in wet paper towels, and refrigerate.

Cut fennel bulbs into ½-inch pieces, removing any brown spots. Place in a colander, wash well, and drain.

After 40 minutes, add fennel and 3 cups water to hot garlic cream. Bring just to a boil, then lower heat. Cover and simmer for 40 minutes, or until fennel is very soft.

Transfer contents to a blender or bowl of a food processor. Puree in several batches until very, very smooth. Return to pot, and add 1 teaspoon salt and finely ground white pepper to taste. Reheat for several minutes, until soup thickens a bit.

Finely chop reserved fennel fronds and scatter on soup before serving.

Serves 6

CHICKEN CONSOMMÉ WITH SHERRY

    4 pounds chicken wings
    4 scallions
    2 tablespoons dry sherry, or more to taste

Cut wings in half through the large joint. Place in a large pot with water to cover. Add ½ teaspoon salt, ½ teaspoon black peppercorns, and 3 thinly sliced scallions, using both white and green parts. Bring to a boil, then reduce heat to medium. Cover pot and cook for 1½ hours.

Strain soup through a fine-mesh sieve into a clean pot. Save chicken wings. Continue to cook soup over low heat until reduced to 4 cups. Using a large spoon, remove as much visible fat as possible. Thinly slice remaining scallion on the bias and add it, along with sherry. Cook 5 minutes more.

Remove as much of the meat as possible from chicken wings. Place chicken meat in bottom of soup plates. Ladle hot soup over chicken.

Serves 4

CARROT-GINGER VELVET

You'll be amazed how easy it is to extract the fresh ginger juice needed in this recipe. Peel the ginger, then grate it on the large holes of a box grater. Place the grated ginger in a paper towel and squeeze hard. That's it!

1½ pounds carrots, plus more for garnish if desired
5-inch piece fresh ginger
½ cup heavy cream, plus more for garnish if desired

Trim carrots, and peel them. Cut them into 1-inch pieces. Put carrots in a medium pot with 4 cups water and 1½ teaspoons salt. Bring to a boil, lower heat, and cook, uncovered, for 35 minutes, or until carrots are very soft.

Meanwhile, peel ginger and grate it on the large holes of a box grater. Place ginger in a paper towel and squeeze hard to extract juice into a small bowl. You should have about 1 tablespoon.

Transfer carrots to bowl of a food processor and puree until very smooth, slowly adding all the cooking water. Add ginger juice and heavy cream, and process to incorporate.

Return soup to the medium pot and add salt and freshly ground black pepper to taste. Reheat before serving. If you want, whip a little extra heavy cream and put a dollop on top, or cook paper-thin slices of additional carrot and scatter on each serving.

Serves 4

POTAGE PARMENTIER

In my version of this typical French soup made with leeks and ordinary white potatoes, I use Yukon golds for deeper color and flavor. I also add bright green swirls of leek puree.

2 pounds Yukon gold potatoes
2 large leeks, about 1¼ pounds
1 cup crème fraîche

Peel potatoes and cut them into large chunks. Remove roots from leeks and discard. Trim dark green part of leeks and set aside. Chop white and lighter green parts, then rinse thoroughly.

Place potatoes and chopped leeks in a medium pot with 5 cups water and 1 teaspoon salt. Bring to a rapid boil. Lower heat and cover pot. Simmer until vegetables are very soft, about 40 minutes.

Puree soup in bowl of a food processor in several batches. Process until very, very smooth. Return soup to pot and whisk in crème fraîche. Add salt and freshly ground white pepper to taste.

Coarsely chop dark green part of leeks to get 2 packed cups. Put in a small saucepan with 1 cup water and a pinch of salt. Bring to a boil. Lower heat, cover, and cook for 10 minutes. Puree contents in bowl of a food processor until very smooth. Reheat soup and ladle into bowls. Using a small spoon, drizzle swirls of dark leek puree on soup.

Serves 6

AUTUMN SOUP WITH CRISPY BACON

Based on two root vegetables, this soup tastes sophisticated nonetheless.

1½ pounds sweet potatoes
1 large rutabaga, about 1½ pounds
6 slices bacon

Peel sweet potatoes with a vegetable peeler. Cut them in half lengthwise, and then cut them cross-wise to make ½-inch slices. Peel rutabaga with a small sharp knife and cut into ½-inch pieces.

Cut 3 slices of bacon into small pieces and place in a medium pot with a cover. Heat gently for a few minutes, until fat is rendered, making sure bacon does not crisp. Add sweet potatoes and rutabagas. Using a large spoon, toss vegetables to coat with bacon fat. Cook over medium heat for 2 minutes.

Add 5 cups water, 1 teaspoon salt, and 12 black peppercorns. Bring to a boil. Lower heat to medium and cover pot. Cook for 45 minutes, or until vegetables are very soft.

Meanwhile, in a nonstick skillet, cook remaining bacon on both sides until just crisp, then place on paper towels to drain.

Working in 2 batches, transfer vegetables and cooking liquid to bowl of a food processor. Process until very, very smooth. Return to pot. Add salt to taste and gently reheat. Ladle soup into bowls and crumble crisp bacon on top.

Serves 6

DEBORAH MADISON'S SUMMER TOMATO SOUP

When Deborah, celebrated cookbook author and vegetarian chef, created this recipe, I'm sure she didn't have 1-2-3 in mind. She merely used three ingredients to express her idea of summer.

3 tablespoons unsalted butter
1 cup finely diced shallots
5 pounds very ripe red juicy tomatoes

Melt butter in a wide soup pot over low heat. Add shallots and let them cook for about 10 minutes while you prepare the tomatoes.

Wash tomatoes and dry them. Remove core and cut into large pieces. Add tomatoes to pot with 1 teaspoon salt and ½ cup water. Cover and cook over low heat for 3 to 4 hours. Stir frequently, making sure tomatoes don't stick to the bottom of pot. Pass the soup, ladle by ladle, through a food mill into a clean pot.

Add salt and freshly ground black pepper to taste. For a little old-fashioned comfort, serve soup piping hot, in mugs or soup bowls with a small pat of additional butter on top.

Serves 4 or more

MUSSEL BISQUE

An unorthodox rendition with surprising results.

    2 pounds small mussels, about 60
    2 cups mild, thick salsa
    1 cup heavy cream

Scrub mussels and remove beards, if any. Place mussels in a large pot with a cover. Add 2 cups water and bring to a boil. Lower heat and cover pot. Cook for approximately 10 minutes, shaking pot back and forth, until the shells open. Discard any mussels that have not opened.

Remove mussels with a slotted spoon. Strain cooking liquid through a fine-mesh sieve. Place half of the liquid in a blender. Add 1 cup salsa and process until smooth. Remove all but 12 mussels from their shells. Add half of shelled mussels to blender and process until very smooth.

Transfer this mixture to a large saucepan. Repeat process with remaining cooking liquid, salsa, and shelled mussels. Add ¾ cup cream and bring soup just to a boil. Lower heat, add salt and freshly ground black pepper to taste, and simmer until hot. Add reserved mussels in their shells to the soup and gently warm them.

Meanwhile, using a wire whisk or electric mixer, whip remaining heavy cream in a mixing bowl until thick.

Place 3 mussels in their shells in each warm soup bowl. Ladle hot soup into the bowls and top with a dollop of whipped cream. Serve immediately.

Serves 4

CREAMY TOMATO SOUP WITH SMOKED MOZZARELLA

This is ultra-satisfying, quick to make, and beautifully textured. A perfect soup when fresh tomatoes are not at their seasonal best.

    28-ounce can plum tomatoes in thick puree
    ¾ cup mascarpone cheese
    6 ounces smoked mozzarella

Put tomatoes and puree in a large saucepan and bring to a rapid boil. Lower heat to medium-high and cover pot. Cook for 10 minutes. Remove cover and, using a potato masher, mash tomatoes thoroughly; you want some small discernible pieces to remain. Whisk in mascarpone and stir over low heat until incorporated. Add salt and freshly ground black pepper to taste, and cook for a few minutes over very low heat.

Meanwhile, dice mozzarella into small even cubes. Pour hot soup into warm soup bowls; garnish with diced mozzarella and coarsely ground black pepper.

Serves 4

PARSNIP SOUP WITH SCOTCH

This is an unbelievably mellow and aromatic soup. The parsnips provide sweetness and acidity; the scotch adds smoky notes. For real drama, flame some additional whisky at the table.

1½ pounds parsnips
4 tablespoons unsalted butter
⅓ cup Scotch whisky, plus more for serving if desired

Peel parsnips and cut into ½-inch pieces. Place in a large pot with a cover. Add 5 cups cold water and 1 teaspoon salt and bring to a boil. Lower heat to medium, and cover pot. Cook for 25 minutes, or until parsnips are very soft.

Working in 2 batches, transfer parsnips and cooking water to bowl of a food processor. Process until very, very smooth. Return puree to pot and set it over very low heat. Cut butter into small pieces and add it, along with ¼ cup Scotch. Cook for 5 minutes, stirring constantly. Add salt and freshly ground black pepper to taste, and remaining Scotch, if desired.

Pour hot soup into individual bowls and serve. Or, if you want to serve soup with flaming Scotch, first pour hot soup into a tureen. Place several additional tablespoons Scotch in a metal ladle and hold it over an open flame on the stove until whisky is warmed. Tip ladle slightly to ignite Scotch; it will flame for about 1 minute, until alcohol evaporates. Carefully pour the flaming Scotch in the tureen and serve.

Serves 6

SOUPE D'ASPERGES AU TRUFFE

Pureed asparagus soup with white truffle oil sounds so good in French.

2¼ pounds medium asparagus
4½ tablespoons unsalted butter
2 teaspoons white truffle oil

Trim woody ends from bottom of asparagus stalks and discard. Remove 8 asparagus tips with 1 inch of stalk attached and boil in salted water for 2 minutes. Drain and set aside.

Using a vegetable peeler and a light touch, peel all the stalks. Cut stalks into 1-inch pieces. Place in a large saucepan and add 1½ cups water, 4 tablespoons butter, and a large pinch of kosher salt. Bring to a boil, then lower heat to medium. Cover pot and cook for 8 minutes, or until the tip of a small sharp knife glides through the asparagus. They should be very yielding, but don't overcook.

Immediately transfer asparagus and cooking liquid to a blender. Let cool for 5 minutes. Starting the blender on low speed, then gradually increasing to high speed, puree for several minutes, until the soup is very, very smooth. Transfer soup to a clean saucepan and add truffle oil. Gently reheat and add salt and freshly ground black pepper to taste.

Place remaining butter in a small nonstick skillet and cook reserved asparagus tips over high heat for 2 minutes, or until hot and lightly browned. Ladle hot soup into bowls and garnish with asparagus tips.

Serves 4

"CREAM" OF SWISS CHARD SOUP

There's not a bit of cream in this ultracreamy, healthful soup.

- 1½ pounds red or Yukon gold potatoes
- 1 very large bunch Swiss chard, about 1½ pounds
- 3½ tablespoons unsalted butter

In a medium pot with a cover, bring 8 cups water and ½ tablespoon kosher salt to a boil.

Peel potatoes and cut them in half lengthwise, and then cut them crosswise to make ½-inch slices. Add potatoes to boiling water. Lower heat to medium-high and cook, covered, for 20 minutes.

Meanwhile, thoroughly wash Swiss chard. Cut off bottom 3 inches of stems and reserve. Tear leaves into small pieces. Add chard leaves to pot after potatoes have cooked for 20 minutes. Cook for 10 minutes longer. Do not overcook or chard will lose its bright green color.

Pour 3 cups of the cooking liquid through a colander into a bowl. Set aside.

Put potatoes, chard, and any remaining cooking liquid in bowl of a food processor and process until smooth. Add butter and process several minutes more, until very smooth. Return mixture to pot. Slowly add up to 3 cups of the reserved broth, stirring constantly, to make a smooth, thick, and creamy soup. Season to taste with kosher salt and freshly ground black pepper. Cook soup for several minutes over medium-high heat, stirring frequently.

Cook reserved chard stems in boiling salted water to cover until tender, about 5 minutes. Cut into fine julienne or fine dice, and scatter over each serving of hot soup.

Serves 6

SIMPLE BREADS TO SERVE WITH SOUP

IMPROBABLE BEER BREAD

This recipe, adapted from chef Scott Allen Terle of Tampa, Florida, is remarkably fragrant, and better still, it works.

- 6½ tablespoons sugar
- 12 ounces beer, at room temperature
- 3 cups self-rising flour, plus more for kneading

Preheat oven to 350°F.

Place sugar in a very large saucepan and cook over medium heat, stirring constantly with a wooden spoon once the sugar begins to melt. Cook until sugar has melted completely into a dark brown liquid. Lower heat to a simmer. Carefully pour in beer, which will bubble and foam. Some of the sugar will harden again so continue to cook, stirring constantly, until melted.

Put flour in the bowl of an electric mixer. Add ½ teaspoon salt and slowly pour in the liquid. Mix until ingredients are thoroughly incorporated and a dough forms; it may be a little sticky at this point.

Place dough on a lightly floured board and knead for several minutes until dough is smooth and no longer sticky, incorporating a little flour as you knead. Coat a nonstick 9 by 5-inch loaf pan with cooking spray. Pat dough into pan and bake for 55 to 60 minutes. The bread is done when a skewer comes out clean. Remove from pan and cool bread on a rack.

Makes 1 loaf

LEMON-POPPY WAFERS

Instead of lavash, a very thin, pliable bread similar to pita, you may substitute large flour tortillas with great results. Cut the tortillas into triangles or wedges instead of squares.

1 large rectangle soft lavash
¼ cup lemon olive oil (page 228)
3 tablespoons poppy seeds

Preheat oven to 300°F.

Cut lavash into 24 squares. Using a pastry brush, spread each square with lemon oil. Press poppy seeds onto each piece and sprinkle lightly with salt.

Place on an ungreased baking sheet and bake for about 15 minutes, or until golden and crisp.

Makes 24

ASIAGO-PESTO TOASTS

1 long, crusty Italian bread
¾ cup prepared pesto
5 ounces Asiago cheese, shredded

Preheat oven to 350°F.

Cut bread on a sharp bias into ¼-inch-thick slices. Place on a rimmed baking sheet and bake for 3 minutes. Turn over and bake 3 minutes longer.

Spread 1 side of each toasted bread slice with about ½ tablespoon pesto. Scatter cheese on bread to cover completely. Return to oven and bake for 10 minutes. Cool slightly and serve warm.

Makes about 24

ELEVEN-INCH PARMESAN STRAWS

6 sheets phyllo dough
4 tablespoons unsalted butter, melted
1 cup freshly grated Parmigiano-Reggiano cheese

Preheat oven to 350°F.

Cut phyllo dough in half across the width. Using a pastry brush, brush each of the 12 pieces lightly with melted butter. Sprinkle each piece with 1½ tablespoons cheese. Roll up each piece tightly, like a cigar, 11 inches long and ½ inch wide. Brush the tops with more melted butter and evenly sprinkle with ½ tablespoon cheese.

Place on ungreased baking sheet. Bake for 12 to 14 minutes, until golden brown and crisp. Let cool to room temperature.

Makes 12

OLIVE OIL BISCUITS

2 cups self-rising flour
¾ cup milk
½ cup extra-virgin olive oil

Preheat oven to 400°F.

Place flour in a medium bowl and make a well in the center. Add milk, 7 tablespoons olive oil, and a large pinch of salt. Stir until just blended. Do not overwork, or biscuits will be tough.

On a lightly floured surface, roll dough out to a ⅓-inch thickness. Cut into 2-inch rounds with a cookie cutter and place on a baking sheet.

Bake for 15 minutes, until biscuits just begin to turn golden. Using a pastry brush, lightly brush tops with remaining olive oil.

Makes 20

ZA'ATAR PITA

More intriguing than oregano or basil, za'atar—a spice blend from the Middle East—is delightful sprinkled on pita or pizza. It is available in Middle Eastern food stores and spice shops.

4 thin pita breads, 6 inches wide
¼ cup extra-virgin olive oil
¼ cup or more za'atar

Preheat oven to 350°F.

Place pita breads on a baking sheet. Using a pastry brush, spread olive oil evenly to coat top of each pita. Sprinkle each pita with 1 or more tablespoons za'atar, and drizzle with a little more oil.

Bake for 8 minutes, or until the edges just begin to turn golden brown. Cut each pita into 8 wedges. Serve warm or at room temperature.

Makes 32

SESAME CRISPS

These crunchy crackers are made from wonton wrappers, available in the refrigerated section of most supermarkets.

    16 square wonton wrappers
    2 tablespoons dark Asian sesame oil
    2 tablespoons white or black sesame seeds

Preheat oven to 400°F.

Place wonton wrappers in 1 layer on a rimmed baking sheet. Using a pastry brush, thoroughly coat each wonton with sesame oil. Evenly sprinkle sesame seeds on each piece, and press them firmly into wontons. Sprinkle lightly with salt.

Bake for 6 to 8 minutes, or until just crisp. Do not overcook. Let cool before serving.

Makes 16

OLD-FASHIONED BUTTERMILK BISCUITS

    3 cups self-rising cake flour
    10 tablespoons unsalted butter, at room temperature
    1 cup buttermilk, at room temperature

Preheat oven to 425°F.

Place flour in a large bowl. Stir in a large pinch of salt. Cut butter into small pieces and, using your fingers, combine it with the flour until butter is incorporated completely. Flour should be slightly damp.

Pour buttermilk into flour mixture all at once, and mix quickly but lightly with a wooden spoon, until dough just comes together.

Turn dough out onto a well-floured board and knead for 1 minute. Using a floured rolling pin, roll out dough to a thickness of ½-inch. Cut out circles with a 3-inch cookie cutter.

Place on a lightly buttered baking sheet and bake for 16 to 18 minutes, until tops of biscuits are golden.

Makes 12 biscuits

BRUSCHETTA, ROMAN STYLE

This preparation is minimal: nothing more than thick slices of charred country bread rubbed with raw garlic, drizzled with good olive oil, and sprinkled with kosher salt. Another fragrant idea: rub the warm bread with a fistful of fresh basil instead of the garlic, then douse with olive oil.

4 thick slices peasant bread, cut from a large crusty loaf
4 small cloves garlic, peeled
⅓ cup extra-virgin olive oil

Grill, broil, or toast bread until charred in many places. (You also can do this in a grill pan lightly coated with olive oil.) Rub each piece of hot bread with a clove of garlic that has been cut in half. Keep bread warm in a 250°F oven until ready to serve. Drizzle each piece with a heaping tablespoon of olive oil and sprinkle with coarse sea salt before serving.

Makes 4

PUFFY CRACKER BREAD

This simple bread, actually more like a big billowy cracker, makes a stunning presentation at the table, especially if you serve it in one large piece. Your guests can break off sections as they please.

8 ounces mascarpone
1 cup all-purpose flour, plus more for dusting
2 tablespoons cumin seeds

Place mascarpone in bowl of an electric mixer. Stir in flour and a large pinch of salt, and mix briefly. Turn dough out onto a clean work surface, lightly dusted with flour, and knead for several minutes until smooth. Pat the dough into a 6-inch square and wrap in plastic. Refrigerate for 1 hour.

Preheat oven to 450°F.

On a lightly floured surface, roll out dough to make a 13 by 15-inch rectangle. Alternatively, divide dough into 2 pieces. Roll each piece into a long, very thin rectangle. One at a time, wrap the rectangles around rolling pin and roll out onto 1 large baking sheet or 2 smaller sheets. Sprinkle lightly and evenly with cumin seeds. Add a very light dusting of salt.

Bake for 14 to 15 minutes, or until pastry is slightly puffy and golden brown. Present to your guests and they can break off pieces themselves.

Serves 6

salads

The true nature of salad can be elusive.

Salad generally implies something leafy, savory, and chilled, but that's not always the case. A salad can begin a meal or serve as an astringent sidekick to some form of protein. It can be a meal in itself, or when thoughtfully paired with cheese, the antecedent to dessert. Sometimes a salad can fill a sandwich. More loosely, a salad is any cold vegetable preparation that's spiked with acidity.

The word *salad*, derived from the Latin *sal* (or salt) transitioned to *salata* (or salted things) in classical times—raw vegetables, for example, dressed with oil and vinegar or with salt. Some of my salads, too, use salt in place of vinegar. In medieval times, salads were composed of green leaves, sometimes with flowers. Later, in England, salads included fruits, such as oranges and lemons. Many of my salads use them, too.

Today it all starts with "the simple green salad," of which there are three essential components: excellent greens (and thankfully there are hundreds of varieties and many leafy mixtures from which to choose); great extra-virgin olive oil; and vinegar, whose varieties rival the options at a perfume counter. You may experiment with other sources of acidity: citrus fruit, verjuice (a sour liquid that's crushed from unripe grapes and is less harsh than vinegar), yogurt, crème fraîche, or simply sea salt; and you may wish to toy with nut oils or flavored olive oils. All lead to greater complexity.

That's how the twentieth century gave rise to anarchy in the salad bowl, witnessing inventions such as oxymoronic warm salad during nouvelle cuisine's reign. Today salad is as salad does, and what each has in common is the need for a fork.

Consider serving some of my vegetable recipes as salads, chilled or at room temperature. Stir-fried Asparagus (page 21), Ruby Beets and Greens with Garlic Oil and Lemon (page 23), Pepper Confit with Sherry Vinegar (page 47), and Fried Zucchini and Lemon Salad (page 65) would all work nicely.

For three-ingredient dressings to drizzle atop your own salad creations, see pages 231 to 233. And choose any of the simple breads (pages 81–85), to add a charming completeness to your salad—wherever in the meal you decide to position it.

FIRST-COURSE SALADS

FANCY GREENS WITH RASPBERRY VINAIGRETTE

Like a basic black dress, the green salad is as versatile as you want it to be. Experiment with different marriages of oil and acid: walnut oil and tarragon vinegar; garlic olive oil (page 228) and fresh lemon; sesame oil and rice vinegar.

6 ounces mixed salad greens
3 tablespoons raspberry vinegar
½ cup hazelnut oil, preferably imported

Wash greens and dry thoroughly; wet lettuce can ruin a salad.

In a small bowl, combine vinegar, a large pinch of salt, and freshly ground black pepper. Slowly drip in hazelnut oil, whisking constantly until dressing emulsifies. Pour as much dressing as is needed over the greens and toss gently. Do not drown the greens in dressing. Serve immediately.

Serves 4

TOMATO, BASIL, AND MOZZARELLA SALAD

8 large ripe tomatoes, about 5 pounds
1½ pounds freshly made mozzarella
1 large bunch fresh basil

Bring a small pot of water to a rapid boil. Cut an *x* in the bottom of 2 tomatoes using a small sharp knife. Plunge these tomatoes into the boiling water and, after 1 minute, remove them with a slotted spoon. Peel them and let cool. Cut in half and squeeze out seeds. Put in a blender and process with a pinch of salt until smooth and frothy.

Cut mozzarella into thick slices and place them in an overlapping layer on a platter. Wash remaining tomatoes and dry thoroughly. Cut the outer wall of tomatoes into julienne strips, saving the inner portion. Place julienne strips in a bowl.

Wash basil and dry very well. Stack large basil leaves on top of each other and finely julienne until you have half the volume of the julienned tomatoes. Add to bowl, season with salt and freshly ground black pepper, and toss to combine. Cut reserved inner portion of tomatoes into chunks or thin wedges. Scatter on top of cheese and top with tomato-basil mixture. Drizzle tomato sauce over tomatoes and basil.

Serves 6

SMOKED TROUT AND WATERCRESS SALAD, WALNUT OIL-GREEN SAUCE

If you can't find smoked trout, you can make this with thick slices of rich smoked sable, or thin slices of luxurious smoked sturgeon. This is a particularly nice starter for a holiday meal.

6 large smoked trout fillets
3 large bunches watercress
6 tablespoons walnut oil

Remove skin, if any, from trout fillets. Cut each fillet in half lengthwise to get 12 pieces. Set aside.

Wash watercress and dry well. Trim all but 1 inch of the stems and discard. Bring 3 cups water to a boil in a medium pot. Add ¼ teaspoon salt and half the watercress. Cook for 1 minute, then, saving ⅔ cup cooking water, drain immediately in a colander under cold running water.

Place cooked watercress in bowl of a food processor and process, adding just enough warm cooking water to make a thick paste. With the machine on, slowly add 4 tablespoons walnut oil, processing until dressing is smooth and fairly thick. Add salt to taste. You should have about ¾ cup dressing.

Portion remaining watercress in center of large plates. Drizzle a little dressing over watercress. Place 2 smoked trout pieces, crisscrossed, on watercress. Drizzle remaining dressing around salad and across the center of the trout. Drizzle with remaining walnut oil and serve immediately.

Serves 6

ROASTED ASPARAGUS AND ORANGE SALAD, ASPARAGUS "FETTUCCINE"

Dazzling and deceptive, the "fettuccine" are actually peelings from the asparagus that have been boiled like pasta.

2 pounds medium-thick asparagus
¼ cup extra-virgin olive oil
4 very large oranges

Preheat oven to 500°F.

Snap off woody bottoms of asparagus and discard. Using a vegetable peeler, gently peel skin from asparagus stalks in long, thin strips. Set strips aside. Cut peeled asparagus spears into 3 pieces on the bias. Place cut asparagus in a bowl with 1 tablespoon olive oil, ½ teaspoon kosher salt, and freshly ground black pepper. Toss to coat thoroughly.

Place asparagus in 1 layer on a rimmed baking sheet. Roast for 12 minutes, shaking several times to prevent sticking.

Meanwhile, grate rind of 1 orange to yield ½ teaspoon zest. Cut 2 oranges in half and squeeze ½ cup juice. Place juice, remaining olive oil, and zest in a blender. Blend until lightly emulsified. Add salt and freshly ground black pepper to taste, and set aside.

Using a small sharp knife, cut off rind from remaining oranges, being sure to remove white pith. Gently cut along the side of each segment, along the membrane, to release segments. Set aside.

Return roasted asparagus to bowl. Cover to keep warm.

Bring a medium pot of salted water to a boil. Add reserved asparagus peelings and cook for 6 to 7 minutes, or until bright green and tender. Drain in a colander and refresh briefly under cool water. Pat dry.

Add orange segments to warm asparagus and toss gently, adding salt and pepper to taste.

Mound in center of large plates. Top with asparagus fettuccine. Pour dressing over salad, and serve slightly warm or at room temperature.

Serves 4

MESCLUN AND ROASTED PEPPER SALAD, CREAMY FETA DRESSING

> 4 large bell peppers, 2 red and 2 yellow
> 5 ounces feta cheese
> 5 ounces mesclun greens

Preheat broiler. Wash peppers and pat dry.

Put whole peppers on a rimmed baking sheet and broil for several minutes on each side, until skins are very black and blistered. Immediately seal peppers in a paper bag to steam for 10 minutes. (You can also use a bowl covered with a lid or plate.)

Remove peppers and carefully peel or scrape away all charred skin. Cut peppers in half, and discard core and all seeds. Place on a platter to collect juices that accumulate from peppers. Let cool, then cut into julienned strips, about ⅓ inch wide.

Crumble cheese into bowl of a food processor. Add freshly ground black pepper to taste. Process, gradually adding up to ½ cup cold water, until very smooth and thick.

Place mound of mesclun in center of 4 large plates. Top with roasted pepper strips and the juices. Drizzle with dressing. Sprinkle with coarsely ground black pepper before serving.

Serves 4

ARUGULA AND MUSSEL SALAD, ANCHOVY VINAIGRETTE

> 1 pound medium-large mussels in their shells
> 2 large bunches arugula
> 2-ounce can rolled anchovies with capers

Wash mussels well in a colander, removing beards, if any. Transfer them to a medium pot with a cover. Add ¼ cup water, cover pot tightly, and cook over high heat for 5 to 6 minutes, shaking pot back and forth several times during cooking. Uncover pot and discard any mussels that have not opened. Let mussels cool, then remove them from their shells and set aside. Strain cooking liquid through a fine-mesh sieve.

Wash arugula and dry well. Keep refrigerated until ready to use.

Put the anchovies, capers, and their oil in a blender. Add 3 to 4 tablespoons mussel cooking liquid and process until very smooth. Add freshly ground black pepper.

Place arugula in a bowl and add cooked cooled mussels. Toss with dressing just to coat leaves. If dressing is too thick, add a little of the mussel cooking liquid to thin it.

Serves 4

HEIRLOOM TOMATO SALAD WITH LEMONY TAHINA

2½ pounds mixed heirloom tomatoes
2 large lemons
½ cup tahina (sesame paste)

Wash tomatoes and dry well. Remove cores and seeds. Cut tomatoes into wedges and place in a large shallow bowl. Sprinkle lightly with salt and freshly ground black pepper.

Grate rind of lemons and set zest aside. Cut lemons in half and squeeze to get 6 tablespoons juice.

Put tahina in bowl of a food processor. Begin to process, adding lemon juice and 5 to 6 tablespoons water until you have a smooth, thick puree. Add salt and pepper to taste. Pour dressing over tomatoes and scatter zest on top.

Serves 4 or more

FRISÉE SALAD WITH LARDONS AND HOT VINEGAR DRESSING

Use wispy jade green heads of frisée lettuce, available in well-stocked produce markets. Chicory makes a more assertive substitute.

2 large heads frisée lettuce, or 1 large head chicory
8 ounces pancetta, sliced ¼-inch thick
¼ cup good-quality red wine vinegar

Wash lettuce and dry well. Tear leaves coarsely and set aside.

Cut pancetta into ¼-inch-wide strips, or lardons. Cook over medium heat in a nonstick skillet, until fat is rendered and pancetta is beginning to crisp. Remove pancetta with a slotted spoon; reserve the rendered fat in skillet.

Divide lettuce among large plates. Divide pancetta evenly over lettuce. Carefully add vinegar to hot fat in pan. Cook over high heat for 1 minute, adding a pinch of salt. Pour hot dressing over lettuce and serve immediately.

Serves 4

TWO-WAY ENDIVE SALAD WITH MARINATED GOAT CHEESE

4 ounces crumbled goat cheese
6 tablespoons extra-virgin olive oil
5 large Belgian endives

Place goat cheese in a shallow bowl and pour ¼ cup olive oil over the cheese. Crush ½ teaspoon black peppercorns and sprinkle over cheese with a large pinch of kosher salt and 1 tablespoon water. Let sit at room temperature for 1 hour.

Trim bottoms from endives. Slice 2 endives very thinly on the bias. Put remaining olive oil in a small nonstick skillet. Add sliced endive and cook over high heat for 5 minutes, or until edges turn dark brown. Add 2 tablespoons water and lower heat to medium. Cook for 10 minutes, until very soft. Set aside.

When ready to serve, trim remaining endives and cut into thin slices on the bias. Place in a large bowl. Add cooked endive with any pan juices. Pour marinated cheese over endive and toss. Adjust seasonings, adding additional salt, pepper, or oil as needed. Serve immediately.

Serves 4

ICEBERG WEDGES WITH BACON AND BLUE CHEESE

An homage to the past when iceberg was at the heart of all salads.

8 ounces crumbly blue cheese
8 slices bacon
1 large head iceberg lettuce

Break blue cheese into chunks and place in bowl of a food processor. Process while adding 7 tablespoons cold water, a little at a time. Blend until very smooth. Add freshly ground black pepper to taste. Cover and refrigerate until ready to use. Makes about 1 cup. If you like your dressing chunky, crumble an additional ⅓ cup cheese into dressing.

Cook bacon until crisp, discarding any fat. Keep bacon warm.

Remove any dark outer leaves from lettuce. Slam bottom of the head on a cutting board and the core will fall out. If not, cut out the core. Cut lettuce into 6 wedges and place on plates. Pour dressing over lettuce and crumble bacon on top. Pass the pepper mill.

Serves 6

SEARED SMOKED SALMON ON PRESSED CUCUMBERS

It may be unusual to cook smoked salmon, but the result provides a warm, intriguing contrast to chilled cucumbers.

1¼ pounds cucumbers
3 tablespoons lemon olive oil (page 228)
8 ounces good-quality smoked salmon, cut in 1 piece from center of fish

Peel cucumbers. Slice into paper-thin rounds and toss in a colander with 2 teaspoons kosher salt. Add a weight, such as a saucepan filled with water, and place colander in a bowl or in the sink to catch liquid.

Let sit for 1 hour, then wash off salt under cold running water. Press cucumber slices between your hands to extract as much liquid as possible. Toss with 1 tablespoon lemon oil and season with freshly ground black pepper. Refrigerate until ready to serve.

Cut salmon into 4 thick strips across the width of fish. Place 1 tablespoon lemon oil in a large nonstick skillet and swirl to coat bottom of pan. Add fish and cook for 2 to 3 minutes. Continue to cook for 2 minutes on 3 remaining surfaces, or until outside turns golden and interior is just barely warm. Do not overcook.

Place cucumbers in center of large plates. Top with warm salmon and drizzle with remaining lemon oil.

Serves 4

BABY SPINACH, BLOOD ORANGE, AND CHORIZO SALAD

7 ounces baby spinach
6 large blood oranges
6 ounces smoked chorizo sausage

Wash spinach and dry very well. Mound spinach in the center of 4 large chilled plates.

Using a small sharp knife, cut rind and all white pith from 4 oranges, then cut in between membranes to release segments. Gather accumulated juices in a small bowl. Tuck orange segments in and on top of spinach leaves and set aside.

Slice chorizo into ⅛-inch-thick rounds and cut those into half-moon shapes. Cook in a nonstick skillet over medium heat until fat is rendered and sausage slices are browned on both sides, about 2 minutes. Cut remaining oranges in half and squeeze their juices over chorizo. Cook for 30 seconds over medium-high heat, adding salt and freshly ground black pepper to taste.

Remove sausages with slotted spoon and place on top of oranges. Pour pan juices evenly over salad and serve immediately.

Serves 4

ESCAROLE AND PEAR SALAD WITH BOURSIN

1 medium head escarole
3 large ripe pears
5 ounces Boursin cheese flavored with garlic and herbs

Wash escarole and dry thoroughly. Tear leaves into small pieces. Using mostly the inner paler leaves, mound escarole in the center of large chilled plates.

Peel pears and cut them in half, saving half a pear for dressing. Remove any seeds from remaining halves and cut into thin wedges. Tuck pears in and on top of escarole.

Break cheese into several pieces and place in bowl of a food processor. Cut reserved pear half into small pieces, discarding seeds. With the machine on, add pear pieces. Add ½ cup cold water and process until smooth, thick, and creamy. Spoon dressing over salads. Sprinkle with salt and coarsely ground black pepper.

Serves 4

SIDE SALADS

LITTLE CUCUMBER SALADS
APPLE CIDER CUCUMBERS

1½ to 2 seedless cucumbers, about 1½ pounds
6 tablespoons apple cider vinegar
¼ cup pure maple syrup

Peel cucumbers. Using a sharp knife, cut into paper-thin slices. Place in a small bowl.

In another bowl, whisk together vinegar and maple syrup. Pour over cucumbers and toss, adding salt and freshly ground black pepper to taste. Cover and refrigerate for at least 1 hour. Adjust seasonings before serving, adding salt, pepper, or vinegar.

Serves 4

CUCUMBERS IN MUSTARD CREAM

8 medium kirby cucumbers, about 1½ pounds
⅓ cup crème fraîche
1½ tablespoons smooth, spicy mustard, such as Colman's

Peel cucumbers and cut into paper-thin slices. In a small bowl, mix crème fraîche and mustard. Mix with cucumbers. Add salt and freshly ground white pepper to taste. Refrigerate until cold.

Serves 4

TURKISH CUCUMBERS

2 medium cucumbers
2 teaspoons dark Asian sesame oil
1 cup plain yogurt

Peel cucumbers. Cut in half lengthwise and remove seeds, using a small spoon. Slice into ¼-inch-thick half-moons. Place in a small bowl. Add sesame oil, yogurt, salt, and freshly ground white pepper to taste. Stir and refrigerate for 1 to 2 hours before serving.

Serves 4

RICE VINEGAR CUCUMBERS

8 kirby cucumbers, about 1½ pounds
¼ cup rice vinegar, or more to taste
¼ cup finely chopped fresh spearmint

Peel cucumbers. Slice half of them paper-thin; cut remaining cucumbers into ¼-inch cubes. Toss with vinegar and mint, and season with salt and freshly ground white pepper to taste. Refrigerate for 1 to 2 hours. Splash with additional vinegar, if desired.

Serves 4

FENNEL AND ORANGE SALAD

2 large fennel bulbs with lots of feathery fronds
4 large navel oranges
6 tablespoons extra-virgin olive oil

Wash fennel. Cut off stalks where they join bulb, reserving feathery fronds. Remove any dark brown spots from bulb. Using a sharp knife, cut bulb in half through root, slice very thin, and place slices in a large bowl.

Grate rind of 2 oranges so you have 1 tablespoon zest. Set aside. Cut 2 oranges in half and squeeze halves to get ½ cup juice. Put orange juice and olive oil in a blender. Add salt and freshly ground black pepper. Process until dressing is creamy.

Cut rind from 2 remaining oranges, using a small, sharp knife. Remove all white pith and cut between membranes to release segments. Add segments to fennel and toss. Add dressing and mix gently.

Chop fennel fronds so you have 6 tablespoons. Scatter chopped fronds and reserved zest on top of salad.

Serves 4 or more

CELERY RÉMOULADE

France's answer to coleslaw is celery en rémoulade. It is made from a gnarled knot of celeriac, an enlarged root of the celery plant. For textural contrast, my version adds unexpected crisps of roasted celeriac.

1½ pounds celeriac (celery root)
½ cup light mayonnaise
2½ tablespoons Dijon mustard

Preheat oven to 400°F.

Peel celery root using a small sharp knife. Cut two-thirds of root into thin slices, about ⅛-inch thick, and then slice these into julienned strips, about ⅛-inch wide and 2 inches long.

Mix mayonnaise and mustard together in a medium bowl, and add julienned celery root. Add salt and freshly ground white pepper to taste, and mix well. Cover and refrigerate for 1 to 2 hours.

Slice remaining celery root paper-thin. Place slices on a rimmed baking sheet, reduce oven temperature to 275°F, and bake for 30 minutes or until crisp, turning once or twice. The celery root chips will brown lightly, but do not let them get too dark. Sprinkle with salt. Serve the celery rémoulade with chips on top.

Serves 4

WHITE BEAN AND ROASTED CHERRY TOMATO SALAD

8 ounces small white beans
1 pint cherry tomatoes
⅓ cup prepared pesto

Put beans in a medium pot with a cover. Add salted water to cover beans. Bring to a rapid boil and boil for 2 minutes. Remove from heat, cover pot, and let sit for 1 hour.

Drain beans and return to pot. Cover with fresh water. Add ½ teaspoon whole black peppercorns. Bring to a boil, skimming any foam. Lower heat and simmer, with cover askew, for 50 to 60 minutes, or until just tender. Be careful not to overcook.

Meanwhile, wash cherry tomatoes and pat dry. Place them in a pie tin and bake at 275°F for 1½ hours, shaking pan several times during baking. Remove from oven and let cool.

When beans are finished, drain them, saving ½ cup cooking liquid. Transfer beans to a medium bowl. Add pesto and enough cooking liquid—about ¼ cup—to coat beans. Add salt and freshly ground black pepper to taste, and toss in roasted tomatoes, mixing gently. Add more cooking liquid to moisten, if necessary. Serve at room temperature.

Serves 6

ROASTED PEPPERS WITH ANCHOVIES AND PINE NUTS

4 large red bell peppers
1 2-ounce can rolled anchovies with capers
⅓ cup pine nuts

Preheat broiler.

Place whole peppers on a rimmed baking sheet 6 inches from heat source. Broil on all sides until peppers blacken, about 10 minutes. Place peppers in a paper bag, seal it, and allow peppers to steam and soften. Or you can put peppers in a bowl and cover it with a plate to steam them.

When peppers are cool, peel off skin using your fingers or a sharp knife. Cut peppers into 6 wedges, lengthwise, and remove seeds. Place peppers on a platter to accumulate juices. Let cool.

Drizzle peppers with oil from anchovies. Using a sharp knife, chop anchovies and capers and sprinkle over roasted peppers. Mix lightly. Put nuts in a small nonstick skillet and cook over medium heat for several minutes, stirring often, until nuts turn golden brown. Scatter nuts over peppers.

Serves 4

ROASTED GARLIC-STRING BEAN SALAD

You can make this doubly appealing by using a mixture of green string beans and yellow wax beans.

1 very large head garlic
2 pounds string beans
¼ cup extra-virgin olive oil

Preheat oven to 400°F.

Wrap garlic in a large piece of foil to make a pouch, and tightly seal the top. Place in a pie tin and roast for 1 hour and 15 minutes, or until very soft. Remove from oven and unwrap. Cut garlic in half horizontally and squeeze out pulp; you should have 2 packed tablespoons. Set aside.

Wash beans and trim tips. Bring a large pot of salted water to a rapid boil. Add beans and cook over high heat for 8 minutes, or until just tender. Drain them in a colander under cold running water until cool.

In a large nonstick skillet, heat olive oil. Add garlic pulp and stir until garlic is incorporated into oil. Add beans and toss with oil so that beans are thoroughly coated. Add salt and freshly ground black pepper. Transfer to a large bowl. Serve at room temperature or chilled.

Serves 6

ARUGULA AND CURRANTS

This is a lovely accompaniment to almost any protein—slightly bitter, slightly salty, slightly sweet.

⅓ cup dried currants
2 large bunches arugula, chilled
¼ cup extra-virgin olive oil or lemon olive oil (page 228)

Place currants in a small bowl. Cover with 1 cup boiling water. Let sit for 15 minutes.

Meanwhile, wash arugula well and dry thoroughly with paper towels or a salad spinner. Place in a bowl. Drain currants, saving 2 tablespoons soaking liquid. Pat currants dry and add to arugula. Add enough olive oil to coat leaves and drizzle with a little of the soaking liquid. Season with salt and freshly ground black pepper. Toss and serve.

Serves 4

JICAMA WITH LIME AND CILANTRO

The interior of jicama, a large tuber covered with a papery tan skin, is bright white, sweet, and crisp. This little side salad is a great palate cleanser.

1 large jicama, about 1½ pounds
2 large limes
1 bunch fresh cilantro

Using a small sharp knife, peel jicama. Cut into julienne, ⅛ inch thick and 3 inches long. Place in a small bowl. Grate rind of 1 lime and add zest to julienned jicama. Squeeze juice of 1 lime over jicama, along with 3 to 4 tablespoons chopped cilantro. Add salt and freshly ground black pepper to taste.

Refrigerate for 30 minutes or longer. Serve very cold with wedges of remaining lime.

Serves 4

SMASHED POTATO SALAD WITH CRÈME FRAÎCHE

2 pounds small-medium red-skinned new potatoes
1 large bunch scallions
8 ounces crème fraîche

Scrub potatoes well, but do not peel. Place in a medium pot with a cover. Add salted water just to cover potatoes. Bring to a boil, lower heat, and cover pot. Cook for 35 to 40 minutes, until potatoes are soft but not falling apart.

Meanwhile, trim scallions. Coarsely chop white part only to get ¼ cup. Reserve green and light green parts. Place chopped scallions in bowl of a food processor with crème fraîche and process until smooth. Add salt to taste. Finely mince green part of scallions to get ¼ packed cup.

When potatoes are cooked, drain in a colander, saving ¼ cup cooking water. Place potatoes in a large bowl and, using a potato masher, mash until some are creamy but some are still in large pieces. While still hot, add scallion-crème fraîche mixture and reserved cooking water. (Potatoes will absorb excess liquid when chilled.) Add salt and freshly ground black pepper to taste. Cover and refrigerate until cold. Adjust salt and pepper, and top with minced green scallions.

Serves 4

CABBAGE "CREAM SLAW"

This time-honored cabbage salad, once know as "cream slaw" has a distinctive cream-and-vinegar dressing that adds a gentle tang.

  1 small green cabbage, about 1½ pounds
  ½ cup heavy cream
  3 tablespoons distilled white vinegar

Shred cabbage very thinly with a sharp knife. Sprinkle with 1 tablespoon kosher salt and put in a colander in the sink. Add a weight on top—a heavy pot filled with water will do. Let sit for 30 minutes. Rinse cabbage well under cold running water. Dry thoroughly with paper towels or a salad spinner.

Put cabbage in a bowl, pour cream over it, and mix well. Add vinegar and freshly ground black pepper, and toss well. Refrigerate for 1 hour. Add salt to taste and toss again.

Serves 4

WARM CABBAGE AND BACON SALAD

This, too, is a kind of slaw, but the cabbage is cooked and served warm.

  1 medium green cabbage, about 2¼ pounds
  1 cup distilled white vinegar
  ½ pound thickly sliced bacon

Cut cabbage in half through the core. Place cut side down on a cutting board and cut into ⅛-inch-thick slices.

Put vinegar in a very large nonreactive pot with a cover. Bring to a boil. Add cabbage and 1 teaspoon salt, and toss to combine. Return to a boil and cover pot. Lower heat to medium and cook for 15 minutes. Cabbage should remain a little crunchy.

Cut bacon across width into ¼-inch pieces. Place in a large skillet and cook until bacon is crisp and brown. Do not overcook or salad will taste bitter. Pour bacon and fat over cabbage. Toss to coat. Add freshly ground black pepper to taste. Serve warm.

Serves 6

fish
and shellfish

It has been said, most succinctly by Alice B. Toklas, "that the only way to learn to cook is to cook." I apply this idea wholeheartedly to the cooking of fish since so many people shy away from it and save their fish eating for restaurants. It's time for a sea change.

To cook fish, one should begin with great ingredients and treat them simply. There is skill involved in the purchasing of seafood, so apply these 1-2-3 rules: 1. Look first. If it's a whole fish, make sure it has clear, shiny eyes, an unblemished layer of scales, and bright red gills. For steaks and fillets, the surface of the fish should be glistening, not dull, and the flesh should be firm and compact with no splits or fissures. Finally, the color should reflect the type of fish you're buying, and the fish should have no splotches or marks. 2. Smell. Fish should never smell fishy or "off"; you can smell bad fish even through a supermarket package. Fine, fresh fish smells like the sea. 3. Ask questions. Don't be afraid to ask your purveyor "How fresh is this?" "How long can I keep it?" "Where does it come from?"

It is hard to give exact times for cooking fish, but you may heed the advice of the ancient Chinese philosopher Lao-tse, who said, "Ruling a large kingdom is like cooking a small fish." This means handle gently and never overdo it. You may also want to rely on your intuition—and your finger. You want the fish to be firm yet yielding to the touch. Intuition will help you avoid overcooking, which is vital in simple fish preparations.

In *Cooking 1-2-3*, there is no room for covering up blunders with lots of sauces and ingredients. The idea is to maximize the unique flavor and the singular texture of each variety of fish, not to overwhelm its virtues.

Salt and pepper and water are integral to fish cooking, so when appropriate, use an excellent sea salt or, in some specific cases, fleur de sel for finishing dishes. The secret to making great shrimp, for example, is to boil them in their shells in water that's as salty as the sea. Always use freshly ground peppercorns, white or black, depending on the taste and look you want.

Fish is good for you. Inherently low in calories and fat, fish contains many beneficial nutrients, including vitamins A and D and omega-3 fatty acids, which can help lower levels of the harmful lipoproteins (LDL) that contribute to heart disease. Omega-3 fatty acids can also help boost the body's immune system.

Learning to cook fish simply at home has many rewards. Thankfully, lots of supermarkets now have top-quality fresh fish—both farmed and wild—that they can cut and fillet right before your eyes. Try, however, to support your local fish store, since it is likely to have fresher and more varied stock. Or, better yet, buy directly from fishermen in season.

The following main-course recipes feature fifteen varieties of fish and shellfish. When portions are halved, many of them make wonderful starters.

SAUTÉED ARCTIC CHAR WITH PARSLEY PUREE

Artic char is a salmonlike fish that lends itself beautifully to simple preparations. Here, the pink fillets are sautéed and topped with a verdant parsley puree.

4 8-ounce arctic char fillets, skin removed
3 large bunches curly parsley
4½ tablespoons unsalted butter, chilled

Using tweezers, remove any bones from fish. Season lightly with salt and freshly ground white pepper.

Bring a medium pot of salted water to a boil. Chop enough parsley to get 3 packed cups, including some of the small stems. Save remaining parsley sprigs for garnish. Boil parsley for 2½ minutes until soft but still bright green. Drain immediately and place in a blender. Puree parsley with 3 tablespoons water and 3 tablespoons butter, cut in small pieces. Add ½ teaspoon salt and freshly ground black pepper. Blend until thick and frothy. Transfer to a small saucepan.

Heat remaining butter in a very large nonstick skillet and add fillets. Sauté on both sides over medium-high heat until cooked through, about 3 minutes per side. Carefully lift fish from pan with a spatula. Gently warm parsley sauce and pour over fish. Garnish with remaining parsley sprigs.

Serves 4

DILL-BAKED ARCTIC CHAR

4 8-ounce arctic char fillets, skin on
1 cup dry vermouth
1 bunch fresh dill

Using tweezers, remove any bones from fish. Place fillets in 1 layer in a shallow casserole. Pour vermouth over fish.

Wash dill and pat dry. Finely chop about ¾ cup and scatter over fish. Coarsely grind 1 teaspoon white peppercorns and sprinkle over fish, along with fine sea salt. Cover and refrigerate for 1 hour.

Preheat oven to 425°F.

Remove fish from marinade. Place fish, skin side down, on a rimmed baking sheet. Bake for 12 to 13 minutes, depending on thickness of fish. Remove from oven. Serve immediately, garnished with tufts of remaining fresh dill.

Serves 4

ROASTED BLUEFISH WITH RED ONION AND SAGE

Oily and rich, meaty bluefish can stand up to strong flavors. But it must be ultrafresh, or don't buy it! Make sure your fishmonger scales, but doesn't skin, the fish.

3-pound bluefish fillet, cut from the center in 1 piece, skin on
1 large bunch fresh sage
1 pound medium red onions

Preheat oven to 500°F.

Using a thin-bladed sharp knife, remove dark strip of flesh from middle of fillet.

Wash sage leaves and pat dry. Remove stems. Fill channel in center of bluefish (where you have removed dark flesh) with sage leaves, packing them tightly. Save some sage leaves for garnish. Season fish with salt and freshly ground black pepper.

Peel onions and slice into very thin rounds. Scatter onions in center of rimmed baking sheet. Place fish, skin-side up, on top of onions, tucking them under fish. Add ¼ cup water to pan.

Roast fish for 22 to 25 minutes, depending on thickness. Skin will become slightly crisp. Turn fish over onto cutting board and cut into 6 portions. Transfer to a warm platter and top with roasted onions. Finely julienne reserved sages leaves and sprinkle over fish. Serve with any pan juices.

Serves 6

TERIYAKI BLUEFISH WITH POACHED SCALLIONS

Scallions do double-duty as a flavoring agent and as a poached vegetable garnish.

4 8-ounce thick bluefish fillets
1 cup teriyaki sauce
3 large bunches thick scallions

Using tweezers, remove any bones from fish. Place fillets in a shallow casserole and cover with teriyaki sauce. Marinate for 20 minutes.

Meanwhile, trim roots from scallions. Remove all but 1 inch of the dark green tops from 2 bunches of scallions. Place trimmed scallions in a skillet with enough salted water to just cover. Bring to a boil, then lower heat and simmer until scallions are soft, about 5 minutes. Keep warm.

Remove fish from marinade. Reserve marinade. Season fish with coarsely ground black pepper. Heat 1 very large or 2 smaller nonstick skillets until very hot. Put fish in pan and place a large heavy skillet on top to act as a weight.

Cook over medium-high heat for 3 minutes. Turn over and cook 3 minutes longer, weighted down with the skillet again.

Finely dice remaining bunch of scallions to yield ½ cup. Add to reserved marinade. Remove weight from fish and add marinade to pan with ½ cup water. Heat for 1 to 2 minutes, or until fish is cooked as desired. Serve immediately with poached scallions that have been quickly warmed in their poaching liquid and thoroughly drained.

Serves 4

CHILEAN SEA BASS WITH LEEK FONDUE

Once known as Patagonian toothfish, Chilean sea bass is fabulously thick and white as snow. Because it's been overfished, your fishmonger should confirm that yours has been legally caught.

> 4 large leeks, about 1¼ pounds
> 8 tablespoons unsalted butter
> 4 8-ounce thick Chilean sea bass fillets

Remove dark green parts from leeks and discard. Slice white parts of leeks paper-thin. Wash well, making sure to remove any dirt. Pat dry.

Melt 6 tablespoons butter in a large saucepan. Add leeks, 6 tablespoons water, ¼ teaspoon salt, and freshly ground white pepper. Bring to a quick boil, then lower heat, cover, and simmer for 25 minutes. Add ¼ cup water, cover again, and cook 10 minutes longer. Leeks should form a fondue, which means they should be so soft they're "melted." Set aside.

Season sea bass with salt and freshly ground white pepper. Melt remaining butter in a very large nonstick skillet. Sauté fish over medium-high heat until golden on each side, making sure it is opaque throughout. Be careful not to overcook.

Gently reheat leek fondue and pour over hot fish. Sprinkle with coarse sea salt.

Serves 4

PESTO-PISTACHIO CHILEAN SEA BASS

This is great for a crowd. Use a good-quality prepared pesto, generally found in the refrigerated section of your supermarket, or use a jarred product imported from Italy. This is a delicious preparation for fresh salmon, too.

> 3-pound Chilean sea bass fillet, cut from the center in 1 piece
> 1 cup shelled unsalted pistachios
> 1 cup best-quality prepared pesto

Preheat oven to 400°F.

Using tweezers, remove any bones running down center of fish. Line a rimmed baking sheet with parchment paper or aluminum foil. Season both sides of fish lightly with salt and place fish on pan.

Place pistachios in bowl of a food processor and process until coarsely ground. Do not over-process; you want small, discernible pieces, not powder.

Spread pesto thickly on top of fish to coat completely, draining most of the oil from the pesto as you go. Dust pesto with freshly ground black pepper. Pack ground pistachios on top of pesto to cover evenly, and press down lightly to create a thick nut crust.

Bake for 35 to 40 minutes, or until fish is cooked as desired. Do not overcook; the fish should be moist and juicy. Remove from oven. Transfer fish to a large warm platter.

Add a little boiling water to the bottom of the pan to develop some pan juices. Strain quickly through a fine-mesh sieve and pour over fish. Serve immediately.

Serves 6

LEMONY COD BAKED IN GRAPE LEAVES

Thick fillets of cod get baked in an "ancestral" wrap of briny grape leaves. Keep the leaves on the fish when you serve it—they become crisp and delicious during baking.

    4 8-ounce thick cod fillets, skin removed
    7 tablespoons lemon olive oil (page 228)
    10 large grape leaves in brine

Preheat oven to 450°F.

Using tweezers, remove any bones from fish. Coat each fillet with 2 teaspoons lemon oil. Season with freshly ground black pepper. Remove grape leaves from brine and rinse thoroughly under cold running water. Pat dry thoroughly. Remove any stems or tough veins.

On a clean surface, arrange 2 grape leaves to make an elongated wrapper. (Pointed tips of leaves will face in opposite directions, with the stem ends overlapping slightly.) Place 1 fillet in center and wrap tightly, tucking in the ends of the leaves to make a tight, neat package. Repeat with remaining fillets. Roll up remaining 2 grape leaves into a tight roll, and cut crosswise to create very thin julienne strips.

Heat 2 tablespoons plus 1 teaspoon lemon oil in a very large skillet. Pan-sear the fish bundles for 20 to 30 seconds on each side so they get crisp. Spread 1 tablespoon lemon oil in center of rimmed baking sheet and place fish on top. Scatter julienned grape leaves around fish. These will become crisp and be used as a garnish.

Bake for 8 to 10 minutes, depending on thickness of fish. Remove from the pan and transfer to warm plates. Scatter the crisp julienned grape leaves over the fish, and drizzle with remaining tablespoon of lemon oil. Serve immediately.

Serves 4

PROSCIUTTO-WRAPPED COD

Prosciutto blankets thick cod fillets with a desirable layer of salt and fat. For a smoky overtone, you may substitute paper-thin slices of speck, which is smoked prosciutto.

    6 8-ounce thick cod fillets, skin removed
    ½ cup garlic olive oil (page 228)
    18 thin slices prosciutto

Preheat oven to 425°F.

Season fish with freshly ground black pepper. Drizzle each fillet lightly with 1 teaspoon garlic oil. Tightly wrap 3 slices prosciutto around each fillet to cover completely. Put 2 tablespoons garlic oil in a large nonstick skillet and pan-sear fish on both sides, 30 to 45 seconds per side.

Place fish on a rimmed baking sheet and drizzle with the remaining 2 tablespoons garlic oil. Bake for 10 to 12 minutes until fish is just firm. Place fish under broiler, about 8 inches away from the heat source, and broil for 2 minutes to crisp the prosciutto a bit. Transfer fish to warm plates. If fillets are very thick, first cut them into thick slices on the bias, then overlap the slices on each plate. Drizzle with pan juices. Sprinkle with coarsely ground black pepper.

Serves 6

PAVÉ OF COD WITH HERBES DE PROVENCE

This is an idea borrowed from chef Paul Minchelli in Paris. A coating of herbes de Provence—a dried spice mixture of rosemary, lavender, fennel, savory, and sage—simulates the skin of the cod. The success of the dish lies in low heat and slow cooking.

    4 8-ounce thick cod fillets, skin removed
    4 tablespoons unsalted butter
    4 tablespoons herbes de Provence

Using tweezers, remove any little bones from cod. Season fillets with salt and freshly ground black pepper.

Melt 2 tablespoons butter in a small pan. With a pastry brush, coat tops of fillets with melted butter. Firmly press 1 tablespoon herbes de Provence onto each buttered fillet to cover completely.

In a very large nonstick skillet, melt remaining butter. Place fillets, herbed side down, in skillet. Cook over low heat for about 10 minutes, then carefully turn fish over. Herb mixture should have formed a crust. Continue to cook over low heat for about 8 minutes, until fish reaches desired doneness.

Carefully transfer fish to plates with a spatula. Serve immediately.

Serves 4

SAUTÉED FLOUNDER WITH ASPARAGUS, ASPARAGUS VELOUTÉ

In this dish, I've spun asparagus stalks into a velvety sauce and used the tips as a garnish. Also terrific made with cod or grouper.

- 1½ pounds medium-thick asparagus
- 4 tablespoons unsalted butter
- 4 8-ounce flounder fillets, as thick as possible

Cut top 3 inches from asparagus and set aside. Trim 1 inch from bottom of stalks and discard.

Peel stalks with a vegetable peeler and cut into 1-inch pieces. Place in a saucepan with enough salted water to cover. Bring to a boil, lower heat, and cook for about 10 minutes, or until stalks are soft. Using a slotted spoon, transfer cooked stalks to a blender. Add ¾ to 1 cup cooking liquid and process until smooth. Add 2 tablespoons butter and continue to process until very smooth. Add salt and freshly ground black pepper to taste. Transfer to a saucepan.

Season fish with salt and pepper. Melt remaining butter in a very large nonstick skillet. Place fish in skillet and cook over medium-high heat for about 2 minutes, until golden. Carefully turn over and cook for 2 minutes more until golden. Cover pan and cook until fish reaches desired doneness (fish should just begin to flake), about 3 minutes on each side, depending on thickness.

Meanwhile, bring a small pan of salted water to a boil. Add asparagus tips and cook for 5 minutes, or until just tender.

Gently reheat sauce and spoon some on each plate. Top with fish and hot, drained asparagus tips. Spoon a little remaining sauce on top. Serve immediately.

Serves 4

FILLET OF FLOUNDER WITH LEMON BUTTER

This is a wonderful preparation with fillets of sole, too.

- 6 tablespoons unsalted butter, chilled
- 4 8-ounce flounder fillets, skin removed
- 2 large lemons

Season fish with salt and freshly ground black pepper. Melt 3 tablespoons butter in a very large nonstick skillet. Cook fish over high heat until golden and slightly crispy, about 3 minutes on each side. Using a spatula, carefully transfer fish to hot plates.

Add juice of 1 lemon to pan and let sauce bubble up. Cook until butter is nut-colored, but not burned. Remove pan from heat and add 3 tablespoons chilled butter. Swirl pan until butter melts. Heat briefly, adding salt and pepper to taste, and more lemon juice, if desired. Pour sauce over fish. Top fish with paper-thin slices of remaining lemon.

Serves 4

SALMON-STUFFED FLOUNDER

In this "fish sandwich," slices of white flounder get a pink filling of fresh salmon. It also is intriguing filled with thick slices of smoked salmon. Leave the skin on the salmon, as this makes it easier to cut horizontally.

   4 thin flounder fillets, as long and wide as possible
   1 thick salmon fillet, same width as flounder
   ⅓ cup crème fraîche

Preheat oven to 450°F.

Using tweezers, remove any little bones from the flounder and salmon. Cut each flounder fillet horizontally in half to create 2 very thin slices. Cut horizontally through the salmon fillet to make 4 thin, flat slices. Discard the skin.

Place a piece of salmon on top of halved flounder and season with salt and freshly ground black pepper. Top with another piece of flounder to make a sandwich. Trim edges with a sharp knife to make a neat package. Repeat with remaining fish.

Place fish on a rimmed baking sheet sprayed with a little nonstick cooking spray. Spread crème fraîche evenly on each sandwich to cover. Sprinkle with salt. Bake 8 minutes, then place under the broiler for 2 minutes until fish is golden brown.

Serves 4

PARMESAN-BAKED HALIBUT

This may seem an unlikely merger of foodstuffs, but when you get it right, you get sweet, moist fish under a blanket of tart cream and the best cheese in the world as a top note. Make sure the Parmesan is grated like sand, not in shreds.

   3 1-pound thick halibut steaks
   1 cup sour cream
   1 cup grated Parmigiano-Reggiano

Preheat oven to 425°F.

Place fish on a rimmed baking sheet lined with parchment paper or aluminum foil. Season with salt. Thickly spread ⅓ cup sour cream on each fish steak to completely cover. Add freshly ground white pepper and sprinkle cheese evenly on top.

Bake for 16 to 18 minutes, until fish is cooked through but not dry. Cheese should be golden brown. If you wish a drier crust, place under the broiler for 30 to 60 seconds.

With a sharp knife, cut each steak along the center bone, separating the fish from the bone to form 2 pieces. Serve immediately.

Serves 6

HALIBUT *EN PAPILLOTE* WITH BLACK OLIVE PUREE

This fish is cooked en papillote—*in parchment paper—a superb way to seal in juices and flavor. Tapenade is a black olive paste that you can purchase in jars or make yourself (page 234).*

4 9-ounce halibut fillets, skin removed
½ cup black olive paste
4 large oranges

Preheat oven to 375°F.

Cut 4 30-inch lengths of parchment paper or aluminum foil. Fold in half lengthwise. Place a fillet on each, slightly off-center.

Spread each fillet with a thin layer of tapenade to cover completely. Grate rind of an orange to get 2 teaspoons zest. Sprinkle each fish with ½ teaspoon zest. Remove skin and all the white pith from oranges and cut the segments into thin slices, being sure to remove seeds. Place overlapping slices of oranges on top of each piece of fish and add any accumulated juices.

Fold parchment paper or foil over fish, crimping edges tightly to make an airtight package and rolling up the edges as you go. The shape should look like a half-moon. Place packets on a rimmed baking sheet and bake for 20 minutes.

Remove from oven. Cut open packets and carefully transfer fish and all the juices to plates.

Serves 4

STEAMED HALIBUT WITH BELL PEPPER CONFETTI

The colorful confetti also makes a great topping for thick grilled swordfish steaks.

4 large bell peppers, 2 red and 2 yellow
⅓ cup garlic olive oil (page 228)
4 8-ounce thick halibut steaks

Core and seed the peppers and meticulously cut them into little ¼-inch squares. Place them in a small nonstick skillet with ¼ cup garlic oil. Add a large pinch of kosher salt and ¼ teaspoon whole black peppercorns. Cover and simmer over very low heat for 10 minutes, or until the peppers are tender.

Brush halibut with remaining oil, and season with salt and freshly ground white pepper. Steam in a large pan fitted with a steamer basket until fish is cooked as desired, about 10 minutes, depending on thickness of fish. Pour warm pepper confetti over fish and serve immediately.

Serves 4

BACON-WRAPPED MONKFISH WITH HERB MUSTARD

Monkfish, known as poor man's lobster, has the requisite firm texture for this dish.

    4 8-ounce monkfish fillets
    ½ cup prepared herb mustard
    8 slices applewood-smoked bacon, or other good-quality bacon

Trim all membranes and any dark spots from fish. Season with salt and freshly ground black pepper. Rub each fillet with 2 tablespoons mustard to coat completely.

Wrap 2 slices of bacon around each fillet. (The edges of bacon slices should touch each other, but not overlap, so that bacon completely envelops fish.) Wrap each fillet tightly with plastic wrap, twisting the ends as if making a thick sausage. This helps create a nice shape. Refrigerate for 1 hour.

Preheat oven to 375°F.

Unwrap fish and place on a rimmed baking sheet. Secure bacon with toothpicks. Bake for 25 minutes, or until cooked through. Place under broiler for 30 seconds to crisp bacon. Transfer fish to plates. Remove toothpicks. Drizzle pan juices over fish and serve immediately.

Serves 4

MUSSELS IN HARD CIDER AND CREAM

Remarkably sophisticated. For a more casual variation, substitute salsa for the cider.

    3 pounds medium-large fresh mussels in their shells
    1¼ cups heavy cream
    1½ cups hard apple cider

Remove beards from mussels and discard. Scrub mussels under cold running water. Pat dry. Discard any mussels that are not tightly closed.

Put cream and cider in a large pot with a cover. Add ½ teaspoon salt and freshly ground black pepper. Bring to a boil for 1 minute. Reduce heat to medium and cook for 2 minutes, or until liquid is slightly reduced.

Add mussels and cover pot. Increase heat to high and cook mussels for 8 to 10 minutes, shaking pot back and forth frequently. Remove cover and, using a slotted spoon, divide mussels among 4 to 6 warm bowls. Quickly reduce liquid in pan and add freshly ground white pepper to taste. Pour sauce over mussels.

Serves 4 or more

CAST-IRON MUSSELS WITH CILANTRO

 2 pounds medium-large mussels
 1 large bunch fresh cilantro
 ¾ cup sake or chardonnay

Preheat oven to 500°F. Place a cast-iron skillet in a hot oven for 10 minutes until it's very hot.

Meanwhile, scrub mussels under cold running water, removing beards if any. Discard any mussels that are not tightly closed. Carefully put mussels in hot skillet and return it to oven. Roast mussels for 6 to 8 minutes, until they've opened.

Wash cilantro and dry well. Coarsely chop to get 1 cup.

Remove mussels from oven and place pan on stovetop over high heat. Pour sake over mussels and add ¾ cup chopped cilantro. Cook for 2 minutes, until some of the alcohol evaporates.

Transfer mussels and broth into 2 or 3 large bowls. Top with remaining chopped cilantro.

Serves 2 or 3

RED SNAPPER BAKED IN SALT

This preparation is suitable for any whole fish of similar size. You'll need at least a five-pound box of kosher salt.

 3 extra-large egg whites
 4-pound red snapper, gutted, scaled, fins removed
 ⅓ cup extra-virgin olive oil

Preheat oven to 400°F.

Whisk egg whites with ½ cup water in a very large bowl. Add 5 pounds of kosher salt and mix with a wooden spoon until salt is evenly moistened. Spread half of salt mixture in a rimmed baking sheet or shallow roasting pan that is 2 inches longer than fish on both ends.

Rinse the fish and pat dry. Place on salt. Cover with the remaining salt mixture, making sure the fish is entirely covered. If needed, make additional salt mixture. Bake for 45 minutes. Turn off oven but leave fish in for 10 minutes longer to set crust. Remove baking pan from oven.

You can present fish to your guests in the pan. Using the back of a chef's knife or a hammer, crack off the top crust. Lift fish from bottom layer of salt and transfer to a cutting board. Fillet as desired, gently carving the fish from the bone. Drizzle with olive oil and add freshly ground black pepper.

Serves 4

SAUTÉED SNAPPER IN CHAMPAGNE SAUCE

6 8-ounce red snapper fillets, skin on
8 tablespoons unsalted butter, chilled
1 cup brut rose champagne

Using tweezers, remove any bones from fish. Season fillets lightly with salt and freshly ground white pepper. Slash skins 3 or 4 times with the tip of a small sharp knife. This prevents the fish from curling.

Melt 2 tablespoons butter in each of 2 large nonstick skillets big enough to hold fish in 1 layer. Place 3 fillets flesh side down in each skillet. Cook over medium heat until opaque and lightly golden, about 3 minutes. Turn fish over with spatula. Increase heat a bit and cook for 2 to 3 minutes, until skin begins to crisp. When fish is cooked, transfer to a warm platter. Cover loosely with aluminum foil.

Quickly combine pan juices into 1 skillet and add champagne. Turn heat to high and reduce liquid to yield ⅓ cup. Reduce heat to a simmer. Cut remaining butter into small pieces and whisk into sauce until thick and creamy. Add salt and white pepper to taste. Pour sauce over fish and serve.

Serves 6

RED SNAPPER IN BURNT ORANGE OIL

I use every edible part of the orange in this dish: juice, rind, and segments.

5 medium oranges or blood oranges, if available
½ cup garlic- or herb-flavored olive oil (page 228)
4 7-ounce thick red snapper fillets, skin removed

Wash oranges. With a vegetable peeler, remove 8 long strips of orange rind (without pith) and reserve. Remove rind and all pith from 4 oranges and discard. Cut in between the membranes to release orange segments. Set aside.

Heat flavored oil in a very large nonstick skillet. Add strips of orange rind. As soon as they become dark brown, remove and set aside.

Sprinkle salt and freshly ground black pepper on both sides of fish. Add fish to the hot oil and sauté on both sides over medium-high heat, until crisp and lightly browned. (You may need to do this in 2 batches.) Transfer the cooked fish to a warm platter and cover loosely with foil.

Add orange segments and the juice of 1 remaining orange to the oil in the pan. Cook over high heat for 1 minute. Add salt and pepper to taste, and pour sauce over the fish. Garnish with the burnt orange peel.

Serves 4

THYME-ROASTED SALMON WITH CRÈME FRAÎCHE

Crème fraîche keeps the salmon meltingly tender; thyme imparts a smoky perfume.

- 4 8-ounce thick salmon fillets, skin on
- 2 large bunches fresh thyme
- 6 tablespoons crème fraîche

Preheat oven to 425°F.

Using tweezers, remove any little bones from fish. Lightly season fish with kosher salt and freshly ground black pepper. Remove 2 tablespoons thyme leaves from stems and set aside.

Scatter stems and remaining thyme in a rimmed baking sheet. Separate thyme stems into 4 flat bundles. Place a salmon fillet on each bundle. Spread crème fraîche thickly on each fillet to cover completely. Sprinkle with kosher salt and scatter with thyme leaves.

Bake for 8 minutes, until just firm. Place under the broiler for 1 minute. Do not overcook. Place fish on warm dinner plates.

Serves 4

THREE-MINUTE WASABI SALMON

Three-minutes refers to the amount of time it takes to prep this dish—one that is truly more than the sum of its parts. For a party, use a three-and-a-half to four-pound side of salmon in its entirety, double the remaining ingredients, and cook for six to eight minutes longer.

- 4 8-ounce thick salmon fillets, skin on
- 3 tablespoons wasabi powder
- ¾ cup mayonnaise

Preheat oven to 450°F.

Using tweezers, remove any little bones from fish. Season with salt and freshly ground black pepper.

Mix wasabi with 2 to 2½ tablespoons water to form a smooth, thick paste. Stir into mayonnaise and mix thoroughly. Add a pinch of salt and freshly ground black pepper.

Spread mixture on top of fillets to cover completely.

Line a rimmed baking sheet with parchment paper or aluminum foil. Place fish in pan and bake for about 15 minutes. It may take a few minutes less or more, depending on the thickness of fish. Do not overcook; the centers should be moist and the top of the fish should be lightly golden. Serve immediately.

Serves 4

SEARED SALMON WITH CORNICHON VINAIGRETTE

Cornichons, tiny French pickled cucumbers, are available in supermarkets and fancy food stores. They provide the acidity for the simple, yet unusual, dressing.

7 tablespoons extra-virgin olive oil
½ cup French cornichons with their pickling liquid
4 8-ounce salmon steaks

In a small saucepan whisk together 6 tablespoons olive oil and 4 tablespoons pickling juice from the cornichons.

Finely mince enough cornichons to yield 6 tablespoons. Add to saucepan with a pinch of freshly ground black pepper. Warm gently over low heat for 30 seconds and set aside.

Season both sides of salmon with salt and freshly ground black pepper. Heat 1 tablespoon olive oil in a very large nonstick skillet. Place salmon steaks in pan and cook over high heat until salmon is browned and crisp on 1 side, about 3 minutes. Carefully turn over with a spatula and cook for 2 to 3 minutes more, or until salmon is cooked to desired doneness. Do not overcook.

Place salmon steaks on individual plates or on a warm platter. Pour vinaigrette into hot skillet to warm it slightly. Pour vinaigrette over fish and serve immediately.

Serves 4

CRISPY SALMON WITH PANCETTA AND SAGE

8 ounces thinly sliced pancetta
4 8-ounce thick salmon fillets, cut from the center of fish
24 fresh sage leaves

Lay pancetta in a large nonstick skillet. Cook over low heat until most of the fat is rendered and the pancetta is just beginning to crisp. Remove pancetta with a spatula and let it cool for 5 minutes. Reserve the rendered fat in the skillet.

Remove skin from fish. Using tweezers, remove any little bones. Holding a sharp knife on the bias, cut 2 deep slits across the width of each piece of fish to make 2 pockets. Do not cut all the way across or all the way down.

Place a thin crisp pancetta slice and 3 sage leaves in each pocket, allowing the edges of the sage and pancetta to show. Reheat rendered fat in skillet. Season fillets with salt and freshly ground black pepper and place them, pocket side down, in the skillet. Cook over medium heat for about 3 minutes, until the fish begins to brown and get crisp. Turn the fillets and cook 3 minutes longer, or to desired doneness. The fish should be crisp on the outside and moist on the inside.

Serves 4

POACHED SALMON WITH CREAMY ZUCCHINI SAUCE

This suave jade green sauce can also be used on other poached or sautéed fish fillets.

1½ pounds medium zucchini
4 8-ounce thick salmon fillets, skin removed
3 tablespoons unsalted butter, chilled

Cut 2 zucchini into paper-thin rounds. Place rounds in a tightly overlapping pattern on top of fish to resemble scales. Sprinkle with salt and freshly ground white pepper, and wrap each fillet tightly in plastic wrap. Refrigerate for 1 hour.

Cut the remaining zucchini into ½-inch chunks. Put in a medium saucepan with ½ cup water and ½ teaspoon salt. Bring to a boil, lower heat, and cover. Cook for 15 minutes, or until zucchini is very soft. Transfer cooked zucchini and liquid to a blender. Cut cold butter into small bits and add it to pureed zucchini. Process until very smooth and thick. Add salt and white pepper to taste, and return to saucepan. Keep warm.

Bring 1 inch of salted water to a simmer in a very large skillet with a cover. Unwrap salmon and zucchini rounds. Place in skillet, cover, and cook approximately 10 minutes, or until salmon is just cooked through. Carefully remove salmon from water and place on plates. Serve with warm zucchini sauce.

Serves 4

SALMON OSSO BUCO

Generally made from a veal shank, osso buco means "bone with a hole." Here, a big sea scallop centered in a rosy salmon steak simulates that bone. Serve with a classic beurre blanc (page 229) or creamy mustard sauce (page 230), or simply as is.

4 10-ounce salmon steaks, skin removed
4 very large sea scallops
4 slices bacon

Preheat oven to 400°F.

Remove any little bones from salmon steaks, including the small center bones.

Insert 1 sea scallop in between the flaps of each salmon steak, where the little center bone was. Cut off a 1-inch piece from the end of one flap so that you can easily wrap flaps around sea scallop. The goal is to make a tight, round shape to resemble traditional osso buco.

Cut each slice of bacon in half lengthwise to make 2 long strips. Wrap 2 bacon strips around edges of salmon package (as though you were replacing the skin) and secure tightly with several toothpicks. Place salmon on a rimmed baking sheet. Sprinkle with salt. Bake for 10 minutes, or until salmon is cooked to desired doneness. Do not overcook. Sprinkle with coarsely cracked black pepper.

Serves 4

SALMON *ARROSTO* WITH ROSEMARY

2 large bunches fresh rosemary
3 large red onions
2½ pound salmon fillet cut from the center, skin on

Preheat oven to 500°F.

Wash rosemary and pat dry. Place 1 bunch on a rimmed baking sheet and distribute so that it approximates the size of the fish. Peel onions and slice thinly. Distribute three-quarters of the onion slices on top of rosemary.

Using tweezers, remove any little bones from fish. Season with salt and freshly ground black pepper, and place fish on onions, skin side down. Scatter remaining onion slices on top of fish. Cover fish with remaining rosemary, saving some sprigs for a garnish.

Roast for 20 minutes. Fish will be moist; do not overcook. Remove fish from oven and transfer to a warm platter along with cooked onions. Garnish with reserved rosemary sprigs.

Serves 4

MAPLE-GLAZED SALMON STEAKS

4 thick 9-ounce salmon steaks, skin on
½ cup pure maple syrup
4 limes

Remove any small bones from fish using tweezers.

Place maple syrup in a small bowl. Grate rind of 1 lime to get 1 teaspoon zest. Cut 2 or 3 limes in half and squeeze to get ¼ cup juice. Whisk maple syrup, lime juice, and zest together with a large pinch of salt. Place salmon in a shallow casserole and pour maple-lime marinade over fish. Let marinate at room temperature for 1 hour, turning fish several times.

Preheat broiler.

Place salmon on a broiler pan or rimmed baking sheet, reserving excess marinade in a small skillet. Broil for about 5 minutes, until fish is golden brown and cooked to desired doneness. Be careful not to overcook; fish should remain moist. Sprinkle lightly with salt.

Reduce marinade over high heat until syrupy, adding a little more lime juice to taste. Using a pastry brush, brush reduced marinade over fish. Serve with wedges or thin slices of lime on top.

Serves 4

SEARED SEA SCALLOPS ON SWEET PEA PUREE

It is crucial that you use "undipped" scallops. Those dipped in preservative absorb large quantities of water that prevent the scallops from browning. This is a good test of your fish store.

20 large sea scallops, about 1¾ pounds
10 ounces frozen petits pois
4 tablespoons unsalted butter

Pat the scallops dry. Season with salt and freshly ground white pepper.

Thaw peas. Put them in a small pot with just enough salted water to cover. Cook briefly over medium-high heat until peas are tender but still bright green. Drain immediately, reserving 6 tablespoons cooking liquid and ¼ cup peas for garnish. Put the rest of the peas in a blender and puree at highest speed. Add 2½ tablespoons butter and enough of the cooking liquid to create a very smooth but thick puree. You should have about 1¼ cups puree. Add salt and pepper to taste, and transfer puree to a small saucepan.

In a large nonstick skillet, melt remaining butter. Add the scallops and cook over high heat on both sides until scallops are golden and centers are opaque, about 2 to 3 minutes on each side. Heat pea puree and spread into circles on large, warm plates. Place scallops on puree, warm the reserved peas, and scatter them on top. Sprinkle with coarse sea salt and serve immediately.

Serves 4

BIG BROILED SCALLOPS

Use a smooth, spicy mustard such as Colman's, imported from England, or those take-out packets of Chinese mustard. The sauce is so good, you may want to double the quantity.

20 to 24 very large sea scallops, about 2¼ pounds
¾ cup crème fraîche
¼ cup smooth, spicy mustard

Preheat broiler.

Pat scallops dry and place them on a rimmed baking sheet.

In a small bowl, mix crème fraîche with mustard until blended. Spoon a little of the mixture on each scallop to cover top. Broil several minutes until scallops turn opaque and tops are golden brown. Transfer scallops to a warm platter. Spoon a little of the remaining sauce over each scallop and serve immediately.

Serves 4

STRIPED BASS ON BRAISED SAVOY CABBAGE

A very comforting fish dish for winter, especially when paired with Pinot Noir.

    1 large head Savoy cabbage, about 3 pounds
    4 ounces slab bacon
    4 8-ounce striped bass fillets, skin removed

Wash cabbage. Remove core and, using a long thin-bladed knife, finely cut cabbage into ¼-inch slices.

Cut bacon into ¼-inch cubes. Place in a very large nonstick skillet with a cover. Cook over medium heat for about 3 minutes, until fat is rendered and bacon begins to crisp.

Add cabbage, ½ cup water, ½ teaspoon kosher salt, and freshly ground black pepper. Cook over medium-high heat for 10 minutes, stirring frequently. Add another ½ cup water and lower heat to medium. Cover skillet and cook 30 minutes more, or until cabbage is browned and soft. If cabbage begins to stick, add a little more water.

Season fish with salt and pepper. Place on cabbage in skillet. Add ¼ cup water and cover skillet. Continue to cook for 10 to 12 minutes, or until fish is cooked through.

Carefully transfer cabbage and fish to large, warm plates. Drizzle with hot pan juices.

Serves 4

SAUTÉED STRIPED BASS WITH BASIL SAUCE

Frozen olive oil is the secret to this fragrant, emulsified bright green sauce.

    5 tablespoons extra-virgin olive oil
    3 large bunches fresh basil
    4 7-to 8-ounce striped bass fillets, skin removed

Place 3 tablespoons olive oil in a small dish and freeze for several hours until solid.

Wash basil and dry well. Coarsely chop enough to get 3 packed cups. Reserve the rest. Bring a pot of salted water to a boil. Add basil and boil for 2½ minutes. Drain immediately and put in a blender with frozen garlic oil and 3 to 4 tablespoons water. Process until thick and creamy. You should have about ¾ cup. Transfer to a small saucepan and add salt and freshly ground black pepper to taste.

Season fish with salt and pepper. Heat remaining 2 tablespoons oil in a very large nonstick skillet until hot. Add fish and cook over medium-high heat, turning once, until fish is opaque inside and golden on both sides. Serve immediately with gently heated sauce, and garnish with small sprigs of remaining basil.

Serves 4

CHILLED SHRIMP WITH WASABI MAYONNAISE

To make perfect poached shrimp, the water must be as salty as the sea, and the shrimp cooked briefly. Wasabi mayonnaise is nothing short of addictive. It also can be served with a pile of crab legs, lobster, stone crab claws, mussels, or jumbo lump crabmeat. A great first course or a summery entrée served alongside a ripe tomato salad.

1½ cups mayonnaise
6 tablespoons wasabi powder
24 very large shrimp in their shells, about 2 pounds

Put mayonnaise in a medium bowl. Stir 5 to 6 tablespoons cold water into wasabi powder until a thick paste is formed. Stir into mayonnaise until thoroughly blended and add salt to taste. Cover and refrigerate until ready to serve.

Wash shrimp in cold water with several tablespoons of kosher salt. Drain. Bring a large pot of water to a rapid boil. Add lots of kosher salt, about ½ cup, so that it tastes very salty. Add shrimp, lower heat to medium, and cook for 3 to 4 minutes, until shrimp are just firm. Using a slotted spoon, transfer shrimp to a bowl of ice cold, heavily salted water to cool. Drain well and chill until ready to serve. Peel shrimp, leaving tails intact. Serve with wasabi mayonnaise.

Serves 4

HERBED SHRIMP AND CRISPY PANCETTA

Boiled shrimp shells make a simple stock that helps meld the diverse flavors. Serve this dish with a mound of Very Lemony Mashed Potatoes (page 48).

24 very large shrimp in their shells, about 2 pounds
6 ounces pancetta, cut into ¼-inch dice
16 fresh sage leaves or large basil leaves

Remove shells from shrimp, leaving tails on. Set shrimp aside. Put shells in a small pot with water to cover. Bring to a boil, lower heat, and cook for 10 minutes.

Bring a medium saucepan of water to a boil. Add diced pancetta and cook for 1 minute. Drain well. Place drained pancetta in large nonstick skillet with a cover and cook over low heat until fat is rendered and pancetta begins to turn golden and crispy.

Add shrimp, raise heat to medium, and cook for 2 minutes, or until shrimp begin to turn opaque.

Coarsely tear 12 sage leaves and add to the skillet, toss gently, and cover. Reduce heat to low and cook for 1 to 2 minutes. Uncover pan. Add coarsely ground black pepper and ¼ cup or more reserved shrimp cooking liquid. Cook for 1 minute more, stirring with a wooden spoon. Garnish with remaining sage leaves. Serve immediately.

Serves 4

POACHED SHRIMP IN CORN MILK SAUCE

Corn milk is extracted from fresh kernels and blended with a broth made from boiled cobs to make a sauce that is demurely sweet and surprisingly healthy.

36 medium-large shrimp in their shells, about 2 pounds
2 large ears corn
6 tablespoons unsalted whipped butter

Remove shells from shrimp, leaving tails on. Place shells in a 4-quart pot with a cover.

Remove husks and silk from corn. Using a thin-bladed, sharp knife, cut corn kernels from cobs, cutting as close to the cob as possible. You should have about 2 cups.

Break cobs into several pieces and add to pot. Cover shells and cobs with cold water. Add 1 teaspoon kosher salt and ½ teaspoon whole black peppercorns. Bring to a boil. Cover pot and cook over medium heat for 20 minutes. Strain broth through a fine-mesh sieve. Add 1 cup broth and 1 cup corn kernels to a blender. Add 4 tablespoons whipped butter. Process until very smooth.

In a large nonstick skillet, add remaining butter. Add shrimp and remaining corn kernels. Cook over medium heat, stirring often, until shrimp turns opaque, about 3 minutes.

Meanwhile, cook sauce over high heat for 2 minutes. Put shrimp and corn mixture in large flat bowls. Spoon hot sauce over the top.

Serves 4

NEW ORLEANS PEPPER SHRIMP

If the preceding recipe has the virtues of being good for you, this buttery dish certainly does not. But it is very, very tasty. Open a six-pack and provide some crusty bread for dunking.

36 very large shrimp in their shells, about 3 pounds
2 sticks (½ pound) unsalted butter, chilled
3 tablespoons Worcestershire sauce

Preheat the oven to 400°F.

Wash shrimp and peel them, leaving tails on. Make a cut along the back of each shrimp and rinse under cold running water to remove vein. Dry on paper towels.

Place shrimp in a single layer in a shallow casserole with 3 tablespoons crushed black peppercorns. Cut butter into small pieces and scatter on shrimp. Bake in the oven for 5 minutes. Toss the shrimp, then add the Worcestershire sauce and 2 teaspoons kosher salt and stir. Bake 2 minutes longer.

Put shrimp, still in the casserole, under the broiler for 1 minute, or until golden. Serve in soup plates with the pan juices.

Serves 6

SWORDFISH "SWORDS" WITH ONION MARINADE

Red onions are used two ways in this dish: they are grated so that their juice impregnates and tenderizes the fish, and they are cut into kebab-style squares and grilled for their look and pleasant charred flavor.

3½ pounds swordfish, cut into 1¼-inch-thick steaks
2 to 3 large red onions
½ cup extra-virgin olive oil, plus more for drizzling

Cut swordfish into large chunks, removing any skin. Peel 1 or 2 onions and cut them into 1-inch pieces. Skewer alternating pieces of fish and onions on 6 12-inch skewers.

Put ½ cup olive oil in a small bowl. Grate 1 onion on the large holes of a box grater to get ¼ cup grated onion and juice. Mix with olive oil. Add 1 teaspoon kosher salt and lots of freshly ground black pepper. Mix well and pour over skewered fish and onions. Cover and marinate for 2 to 4 hours.

Heat a charcoal fire or gas grill, or preheat the broiler.

Cook skewered swordfish on all sides until slightly charred but still moist inside, about 5 minutes total. Serve 1 fish-and-onion sword per person. Drizzle with a little more olive oil and sprinkle with kosher salt.

Serves 6

PAN-GRILLED SWORDFISH WITH LIME-PEPPER SAUCE

4 8-ounce swordfish steaks
7 large limes
8 tablespoons unsalted butter, chilled

Place swordfish on a platter. Cut 1 lime in half and squeeze juice over fish. Sprinkle each piece of fish with salt. Let sit 20 minutes at room temperature.

Cut rind from 3 limes using a small sharp knife. Cut along edge of membranes to release lime segments. Cut remaining 3 limes in half and squeeze them so that you have ⅓ cup juice. Set aside.

Heat a very large nonstick skillet until very hot. Add fish and cook over medium-high heat until golden, 2 to 3 minutes. Turn fish carefully and cook for 2 to 3 minutes more, until fish is cooked through but still very moist. Transfer fish to a warm platter and keep warm under tented aluminum foil.

To juices in pan add lime juice, butter cut into small pieces, and ½ teaspoon coarsely ground black pepper. Cook for 1 minute over high heat, or until sauce gets creamy, stirring constantly. Add lime segments and swirl into sauce for a few seconds over high heat. Pour sauce over fish and serve immediately.

Serves 4

BRAISED SWORDFISH STUFFED WITH WATERCRESS

This technique, marinating fish in lots of olive oil, yields extraordinarily tender results.

> 4 10-ounce swordfish steaks, cut 1 inch thick
> 1 cup extra-virgin olive oil
> 2 bunches watercress

Place fish in a shallow casserole. Pour olive oil over fish to cover. Let marinate for 1 hour at room temperature.

Remove fish from olive oil. Set oil aside. Make a pocket in each steak by cutting horizontally through the center of the fish, being careful not to cut all the way through.

Wash watercress well and pat dry, saving 4 large sprigs for garnish. Discard stems from remaining watercress. Roll watercress leaves in olive oil and sprinkle lightly with salt. Stuff fish pockets with watercress, packing tightly.

Place fish in a very large nonstick skillet. Add 3 to 4 tablespoons of the reserved oil. Cook fish over low heat for 2 minutes. Cover pan and continue cooking very slowly, until fish is cooked through and tender, turning once with a spatula. This will take about 5 to 6 minutes on each side.

Transfer fish to a warm platter and pour any pan juices over the fish. Sprinkle with salt and freshly ground black pepper. Serve immediately with remaining sprigs of watercress.

Serves 4

TUNA STEAK *AU POIVRE*

Serve this with Ultimate Potato Puree (page 19), for a meat-and-potatoes kind of experience. The thick balsamic vinegar sauce is so good, you will want to put it on everything! It looks like chocolatey ketchup.

> ½ cup good-quality balsamic vinegar
> 4 8-ounce tuna medallions, each 1 inch thick
> 4 tablespoons unsalted butter, chilled

Put vinegar in a small nonreactive saucepan. Bring to a boil. Lower heat and cook until vinegar is reduced to 3 tablespoons. Set aside.

Crush 2 tablespoons black peppercorns and press firmly into one side of each tuna medallion. Sprinkle tuna lightly with salt. Melt 1 tablespoon butter in a very large nonstick skillet and cook fish, pepper side down, over high heat for 3 minutes. Turn over and cook for 45 seconds to 1 minute, until fish is still very pink in the center. Transfer fish to a warm platter and keep warm under tented aluminum foil.

Quickly add remaining butter and reduced vinegar to pan and cook over high heat, whisking constantly, until thick, 1 to 2 minutes. Pour sauce around fish.

Serves 4

PEPPER-SEARED TUNA, COOL MANGO RELISH

2 large ripe mangoes
1 large bunch cilantro
4 8-ounce tuna steaks

Peel the mangoes with a small sharp knife. Cut the flesh away from the pit, dice it into ¼-inch pieces, and put it in a small bowl. Finely chop enough cilantro to get ⅓ cup and reserve the rest. Add chopped cilantro, a pinch of salt, and freshly ground black pepper to chopped mangoes. Refrigerate for 30 minutes to 1 hour. Transfer one-third of the mixture to a food processor or blender with a few tablespoons water. Process until very smooth.

Coat a large nonstick skillet with cooking spray. Press ½ teaspoon very coarsely ground black pepper into 1 side of each tuna steak. Sprinkle lightly with salt. Preheat skillet. Place fish, pepper side down, in hot skillet. Cook on both sides over medium-high heat until the fish is seared on the outside, about 2 minutes per side, but still quite rare in the center. Serve hot tuna with mango relish. Drizzle with mango puree and garnish with remaining sprigs of cilantro.

Serves 4

TERIYAKI TUNA ROAST

This high-temperature approach to cooking one huge piece of top-quality tuna was inspired by a recipe from Barbara Kafka in her acclaimed book Roasting: A Simple Art. *Think of this tuna as filet mignon: rich and rare and slightly glazed on the outside.*

2 tablespoons plus 1 teaspoon dark Asian sesame oil, plus more for drizzling
½ cup prepared teriyaki sauce, plus more for drizzling
2½- to 3-pound piece tuna fillet, about 4 inches thick

Place rack in center of oven. Preheat oven to 500°F.

In a small bowl, whisk together 2 tablespoons sesame oil and teriyaki sauce. Gently tie kitchen string around fish in several places to help shape it like a roast. Do not pull the strings too tightly, as the tuna flesh is soft. Place fish in a shallow roasting pan and pour oil-teriyaki mixture over it. Massage the mixture into the fish. Marinate at room temperature for 1 hour, rolling the fish around in the marinade occasionally.

Lightly coat center of a rimmed baking sheet with 1 teaspoon sesame oil. Place fish in pan (the triangular tip of the fish should be pointing up) and roast for 15 minutes for rare. For medium rare, cook 5 minutes longer; for medium, cook 10 minutes longer.

Meanwhile, transfer marinade to a small saucepan and reduce over high heat until syrupy. When fish is cooked to desired doneness, carefully transfer it to a cutting board using 2 spatulas. Using a pastry brush, brush outside of tuna roast with reduced marinade, reserving ¼ cup for serving.

Slice tuna into thick slices across the width of the roast. Sprinkle slices with coarse sea salt and coarsely ground black pepper. Serve with a spoonful of the reduced marinade or, if you want, mix fresh teriyaki sauce and sesame oil together and drizzle on fish.

Serves 4

poultry

When my mother was a barefoot child in Pahokee, Florida, no one cooked *just* a chicken breast. When the family wanted Sunday dinner, she fetched an entire bird from the backyard, which my grandfather then dispatched and mumma (my grandma) cooked.

Tough, tender, stringy, juicy, dry—it was all chance back then. But one thing was certain: that chicken had flavor.

Today you can buy almost any part of the chicken you desire, and since virtually all these birds have swum in the same gene pool, we're guaranteed that they'll be tender, moist—and bland to a fault. For more flavor, look for natural, organic, free-range, or farm-raised birds from boutique producers.

The essence of cooking all poultry these days—since even turkey and capon have moved a few rungs down the flavor ladder—is to compensate for this gastronomic neutrality. That said, the objective of this chapter is to prod and provoke your taste buds with bright, simple flavor overlays—herbs and spices, olives and grapes, cured meats—and with "new" ingredients from faraway, such as pomegranate molasses, chipotle peppers in adobo, and tandoori rubs.

Poultry was a costly treat when my mother was growing up in Pahokee. (Remember, Herbert Hoover's presidential campaign promise was "a chicken in every pot.") My late mother-in-law said that when she was a girl, chicken salad was such a luxury that it was often augmented with veal. But now poultry is cheap, everyday fare. And because most people buy specific parts of birds, cooking is rapid, which to me signifies how easy it is to convert this everydayness into a culinary celebration.

Speaking of celebrations, I encourage you to try my recipes for duck, a bird that's rarely cooked at home these days. Duck has deep, rich flavor, lots of yummy fat (which you can save for other uses), and I assure you, it can be cooked without fear of failure.

STUFFED CORNISH HENS WITH PANCETTA AND ROSEMARY

2 Cornish hens, 1½ pounds each
8 ounces pancetta, cut into ¼-inch-thick cubes
2 bunches fresh rosemary

Preheat oven to 375°F.

Remove giblets from hens, discarding livers. Wash hens thoroughly and pat dry with paper towels. Cut off wing tips and set aside.

Put pancetta cubes in a bowl. Finely chop enough rosemary leaves to get 2½ tablespoons. Reserve the rest. Add chopped rosemary to pancetta with several pinches of freshly ground black pepper. Mix well.

Fill cavities of hens with all but ¼ cup of the pancetta mixture. Lightly salt hens, then truss them with kitchen string. Place in a large shallow roasting pan and bake for 40 minutes, basting with any pan juices.

Meanwhile, prepare stock. Place giblets and wing tips in a small saucepan with reserved pancetta mixture. Add several sprigs of rosemary and ½ teaspoon black peppercorns. Add cold water just to cover and bring to a boil. Lower heat and simmer for 30 minutes. Strain through a fine-mesh sieve into a clean saucepan and reduce over medium-high heat until you have ½ cup stock.

When cooked, transfer hens to a warm platter. Add stock to roasting pan, scraping up browned bits. Cook over high heat for 1 minute or until sauce gets a bit syrupy. Pour over halved hens. Garnish with rosemary sprigs.

Serves 4

CORNISH HEN UNDER A BRICK

You'll need a brick or two for making this dish, since the hen needs to lie completely flat while cooking. This preparation is Italian in its flavors, but if you substitute clarified butter and paint the hens with sour cream during cooking, you would have Chicken Tabaka, *an authentic Georgian-Russian recipe.*

1½-pound Cornish hen or squab chicken
3 tablespoons garlic olive oil (page 228), plus more for drizzling
½ cup dry white wine

Preheat oven to 450°F.

Wrap 1 or 2 bricks in foil. Remove giblets from hen and discard. Wash hens thoroughly and pat dry with paper towels. With kitchen shears, cut hen along the length of the backbone and remove the backbone. Also remove first wing joint. With your fist, pound the bird flat so that it is butterflied. Season with salt and freshly ground black pepper.

Heat garlic oil in a large nonstick skillet. Place hen, skin side down, in the oil and place a brick or bricks on top. (You can also use a cast-iron skillet as a weight.) Cook over medium-high heat for 10 minutes, until hen is golden brown. Turn it over, weight it again, and cook 8 to 10 minutes longer. Remove brick. Transfer hen to an ovenproof plate and put in hot oven for a few minutes while you prepare the sauce.

Add wine to pan juices in the skillet and reduce over high heat, scraping up browned bits. When the sauce has thickened, add salt and pepper to taste. Pour sauce over hen and serve immediately. Drizzle with additional garlic oil, if desired.

Serves 1 or 2

TARRAGON-ROASTED CORNISH HENS

Cooking buttered hens at a very high temperature—somewhere between broiling and roasting—crisps their exterior while keeping their insides moist.

> 6 tablespoons unsalted butter, chilled
> 2 Cornish hens, about 1½ pounds each
> 2 bunches fresh tarragon

Preheat oven to 475°F.

Melt 4 tablespoons butter. Keep 2 tablespoons chilled.

Remove giblets from hens and discard, or save for another use. Wash hens thoroughly and pat dry with paper towels. Fill cavities with lots of tarragon, including the stems, saving some leaves for later. Using a pastry brush, brush hens on all sides with melted butter. Sprinkle liberally with salt and freshly ground black pepper. Place hens in a shallow roasting pan or rimmed baking sheet. Roast hens for 40 minutes, basting often with melted butter. When hens are golden and juices run clear, remove from oven. Transfer hens to a cutting board.

Add ⅔ cup boiling water to pan juices and scrape up any browned bits. Pour liquid through a fine-mesh sieve into a small skillet. Add 1 tablespoon finely chopped tarragon leaves and bring to a boil. Boil for several minutes, until reduced to ⅓ cup. Whisk in remaining cold butter, adding salt and pepper to taste. Continue to cook until sauce thickens. Cut hens in half along the breast and backbones, and transfer to a platter. Pour sauce alongside hens, and serve immediately.

Serves 4

BROILED CORNISH HENS WITH LEMON CREAM

2 Cornish hens, about 1½ pounds each
2 lemons
¾ cup sour cream

Preheat oven to 400°F.

Remove giblets from hens and discard. Wash hens thoroughly and pat dry with paper towels. Remove wings from hens using a sharp knife or poultry shears. Cut hens in half along the breast and backbones. Place hens, cut side down, on a cutting board and press so that the legs lie flat.

Heat a very large nonstick skillet until very hot. Add hens, skin side down, and cook over medium high heat for 3 to 4 minutes. Turn over and cook 3 minutes more. Transfer hens to a rimmed baking sheet, leaving any fat in the skillet. Bake hens for 15 minutes, then place hens under the broiler and broil until golden brown and crisp, 1 to 2 minutes.

Meanwhile, grate zest of lemons and set aside. Cut lemons in half and squeeze to get ¼ cup juice. Place skillet with the fat over high heat and whisk in 3 tablespoons lemon juice and 2 tablespoons water. Heat, whisking constantly, for 1 minute. Reduce heat to low, add sour cream, and, whisking constantly, cook for a few minutes until sauce thickens a bit. If it's too thick, add a little more lemon juice or water. Add salt and freshly ground white pepper to taste. Keep warm.

Remove hens from broiler and transfer to a warm platter. Spoon warm sauce over hens (reheat sauce if necessary) and sprinkle with lemon zest.

Serves 4

WHOLE TANDOORI CORNISH HENS

Tandoori paste, which hails from India, is sure to become a new staple in the twenty-first-century pantry. This thick, spicy, and aromatic mixture of ginger, garlic, and many exotic spices is, thankfully, available in jars in specialty food stores and many supermarkets. I like to serve one tandoori hen per person, but if you cannot find small hens, use one large one, about one and three-quarters pounds, and cut it in half. The hens must marinate for twelve to twenty-four hours, so plan ahead.

2 Cornish hens, about 1 pound each
⅓ cup tandoori paste
2 cups plain yogurt

Remove giblets from hens and discard, or save for another use. Wash hens thoroughly and pat dry with paper towels. Slash hens down the center of each breast and down each leg. Rub about 2 tablespoons tandoori paste into the slashes and all over the front and back of hens. Place hens in a large bowl and spread 1½ cups yogurt over them. Toss to coat hens completely in yogurt. Cover and refrigerate for 12 to 24 hours.

Mix remaining yogurt with ½ tablespoon tandoori paste and a large pinch of salt. Refrigerate until ready to use.

When ready to cook, preheat oven to 400°F.

Remove all the marinade from the hens and pat hens dry. Rub each breast with remaining tandoori paste to cover completely. Place hens on a rimmed baking sheet and bake 25 minutes, or longer if using a larger hen. Remove from oven and pour any pan juices over hens.

Preheat broiler.

Place hens under broiler for 2 minutes or longer, until blackened in many spots. Remove from broiler and sprinkle with salt. Serve with yogurt sauce.

Serves 2

LIME-ROASTED CHICKEN

A lovely dinner for two.

2¾-pound chicken
4 limes
3 tablespoons extra-virgin olive oil

Preheat oven to 375°F.

Remove giblets and set aside; discard liver. Place giblets in a small saucepan with 1 cup water. Bring to a boil. Lower heat and simmer for 25 minutes. Remove from heat and strain broth through a fine-mesh sieve. Set aside.

Wash chicken thoroughly and pat dry with paper towels. Using a small sharp knife, make a dozen slits in each of 2 limes and place in cavity of chicken. Truss chicken with kitchen string and place in a shallow roasting pan. In a small bowl, mix olive oil and ½ teaspoon salt, and pour mixture all over chicken, spreading it with your hands. Roast for 50 minutes, or until meat thermometer reaches 160°F in the thigh, basting frequently.

Transfer chicken to a cutting board. Pour off most of fat from pan. Scrape up all the brown bits from pan with ½ cup boiling water and strain into saucepan with reserved broth. Add the zest of 1 lime and 1 tablespoon lime juice. Bring to a boil and cook until reduced a bit. Add salt and freshly ground black pepper to taste. Remove limes from cavity and carve chicken as desired. Serve with sauce and fresh lime wedges.

Serves 2

BISTRO CHICKEN WITH WILD MUSHROOMS

5-pound roasting chicken
1 cup dried porcini mushrooms
5½ tablespoons unsalted butter

Preheat oven to 375°F.

Wash chicken thoroughly and pat dry with paper towels. Remove giblets and set aside; discard liver. Season chicken, inside and out, with salt and freshly ground black pepper.

Soak mushrooms in 2 cups of boiling water for 20 minutes. Drain mushrooms, saving the soaking liquid. Melt 1 tablespoon butter in a small skillet and sauté mushrooms for 5 minutes. Fill cavity of chicken with mushrooms and truss chicken with kitchen string.

Spread 2 tablespoons butter on chicken breasts. Place chicken in a heavy, shallow roasting or broiler pan, and roast for about 1 hour and 30 minutes, or until chicken thigh reaches an internal temperature of 160°F.

Meanwhile, put giblets in a small saucepan with ½ cup water. Pour mushroom liquid through a fine-mesh sieve and add it to the saucepan. Bring to a boil, then simmer for 25 minutes. Discard giblets. Pour liquid through a strainer into a clean saucepan.

Remove chicken from oven and transfer to a cutting board. Using a large spoon, scoop mushrooms out of the chicken cavity and add to mushroom liquid. Add ½ cup boiling water to pan juices and cook for 1 minute over high heat, scraping up any browned bits. Strain pan juices into mushroom liquid. Cook over high heat until reduced by two thirds. (You should have about 1 cup.) Add remaining butter and cook for 1 minute, whisking constantly, until sauce emulsifies. Add salt and freshly ground black pepper to taste. Carve chicken and serve with mushroom sauce.

Serves 4

GOAT CHEESE-AND-BASIL STUFFED CHICKEN

This unorthodox stuffing goes under the skin rather than in the chicken's cavity. It makes an extraordinarily plump bird.

2 large bunches fresh basil
8 ounces fresh goat cheese
5-pound roasting chicken

Preheat oven to 375°F.

Wash basil well and pat dry. Remove enough basil leaves to make 3 packed cups. Place basil and goat cheese in bowl of a food processor. Add a pinch of salt and a generous amount of coarsely ground black pepper. Process until cheese is smooth, being careful not to overprocess.

Remove giblets from chicken, discarding or saving for another use. Wash chicken thoroughly and pat dry with paper towels. Starting at neck of chicken, slip your fingers under the breast skin, carefully separating the skin from the flesh. Continue downward and, with your index finger, separate the skin around the thighs.

With your fingers or a spoon, push cheese mixture under skin to cover entire breast and thighs. Use all of the mixture. You should have, approximately, a ¼-inch layer of cheese under the skin. (Press on skin to evenly distribute cheese.)

Truss chicken with kitchen string. Sprinkle lightly with salt and freshly ground black pepper. Roast in a heavy, shallow roasting pan for 1½ hours, or until meat thermometer reaches 160°F in the thigh. Baste several times during roasting. Remove from oven. Let rest for 10 minutes before carving.

Serves 6

SALT-BAKED CHICKEN WITH THYME AND LEMON OIL

Chicken baked in an impenetrable salt crust seals in natural juices and is fun to present at the table. You will need about four pounds of kosher salt.

> 4-pound chicken
> 2 large bunches fresh thyme
> ¼ cup lemon olive oil (page 228)

Preheat oven to 450°F.

Wash chicken thoroughly and pat dry with paper towels. Discard giblets or save for another use. Fill cavity with thyme, saving some sprigs for a garnish.

Pour 3 cups kosher salt into the bottom of a deep casserole with a cover. Put chicken on salt, breast side up. Add enough salt to cover top and sides of chicken, about 10 cups. Sprinkle with 1 cup water, patting the salt down to make a solid crust.

Bake, covered, for 45 minutes. Remove cover and bake chicken 20 minutes more. Remove casserole from oven and let rest for 10 minutes.

Meanwhile, mix lemon oil with 1 teaspoon coarsely ground black pepper and a pinch of salt. Set aside.

Present chicken to guests, then return to kitchen. Crack off the salt crust with the back of a heavy chef's knife to remove the chicken. Remove remaining salt with a pastry brush. Cut chicken as desired. Serve with lemon-pepper oil and reserved sprigs of thyme.

Serves 4

POULE AU POT WITH BEEF SHIN AND LEEKS

This is chicken-in-the-pot made with gelatinous beef shin and leeks, all slowly simmered for hours. It is the ultimate comfort dish. Sprinkle with fleur de sel—the best coarse sea salt.

  3½-pound chicken
  5 pounds beef shin, cut into ¾-inch-thick slices
  4 large leeks

Wash chicken thoroughly and pat dry with paper towels. Place chicken and beef shin into an 8- to 10-quart soup pot or flameproof casserole with a cover.

Trim 2 inches off green tops of leeks and discard. Trim roots. Wash leeks, removing any grit between leaves. Cut leeks into 3 sections and add to pot. Add enough cold water to cover chicken. Add 1 teaspoon whole black peppercorns.

Bring to a boil. This will take approximately 15 minutes. Cover pot, lower heat, and simmer for 4 hours or longer, until beef is very tender. Check occasionally to make sure chicken is covered with liquid, adding more water if necessary. Remove from heat.

Transfer chicken, beef, and leeks to a platter. Remove some of the fat from top of broth. Increase heat to high and reduce liquid by half. Return chicken, beef, and leeks to pot and reheat gently. Remove chicken and carve as desired. Arrange chicken, beef, and leeks in large flat soup plates. Pour hot broth over them and sprinkle with kosher salt.

Serves 6

LEMON ZA'ATAR CHICKEN

Za'atar, a spice mixture redolent of biblical antiquity, is an intoxicating blend of dried hyssop, sumac, and sesame seeds. You can find it in any Middle Eastern food market. Buy a lot—it lasts a long time in a covered jar.

  4½-pound roasting chicken
  ½ cup za'atar
  4 lemons

Wash chicken thoroughly and pat dry with paper towels. Cut chicken into quarters so you have 2 breast and 2 leg-and-thigh pieces. Remove chicken wings for making stock. Remove and save giblets, discarding liver.

Place chicken in a shallow casserole. Rub well with za'atar. Grate the rind of 2 lemons and sprinkle zest over chicken. Cut these lemons in half and squeeze juice over chicken. Add freshly ground black pepper and mix well. Cover and refrigerate for 3 to 4 hours.

Meanwhile, make stock. Place chicken wings and giblets in a large saucepan. Cover with cold water, and add ¼ teaspoon salt. Bring to a boil, lower heat, and simmer, uncovered for 30 minutes, skimming often. Strain through a fine-mesh sieve into a small saucepan. Over low heat, reduce stock so you have about ¾ cup. Set aside.

Preheat oven to 375°F.

Place chicken pieces on a heavy rimmed baking sheet or in a shallow broiler pan. Sprinkle lightly with salt. Bake for 45 minutes. Transfer chicken to a warm platter.

Add chicken stock to baking sheet, scraping up browned bits. Quickly strain through a fine-mesh sieve back into the saucepan. Cook over high heat for a few minutes, until syrupy. Add salt and pepper to taste. Pour over chicken and serve with wedges of remaining lemon.

Serves 4

CRISPY FRIED CHICKEN

Brining the chicken pieces for 6 hours makes for a very moist bird. Self-rising flour ensures a crispy crust, and solid vegetable shortening is essential for supernal crispness.

- 2 2¾-pound frying chickens
- 4 cups self-rising flour
- 2 cups solid vegetable shortening

Cut each chicken into 8 pieces: 2 legs, 2 thighs, 2 wings, and 2 half breasts. Remove backbone. Wash chicken pieces. Put them in a large pot with a cover. Add cold water to cover and stir in 1 cup kosher salt until it dissolves. Cover and refrigerate for 6 hours.

Remove chicken pieces from brine. Pat each piece dry with paper towels. Mix flour with 1½ teaspoons salt and 1 tablespoon freshly ground black pepper. Dredge each piece of chicken in flour mixture.

Heat 1 cup shortening in each of 2 large heavy frying pans with covers until thoroughly melted and hot. Add chicken, skin side down, and fry over high heat for 5 minutes. Lower heat to medium and cook for 5 minutes longer. Cover pans and fry for 5 minutes longer. Adjust the heat during cooking so the chicken continues to sizzle without spattering.

Uncover and turn the chicken pieces. Turn heat to medium-high and cook for 10 minutes. Lower heat to medium and cover; cook for 5 minutes. Uncover and turn pieces again so they are skin side down; cook, uncovered, for 5 minutes, or until chicken is crisp and the juices run clear. Transfer to a platter lined with paper towels to drain. Serve immediately.

Serves 6

SAUTÉED CHICKEN BREASTS WITH OVEN-DRIED GRAPES

This surprising sauce, fashioned from fresh grape juice and a little chilled butter, makes for a very elegant and low-calorie dish (under 350 calories). The sauce and preparation are terrific with duck breasts and pork chops, too.

1½ pounds dark red seedless grapes
3½ tablespoons unsalted butter, chilled
4 6-ounce skinless, boneless chicken breasts

Preheat oven to 275°F.

Wash grapes and remove from stems. Place half of the grapes on a rimmed baking sheet. Bake for 1½ hours, shaking pan frequently. Remove from oven and set aside.

Place uncooked grapes in a blender and puree until very smooth. Strain through a coarse-mesh sieve, pressing down hard on the skins. You should get about ¾ cup juice.

In a large nonstick skillet, melt 2 tablespoons butter. Wash chicken breasts thoroughly and pat dry with paper towels. Season chicken with salt and freshly ground black pepper. Add to pan and cook over medium-high heat for 5 minutes on each side, or until golden.

Add grape juice and cook 5 minutes longer, or until chicken is cooked through and just firm to the touch. Be careful not to overcook. The grape juices will darken into a mahogany-colored sauce. Transfer breasts to a platter.

Add remaining butter to skillet and cook over high heat for 1 minute. Add oven-dried grapes and cook 1 minute longer. Add salt and pepper to taste and pour sauce over chicken. Serve immediately.

Serves 4

CHICKEN *ROULADES* WITH SOPPRESSATA AND ROASTED PEPPERS

Instead of soppressata, which is a flavorful pepper-studded Italian salami, you may substitute Genoa or Hungarian salami. In a pinch, you may use good-quality jarred roasted peppers instead of roasting your own.

2 red bell peppers
4 8-ounce boneless chicken breasts, skin on
4 ounces very thinly sliced soppressata

To roast peppers: Preheat broiler. Place whole peppers on a rimmed baking sheet 6 inches from heat source. Broil on all sides until blackened, about 10 minutes. Place peppers in a paper bag, then seal bag and allow peppers to steam and soften. Peel away charred skin.

Preheat oven to 350°F.

Wash chicken breasts thoroughly and pat dry with paper towels. Remove tenders from breasts and set aside. (Tenders are the small muscles, approximately ½ inch in diameter, running the length of each breast half.) Place breasts on a flat surface, skin side down. Flatten slightly with a cleaver or mallet and season with salt and freshly ground black pepper.

Place an overlapping layer of soppressata on each chicken breast to cover the flesh. Place a strip of red pepper, about ½ inch wide by 3 inches long, down the center of each breast. Place chicken tender on top of pepper. Roll chicken breasts tightly, jelly-roll style, to completely envelop the filling.

Season *roulades* with salt and pepper and place them on a rimmed baking sheet. Bake for 25 minutes, and then place under a broiler for 30 seconds to crisp the skin.

Remove from oven. Let rest for 5 minutes. Cut each breast, on a slight bias, into 5 thick slices. Serve overlapping slices with pan juices drizzled on top.

Serves 4

CHICKEN BREASTS IN WALNUT AND POMEGRANATE SAUCE

This beguiling chicken dish, with its sweet, sour, salty, and bitter flavors, is an adaptation of a Persian dish known as fesenjune. *It's even better the second day . . . and the third. Pomegranate molasses can be purchased in Middle Eastern food stores.*

    12 ounces walnut pieces, about 3 cups
    3 whole chicken breasts, bone in, skin on, about 4½ pounds
    ½ cup or more pomegranate molasses

Put walnuts in bowl of a food processor and process until finely ground but not quite a paste. In a large nonstick skillet, brown walnuts slowly over medium heat, stirring constantly with a wooden spoon. Adjust heat so they do not burn but turn dark very slowly; it will take about 15 minutes. Remove from heat and place in a flameproof casserole or heavy pot, large enough to accommodate chicken in a single layer.

Wipe the nonstick skillet clean with a paper towel. Wash chicken breasts thoroughly and pat dry with paper towels. Cut each breast in half through the breastbone. Heat skillet and add chicken, skin side down. Brown over medium heat until chicken is almost cooked through, about 10 minutes on each side. Season with salt and freshly ground pepper.

Meanwhile, add 3½ cups water to casserole with the nuts. When chicken is browned, transfer chicken and all the pan juices to casserole. Bring to a boil then lower heat and simmer until thickened, about 15 minutes. Remove chicken with a slotted spoon and continue cooking until sauce is thick; the time will vary.

Once sauce is thick, add pomegranate molasses. Cook over medium-high heat for 5 minutes to reduce sauce. You can adjust sauce until balanced, adding more molasses, salt, and pepper to taste. Return chicken to casserole and heat for a few minutes until hot.

Serves 6

CHICKEN RUSTICA WITH CHORIZO AND DICED LEMON

You will want a piece of crusty bread for mopping up the fabulous juices. Chorizo is my first choice, but you can substitute pepperoni.

> 8 medium-large chicken thighs, about 3¼ pounds
> 3 large lemons
> 8 ounces chorizo sausage, about ¾ inch in diameter

Wash chicken thighs thoroughly and pat dry with paper towels. Place them in a large nonreactive bowl. Grate rind of lemons and add the zest to the chicken with ½ teaspoon kosher salt and freshly ground black pepper. Slice the chorizo into ¼-inch-thick rounds. Add to chicken, toss, and refrigerate for 4 to 6 hours.

Cut rest of rind and pith from the lemons with a small sharp knife. Cut lemon flesh into ¼-inch dice, removing any seeds. Set aside.

Heat a very large nonstick skillet. Place the chicken, skin side down, in pan, along with the chorizo. Cook over medium-high heat until chicken is golden, about 10 minutes. Turn over and cook until chicken is cooked through and chorizo is browned, about 10 minutes longer. Add diced lemon and increase heat to high. Cook for 3 to 4 minutes more. The lemon will thicken the pan juices. Add salt and pepper to taste.

Serves 4

CHIPOTLE AND RED ONION CHICKEN

Serve with 1-2-3 tostones: fry thick slices of plantains in corn oil and serve with wedges of lime.

> 4 large chicken breast halves, bone in, skin on, about 3 pounds
> 3 medium-large red onions
> 4 chipotle peppers in adobo sauce

Wash chicken thoroughly and pat dry with paper towels. Place it in a large nonreactive bowl. Peel onions. Grate 1 onion on the large holes of a box grater. Add grated onion and juice to chicken. Thinly slice remaining onions and add to chicken. Chop chipotle peppers with a little of their sauce and add to chicken. Add ½ teaspoon kosher salt and toss well. Cover and refrigerate for 1 hour.

Preheat oven to 350°F.

Transfer chicken and marinade to a rimmed baking sheet or shallow broiler pan, slipping onion slices under breasts. Bake for 40 minutes, or until chicken is cooked through. Do not overcook. You want chicken to be juicy and moist. Serve chicken on warm plates with onions on top. Add salt to taste.

Serves 4

PESTO-CRUSTED CHICKEN BREASTS

The interesting technique here is not to bake the chicken with the skin, but rather render the fat from the skin to drizzle on the crust. This quick crust can be made with toasted pecans or grated cheese, provided you use real Parmigiano-Reggiano. You choose.

4 large chicken breasts halves, bone in, skin on, about 3 pounds
¾ cup prepared pesto
¾ cup finely ground toasted pecans or grated Parmigiano-Reggiano

Preheat oven to 425°F.

Wash chicken thoroughly and pat dry with paper towels. Remove skin and fat from chicken and place it in a nonstick skillet. Heat over medium heat for 10 minutes, until fat is rendered.

Thickly coat the top of each breast with pesto. Pack on nuts thoroughly to coat top of each breast. Place chicken on a rimmed baking sheet. Drizzle each piece with 1 to 2 tablespoons melted chicken fat. Sprinkle with salt and freshly ground black pepper. Bake for 30 minutes. Drizzle any pan juices on top.

Serves 4

ROOT BEER CHICKEN

A thoroughly retro recipe, chicken made with Coca-Cola recently became a rage in Paris. This is my version. Root beer adds more character to this fun dish, which your kids will love. My husband loves it, too—hot, cold, or in between.

1 cup ketchup
1 cup root beer, the best you can find
3½-pound chicken, quartered

Preheat oven to 350°F.

In large bowl, whisk together ketchup and root beer until thoroughly blended. Add a large pinch of kosher salt and sprinkle liberally with freshly ground black pepper. Wash chicken and thoroughly pat dry with paper towels. Add chicken to bowl and toss to coat thoroughly. Let sit for 15 minutes.

Remove chicken, reserving marinade. Place chicken pieces, skin side up, on a rimmed baking sheet. Bake for 1 hour and 10 minutes. Meanwhile, put marinade in a small saucepan. Bring to a boil, then lower heat to medium and cook until marinade is reduced to about ¾ cup. During baking, baste chicken several times, alternating with the marinade and with some of the fat that accumulates in the pan. Drain the fat once during baking.

When chicken is done, transfer it to a warm platter or plates. Drizzle with a little more warm marinade, and serve extra marinade on the side.

Serves 4

GARLICKY CUMIN CHICKEN

This can be made in a hot oven or on a charcoal grill. Serve with corn on the cob and a plate of sliced heirloom tomatoes.

4 large chicken breast halves, bone in, skin on, about 3 pounds
⅓ cup garlic olive oil (page 228), plus more for drizzling
2½ tablespoons ground cumin

Wash chicken thoroughly and pat dry with paper towels. Make 3 or 4 slits about ¼-inch deep across width of each chicken breast. Place chicken in a shallow casserole. Add garlic oil, 2 tablespoons cumin, 1 teaspoon kosher salt, and lots of freshly ground black pepper, making sure that the mixture gets into the slits and coats the chicken. Cover and refrigerate for 3 to 4 hours.

Preheat oven to 425°F, or light a charcoal grill. If grilling, add the chicken pieces to the hot grill and cook until done, turning as necessary, about 10 minutes per side.

If using oven, remove chicken from marinade and place on a rimmed baking sheet. Let come to room temperature. Bake for 30 minutes, then place under broiler for 1 minute, or until crisp and brown.

Remove from broiler or grill when done. Drizzle with additional garlic oil and dust with the rest of the cumin. Sprinkle with salt and pepper.

Serves 4

WARM POACHED CHICKEN WITH SUN-DRIED TOMATOES AND CAPERS

The following method, adapted from a Chinese technique, is meant to save both fuel and effort. A pot of water with a chicken in it is brought to a rapid boil, then removed from the heat. The pot stays covered until cooled. The result is succulent, velvety meat.

4-pound chicken
¾ cup sun-dried tomatoes in oil
3 tablespoons capers, brine reserved

Discard giblets from chicken, or save for another use. Wash chicken thoroughly and pat dry with paper towels. Truss chicken with kitchen string. Place chicken in a covered pot large enough to comfortably accommodate it. Add 3 tablespoons kosher salt and 1 tablespoon whole black peppercorns. Cover pot and bring to a rapid boil, 20 to 25 minutes. Do not lift cover; listen for the water to boil, then turn off heat. Do not lift cover. Let sit for 3 hours.

Immediately remove chicken from pot and discard skin and fat. Remove meat in large pieces from bones. Arrange chicken pieces on a warm platter and cover with aluminum foil.

Coarsely chop or julienne sun-dried tomatoes and put them, with their oil, in a small saucepan. Add 2 to 3 tablespoons capers plus a little brine to taste, and warm gently. Pour over chicken and serve immediately.

Serves 4

LACQUERED CHICKEN

½ cup blackstrap molasses
⅔ cup red wine vinegar
8 chicken thighs, about 3 pounds

In a large bowl, whisk together molasses, vinegar, ½ teaspoon salt, and lots of freshly ground black pepper. Wash chicken thoroughly and pat dry with paper towels. Add thighs to marinade and coat well. Let sit at room temperature for 1 hour, turning often.

Preheat oven to 400°F.

Shake excess marinade from chicken thighs and place them on a rimmed baking sheet. Heat marinade a in small skillet until reduced by half.

Bake chicken for 35 minutes, turning twice and basting several times with reduced glaze. After 35 minutes, put thighs briefly under broiler to brown.

Serves 4

YOGURT CHICKEN WITH BLACKENED ONIONS

Onions are used three ways here: grated, diced, and sautéed. Yogurt tenderizes the meat, which is delicious hot or cold.

8 very large chicken thighs, about 3½ pounds
3 large yellow onions
2 cups plain yogurt

Wash chicken thoroughly and pat dry with paper towels. With a sharp knife, remove any extra lobes of fat or skin from the thighs and set aside. Place chicken in a shallow casserole. Peel onions and cut in half. Grate one half of an onion on the large holes of a box grater and add grated onion and juice to chicken. Set other half onion aside for later. Dice a second onion into ⅛-inch pieces. You should have 2 heaping cups. Add diced onions, yogurt, 1 teaspoon salt, and freshly ground black pepper to chicken. Toss to coat. Cover and refrigerate for 8 to 12 hours.

Preheat oven to 350°F.

Place chicken and marinade on a rimmed baking sheet, making sure the pieces are in 1 layer and well covered with yogurt and onions. Bake for 45 minutes. Then broil, placing the pan the farthest away from heat source, until onions are somewhat blackened, about 4 minutes.

Meanwhile, put reserved fat and skin in a medium nonstick skillet and heat until fat is rendered. Remove skin. Slice remaining onion half paper-thin. Add onion to hot chicken fat and cook over high heat until dark brown, stirring often.

Remove chicken from broiler. Spoon pan juices over chicken and top with sautéed onions.

Serves 4

CHICKEN-IN-A-WATERMELON

This positively wacky idea results in a succulent bird with sweet juices. However improbable, it will make a big hit at your beach house. Or serve it on April Fool's Day—a holiday strangely bereft of a single signature dish—providing you can find a watermelon. Five-spice powder is a combination of Szechuan peppercorns, star anise, cloves, cinnamon, and fennel. It's available in most supermarkets.

1 very large watermelon
5- to 6-pound roasting chicken
1 or more tablespoons five-spice powder

Preheat oven to 400°F.

Cut off a ¼-inch-thick slice of rind the length of the watermelon so it can sit without wobbling. Cut off top third of melon in one long horizontal slice; this piece will become the cover. Scoop out enough of the flesh from the inside of the melon and the cover to make room for whole chicken.

Wash chicken thoroughly and pat dry with paper towels. Season chicken with salt and freshly ground black pepper, then liberally rub five-spice powder into skin of chicken. Place chicken in melon and then place the melon cover on top, securing with long skewers. Put a rimmed baking sheet on bottom rack of oven to catch any juices. Bake watermelon directly on the middle rack for 2 hours. Reduce temperature to 300°F and cook 1½ hours longer.

Carefully put the watermelon on a tray and present it to your guests, but return to kitchen to remove chicken from watermelon. Carve as desired. Tip juices out of watermelon into a nonstick skillet and cook over high heat until juices thicken. Add more five-spice powder to sauce, if desired, and salt and pepper to taste. Serve chicken on a warm platter, accompanied by sauce in a sauceboat.

Serves 6

ROAST CAPON WITH FORTY CLOVES OF GARLIC

A capon is a castrated rooster that has been fattened for eating. The pan juices are enhanced with dry (fino) sherry or a slightly sweeter sherry like Dry Sack.

7¾- to 8-pound capon
40 large garlic cloves
¾ cup dry sherry

Preheat oven to 400°F.

Remove giblets and discard liver. Wash capon thoroughly and dry with paper towels. Set aside. Put giblets in a medium saucepan with water to cover. Add 1 clove garlic, slightly smashed, and ¼ teaspoon black peppercorns. Bring to a boil. Lower heat and simmer for 45 minutes. Strain through a fine-mesh sieve into a clean saucepan. Reduce liquid over medium heat to get about 1 cup stock.

Peel 2 garlic cloves, press through a garlic press, and rub garlic all over capon. Season with salt and freshly ground black pepper. Truss with kitchen string.

Place capon, breast side up, in a shallow roasting pan. Surround capon with remaining unpeeled garlic cloves. Roast for 30 minutes, lower temperature to 350°F, and roast 50 minutes longer, basting often, or until internal temperature of thigh is 155°F and juices run clear. Transfer capon and garlic to cutting board and tent with aluminum foil while you prepare sauce.

Pour off most of fat from roasting pan. Place pan on stovetop over high heat, add stock and sherry, and scrape up browned bits with a spatula. Pour liquid through a fine-mesh sieve into a clean saucepan and bring to a boil. Lower heat and simmer until sauce is a bit syrupy. Carve capon as desired and serve with roasted garlic cloves and sauce.

Serves 6

BREAST OF CAPON WITH FENNEL SAUSAGE AND PRUNES

You need a large capon, with a breast that weighs about six pounds. Ask your butcher to bone the breast, leaving the lobes attached. It will look very pretty when sliced. You can roast the legs and thighs alongside the breast, or save them for another use.

16 large pitted prunes
9- to 10-pound capon, breast boned, legs and thighs removed
12 ounces fennel sausage

Preheat oven to 400°F.

Place prunes in a bowl and cover with boiling water. Let sit for 5 minutes, then drain.

Pat prunes dry.

Wash capon thoroughly and pat dry with paper towels. Place capon breast on work surface, skin side down. Season with salt and freshly ground black pepper. Remove sausage from casing and place in a long row down the center of the breast, between the halves. Place a row of prunes alongside sausage. Roll up breast tightly, jelly-roll style, to enclose filling. Tie with kitchen string at 1-inch intervals to hold shape.

Place capon in a shallow roasting pan. Add ¼ cup water to bottom of pan. Roast, basting often, for 1 hour and 20 minutes, or until internal temperature is 155°F. Transfer capon to a cutting board. Add ¾ cup boiling water to pan, scraping up any browned bits.

Strain liquid through a fine-mesh sieve into a small saucepan. Bring to a boil and cook for several minutes until syrupy, adding salt and pepper to taste. Cut capon into thick slices and serve with reduced pan juices.

Serves 6

BRINED-CURED TURKEY BREAST WITH TURKEY BACON

Immersing a turkey breast in salted water creates moist, smoothly textured flesh. A mantle of turkey bacon adds a subtle smoky flavor and makes the roast self-basting. This recipe is also appropriate for those with a kosher kitchen.

6½- to 7-pound all-natural turkey breast
12 ounces thinly sliced turkey bacon
6 large thick leeks

Put turkey breast in a large pot with cold water to cover. Add 2 cups kosher salt and stir to dissolve. Cover and refrigerate for 6 hours.

Preheat oven to 350°F.

Season turkey with freshly ground black pepper. Remove pop-up thermometer if there is one. Lay strips of turkey bacon in a tightly overlapping pattern to cover entire breast. Secure with toothpicks. Wrap breast securely with a double layer of cheesecloth: first wrap around breast, then wrap front to back, making sure the entire breast is covered.

Remove roots from leeks and cut in half lengthwise. Wash well between layers to remove any dirt. Pat leeks dry and place side by side, cut side down, in a large shallow roasting pan. Place turkey on leeks and cover breast tightly with foil.

Roast turkey for about 1 hour and 45 minutes. Remove foil and roast 40 minutes longer, or until internal temperature is 150°F. Remove from oven and transfer leeks and turkey to a warm platter. Cut leeks in half crosswise and remove cheesecloth from turkey. Pour 1 cup boiling water into roasting pan and scrape up any browned bits. Pour pan juices through a fine-mesh sieve into a small saucepan. Bring to a boil and cook for several minutes until syrupy, adding salt and pepper to taste. Present turkey to guests, then return to kitchen. Remove bacon and carve turkey as desired. Serve with bacon, leeks, and hot pan juices.

Serves 8

ROLLED-AND-TIED TURKEY ROAST WITH PEARS

Half of a large turkey breast, skin on and bones removed, resembles and can be used as London broil. I love this cut of turkey, which most butchers carry. Here it is rubbed with herbs, rolled, and tied like a roast. Baked pears become a delectable sauce.

1 large bunch fresh basil
2½ pound turkey London broil (half a breast with bones removed)
3 large ripe Comice pears

Preheat oven to 400°F.

Chop enough basil to get ½ cup. Reserve remaining sprigs.

Wash turkey thoroughly and pat dry with paper towels. Place turkey, skin side down, on a board. Spread chopped basil on flesh, and season with salt and freshly ground black pepper. Roll turkey breast lengthwise to make a cylindrical shape, about 10 inches long by 4 inches wide at the widest point. Tie with kitchen string at 1½-inch intervals. Season turkey with salt and pepper. Tuck enough whole basil leaves under strings to cover top. Place turkey in a shallow roasting pan.

Peel pears and cut in half lengthwise, removing seeds. Arrange pears, cut side down, around turkey.

Bake turkey for 45 to 50 minutes, or until the internal temperature reaches 150°F. Transfer turkey and roasted pears to a cutting board.

Pour ½ cup boiling water into roasting pan and scrape up browned bits over medium-high heat. Pour pan juices into a blender, and add 3 pear halves that have been cut in pieces and a few basil leaves. Puree until very smooth. Strain through a coarse-mesh sieve into a small saucepan. Add salt and pepper to taste and warm over low heat. Cut remaining pears in half lengthwise. Slice turkey and serve with pear quarters, pear sauce, and remaining basil sprigs.

Serves 6

TURKEY BALLOTINE WITH SAGE AND GARLIC JUS

Ballotines can be made from poultry, meat, or fish; the flesh is boned, stuffed, and rolled into a large cylindrical shape. However labor-intensive, they are an ideal way to serve lots of guests since they are easily carved and spectacularly showy. Have butcher prepare turkey as follows: Remove wings and separate tips from wings. Remove legs with thighs, separating these pieces at the joint. Remove breastbone but keep breast and back skin intact. Keep turkey carcass for making stock.

    16-pound turkey, prepared as above (breast will weigh about 7½ pounds)
    2 large heads garlic
    2 large bunches fresh sage

Wash turkey thoroughly and pat dry with paper towels.

Early in the day, prepare turkey broth. Place turkey carcass in a large heavy pot. Add giblets, except liver, and wing tips. Add cold water to cover, plus ½ teaspoon whole black peppercorns, 1 head garlic, cut in half horizontally, and 6 sage sprigs. Bring to a boil, skimming any fat and foam. Lower heat to medium and cook for 2 hours, skimming periodically. Discard carcass and giblets. Strain broth through a fine-mesh sieve into a large clean pot. Bring to a boil. Lower heat and simmer until broth is reduced to 6 cups. Add salt to taste.

To prepare ballotine, remove skin from turkey thighs and reserve. Cut meat from thighs into ¼- to ½-inch cubes. You should have about 4 cups. Placed diced turkey in a large bowl. Finely chop enough sage to make ½ packed cup, reserving remaining sprigs. Add to diced turkey. Press 4 cloves garlic through garlic press and add to bowl with 1 teaspoon salt and ½ teaspoon freshly ground black pepper. Mix well and let sit while you preheat oven to 325°F.

Lay boned breast, flesh side up, on a clean work surface. Position it with a lobe to your left and a lobe to your right. Butterfly breast meat so that breast lies as flat as possible. Sprinkle with salt and pepper. Arrange diced turkey mixture in a row across lobes. You want the mixture to go from end to end. Roll up breast tightly, top to bottom, like a jelly roll. Use reserved thigh and leg skin, if necessary, to cover any exposed meat.

Tie kitchen string tightly around rolled breast at 1-inch intervals. Your ballotine should be about 16 inches long. Sprinkle with salt.

Place in a large shallow roasting pan. Add ½ cup broth to pan. Bake for 50 minutes. Baste with pan juices and place turkey wings and legs in pan. Add ½ cup broth. Bake 50 to 55 minutes longer, or until a meat thermometer stuck in center of ballotine registers 145°F. Remove pan from oven. Transfer ballotine, wings, and legs to a large platter. Ballotine will continue to cook.

Add 5 cups broth to roasting pan, scraping up browned bits. Strain through a fine-mesh sieve into a medium saucepan. Add 1 clove garlic, pushed through a press, and salt and pepper to taste. Cook over medium-high heat until reduced to 3 cups.

Remove strings from turkey. Cut into thin slices and serve with wings, legs, and hot garlic jus. Garnish with remaining sage sprigs.

Serves 12

ONE DUCK, TWO DINNERS

If "poultry is to the cook what canvas is to the painter," as the gastronome Brillat-Savarin once said, then these dishes are artistic proof: a dinner of Braised Duck Legs with Apples and Sauerkraut, and another of Sautéed Duck Breasts with Green Olives and Port.

BRAISED DUCK LEGS WITH APPLES AND SAUERKRAUT

> 5½-pound duck
> 1 pound sauerkraut, sold in a plastic bag
> 3 large tart apples

Wash duck thoroughly and pat dry with paper towels. Cut the duck into the following pieces: 2 breast halves with wings and back removed; 2 legs with thighs attached. Reserve the breasts for the next recipe.

Put neck, back, wings, and gizzards (discard liver) and 4 cups water in a medium pot with a cover. Add 1 teaspoon whole black peppercorns. Simmer for 1 hour with the cover askew. Then strain through a fine-mesh sieve. Return to pot and reduce stock to 1 cup over high heat. Add kosher salt to taste.

Preheat oven to 350°F.

Heat a large nonstick skillet until hot. Season duck legs with salt and freshly ground black pepper and place, skin side down, in skillet. Cook for 10 minutes over medium-high heat, turning several times, until skin is golden brown. Pour off fat and set aside.

Drain the sauerkraut. Core 2 apples and dice them into ¼-inch cubes. Mix diced apples with sauerkraut and put in the bottom of a shallow casserole. Add ½ teaspoon kosher salt, freshly ground black pepper, and ½ cup duck stock. (Reserve remaining stock for next recipe.) Place legs on top of sauerkraut and bake for 45 minutes. Pour 3 tablespoons reserved duck fat over the legs and sauerkraut and bake 15 minutes longer.

Meanwhile, cut remaining apples into 12 wedges, discarding any seeds. Heat 1 tablespoon reserved duck fat in a small nonstick skillet and cook apple wedges over high heat until browned and soft. Remove casserole from oven. Put the sauerkraut and duck legs on a warm platter and top with sautéed apple wedges.

Serves 2

SAUTÉED DUCK BREASTS WITH GREEN OLIVES AND PORT

> 2 duck breasts and ½ cup duck stock (from preceding recipe)
> ½ cup tawny port
> ½ cup French picholine or Spanish green olives

Remove bones from duck breasts. Using a sharp knife, make several cross-hatch slashes in skin of duck, being careful not to pierce flesh. Season breasts with kosher salt and freshly ground white pepper. Wrap in plastic wrap and refrigerate for several hours.

Put duck breasts, skin side down, in a cold, large nonstick skillet. Cook slowly over medium heat until fat is rendered, about 10 minutes. Pour fat from pan. Turn duck over and continue to cook for about 8 minutes.

Preheat broiler.

Add reserved duck stock, port, and olives to pan. Increase heat to high and cook until sauce has reduced by half. It should be thick and syrupy. Keep warm.

Transfer duck breasts to a heavy pie tin or a rimmed baking sheet and place under broiler to crisp skin. Transfer duck breasts to warm dinner plates and pour sauce and olives over and around duck.

Serves 2

SIMPLE ROAST DUCK WITH CHUTNEY

Garam masala—an Indian spice mixture of cumin, cinnamon, pepper, and cloves—contributes a special flavor to this roast duck. It is available in many supermarkets and all spice stores. Roasting the duck for a long time at a low temperature results in moist flesh. Raising the temperature ensures crisp skin. One duck feeds two, amply. So make two ducks to serve four, not one large one.

2 small Long Island or Muscovy ducks, about 4½ pounds each
⅓ cup garam masala
1 cup mango chutney

Preheat oven to 275°F.

Wash ducks thoroughly and pat dry with paper towels. Remove giblets from ducks. Discard liver or save for another use. Remove wings up to the first wing joint, and put wing tips and giblets in a saucepan with water to cover. Add a large pinch of garam masala, ½ teaspoon black peppercorns, and a large pinch of salt. Bring to a boil, lower heat, and simmer for 1 hour. Strain liquid through a fine-mesh sieve into a clean saucepan. Reduce over medium-high heat to 1 cup.

Using a fork, prick the skin of the ducks all over. Season ducks with salt and pepper, and then liberally rub ducks on all sides with about 2 tablespoons garam masala. Tie legs together with kitchen string.

Place ducks, breast side up, on a rack in a roasting pan and roast for 2 hours, frequently removing fat. Increase heat to 400°F and roast 30 minutes longer, or until skin is crisp. Cut ducks in half through the breastbone and back with a sharp knife or kitchen shears. You may remove the back, cutting along each side of the spine. Sprinkle duck halves with salt and remaining garam masala.

Add ¼ cup chutney to reduced stock and bring to a boil. Cook for 5 minutes over medium heat. Serve ducks with some of the duck stock and remaining chutney.

Serves 4

ROSEMARY-ROASTED DUCK WITH POMEGRANATES

This fragrant duck has a celebratory air that is perfect for winter holidays, when pomegranates are available. Use some of the duck fat to sauté little potatoes with garlic and kosher salt—for another three-ingredient recipe.

2 5½-pound ducks
2 large bunches fresh rosemary
2 large pomegranates

Wash ducks thoroughly and pat dry with paper towels. Remove wings and giblets from the ducks. Discard livers or save for another use. Place wings and giblets in a large saucepan with 4 cups water, or to cover. Add 1 large branch rosemary, 1 teaspoon black peppercorns, and 1 teaspoon salt. Bring to a boil and skim off any foam. Lower heat and simmer for 45 minutes. Strain through a fine-mesh sieve into a clean saucepan. Bring to a boil and cook until reduced to 2 cups.

Preheat oven to 375°F.

Scatter 1½ bunches rosemary on bottom of heavy shallow roasting pan. Mince enough of remaining rosemary to get 1 tablespoon and set aside.

Prick ducks all over with a fork. Rub skin with salt and freshly ground black pepper. Place ducks, breasts side up, on rosemary and roast for about 2 hours, frequently removing fat. Skin should be crisp and duck meat juicy and tender.

While ducks are cooking, cut 1 pomegranate in half through the equator. With a hand juicer, squeeze pomegranate halves to get ½ cup or more juice. Cut remaining pomegranate in half and remove and reserve seeds, adding any juice to squeezed juice.

When ducks are cooked, place on a large cutting board and transfer rosemary to a platter.

Drain off fat from roasting pan and place pan on stovetop. Add reserved duck broth and pomegranate juice. Over high heat, scrape up browned bits with a spatula, and cook until sauce is syrupy and reduced to 1⅓ cups. Pour through a fine-mesh sieve into a saucepan and season with salt and freshly ground black pepper.

Cut ducks into 6 pieces. Place on top of rosemary on platter. Scatter with pomegranate seeds. Pour warm sauce around duck, drizzling a little on top. Sprinkle with the minced rosemary and serve immediately.

Serves 6

pork, lamb, and beef

Humans are the only carnivores capable of deciding to become vegetarians for religious, social, or political reasons. But I, for one, would no more suppress my primordial instinct for a succulent hunk of animal protein than I'd tell a tiger to graze on wheat grass. I'm not in the high-protein diet camp, mind you, but meat offers me gastronomic satisfaction that can't be matched any other way.

There are two contrasting ways to cook meat: There are flash-in-the-pan recipes such as searing a steak, grilling a veal chop, or sautéing pork medallions. Great for getting dinner on the table quickly, each of these techniques chars and caramelizes the surface, leaving a slightly chewy interior. And then there's slow cooking in moist, unattended heat that transforms hefty pork shoulders, sinewy beef, and gelatinous roasts into spoon-tender flesh bathed in natural juices. This chapter contains both.

I'm thrilled by the growing variety of cuts of meat available in food markets these days and delighted by the jump in quality of these products. I'm all for buying the best, even if it entails a side trip or two. Befriend a neighborhood butcher who can French a rack of lamb, prepare a standing rib roast, or bone your holiday turkey.

Those with deeper pockets may head for the natural or organic sections of their supermarkets' meat department where they'll find products from a growing number of producers who are raising animals in environmentally sensitive ways, usually with no hormones, colors, or artificial ingredients and little or no use of antibiotics.

The essence of meat cookery is applying the proper technique to the right cut of meat, and then serving it at the right temperature. You wouldn't pan-sear a thick short rib or stew a porterhouse steak, nor should you risk overcooking a costly veal chop. But you want a pork shoulder simply to collapse into tenderness after eight hours in the pot.

Professional chefs and smart home cooks keep an instant-read thermometer within easy reach. Use it to tell when your filet mignon or prime rib of beef is rare (an internal temperature of 125°F) or medium-rare (135°F).

Non-Atkins nutritionists these days suggest downsizing the portions of protein we consume; their idea of a great piece of steak is positively monastic. If that satisfies you, go ahead and plan your meals accordingly, but I've been more generous in my recipes. For me, either there's enough Eighteen-Hour Roast Pork, Spiced Lamb with Ginger and Mint, or Rib Steak with Gorgonzola to go with that special bottle of Cabernet—or there isn't.

Tomorrow's the day for a tidbit of chicken on a bed of roughage. Today I am a tiger.

PORK TENDERLOIN WITH SWEET MUSTARD AND ROSEMARY

This is surprisingly low-cal (about 350 calories per serving) and flavor-packed to boot. The rosemary perfumes the pork and keeps it from sticking to the pan.

> 2 14-ounce pork tenderloins
> ¾ cup good-quality honey mustard
> 2 large bunches fresh rosemary

Trim any excess fat from pork.

In a small bowl, mix mustard with 3 tablespoons finely chopped rosemary needles. Add coarsely ground black pepper and spread mustard mixture over tenderloins, rolling them around in mixture so they are completely coated. Place in a shallow casserole and cover with plastic wrap. Refrigerate for 6 to 8 hours.

Preheat oven to 375°F.

Remove most of marinade from pork. Season with salt and pepper. Remove several rosemary sprigs from branches and set aside. Distribute remaining rosemary branches down the center of a rimmed baking sheet and place tenderloins on top. Bake for 12 minutes, turn over, and bake 12 minutes longer. Pork should be slightly pink. Remove from oven. Transfer pork to a cutting board. Let rest for 5 minutes.

Slice thinly, placing pork in overlapping slices on a warm platter. Pour any pan juices over pork. Garnish with reserved rosemary branches.

Serves 4

STUFFED PORK LOIN WITH SAUSAGE AND DRIED FRUIT

Not quite a Norman Rockwell centerpiece, but very close.

> 4 ounces mixed dried fruit, including apricots, prunes, and apples
> 6 ounces sweet Italian sausage
> 2½-pound boned center-cut pork loin

Preheat oven to 375°F.

Cut fruit into ¼-inch dice. Remove sausage from casing and crumble into a medium bowl. Add fruit and mix well. Slit pork from end to end, cutting deeply down to the center of meat; make sure to leave bottom half intact. Season resulting channel with salt and freshly ground black pepper. Fill with sausage mixture, packing it in tightly. Using kitchen string, tie pork tightly at ½-inch intervals, then wrap string once around length of pork.

Season pork with salt and pepper. Spray a shallow roasting pan or rimmed baking sheet with nonstick cooking spray, and place roast in pan, cut side down. Roast for 25 minutes, then turn pork over. Cook 30 minutes longer, or until a meat thermometer reads 145 to 150°F. Transfer roast to a cutting board. Add ½ cup boiling water to pan juices and scrape up browned bits.

Strain liquid through a fine-mesh sieve into a clean saucepan. Add salt to taste and cook liquid over high heat for a few minutes. Carve pork into thick slices and serve with pan juices.

Serves 6

PORK LOIN WITH PRUNES AND BAY LEAVES

This dish is impressive enough for company, comforting enough for family. I like to use big, sour prunes from a Middle Eastern or Russian food store.

    10 long California bay leaves
    16 very large prunes, pitted
    2-pound center-cut pork loin

Place bay leaves and prunes in a bowl. Pour boiling water over them to cover and let sit for 15 minutes.

Preheat oven to 400°F.

Using a small sharp knife, cut a deep slit along the length of the roast to make a channel that goes halfway through the pork. Make sure to leave ½ inch uncut on each end and at least 1 inch on bottom of roast. Season inside of channel with salt and freshly ground black pepper.

Drain prunes and bay leaves and pat dry with paper towels. Place prunes in channel, filling it from end to end. Mince 1 bay leaf very, very fine, removing the center vein, and sprinkle it over prunes.

Using kitchen string, tie pork tightly at 1-inch intervals. Sprinkle with salt and freshly ground black pepper. Tuck remaining bay leaves under strings in 1 long line.

Spray a rimmed baking sheet with nonstick cooking spray and place roast in the center, bay leaf side up.

Bake for 45 to 50 minutes for medium, or until a meat thermometer reads 145 to 150°F. (Do not overcook; pork should be moist and slightly pink.) Transfer to a cutting board and let rest for 5 minutes. Remove bay leaves and cut pork into ½-inch slices.

Serves 4 or more

ROAST RACK OF PORK *ARISTA*

This streamlined preparation of the classic Tuscan pork roast is delicious served with a tangle of bitter broccoli rabe.

¼ cup finely chopped fresh rosemary
3 tablespoons finely chopped garlic, 8 or 9 large cloves
4-pound rack of pork, bones trimmed but not removed

With a mortar and pestle or using a very sharp knife, make a coarse paste from 3½ tablespoons rosemary, garlic, 1 teaspoon kosher salt, and ½ teaspoon coarsely ground black pepper.

Pat the pork dry with paper towels. Using the tip of a sharp knife, make small incisions in the meat and insert the garlic mixture. Spread remaining mixture over the surface of the pork and let it stand for 1 hour.

Preheat oven to 325°F.

Roast pork in a heavy shallow roasting pan for 1½ hours (about 25 minutes per pound), or until a meat thermometer reads 145 to 150°F. Transfer pork to a cutting board and let rest for 5 minutes.

Add 1 cup boiling water and remaining chopped rosemary leaves to pan. Scrape up any browned bits and pass cooking liquid through a fine-mesh sieve into a small saucepan. Cook over high heat until syrupy. Slice pork and serve with hot pan juices.

Serves 6

PORK MEDALLIONS WITH SHERRY AND CRACKED PEPPER

Dry Marsala can be substituted, but a bone-dry fino sherry will yield the most sophisticated results.

2 pounds whole boneless pork loin
½ cup roasted garlic olive oil (page 228)
1½ cups dry sherry

Cut pork loin into 8 ¾-inch-thick slices. Place slices in 1 layer on a cutting board. Coarsely crush 3½ tablespoons black peppercorns with the bottom of a glass or the flat side of a heavy chef's knife. Liberally rub cracked pepper into 1 side of each medallion. Place them in a shallow casserole. Drizzle each with ½ tablespoon garlic oil. Cover and refrigerate for up to 8 hours.

Heat 3 tablespoons garlic oil in a very large nonstick skillet. When hot, add medallions, pepper side down. Cook over medium heat, turning once, until pork is just cooked through but still moist, approximately 4 minutes on each side. Quickly remove medallions to a platter. Sprinkle them with salt and cover with aluminum foil.

Add sherry to the hot pan and a large pinch of salt. Cook over high heat until sherry is reduced to a syrupy sauce. Spoon sauce over medallions and drizzle with remaining garlic oil.

Serves 4

CHEDDAR-STUFFED PORK CHOPS WITH CIDER REDUCTION

The better the cheese, the better this dish, so select a very sharp cheddar from England or a great domestic producer or use a crumbly English Cheshire. The reduced cider adds finesse to this simple partnership of meat and cheese.

    1 quart apple cider
    8 very thick (about 1½ inches) rib pork chops, 10 to 12 ounces each
    12 ounces very sharp cheddar or Cheshire cheese

Place cider in a large saucepan and bring to a boil. Lower heat to medium and cook until reduced to 1 cup. This will take about 40 minutes. Set aside.

With a very sharp chef's knife, make a deep horizontal pocket in each pork chop. Cut cheese into 8 slices and pack one slice into each pocket so that no cheese is showing. Press down lightly on each pork chop, and season lightly with salt and freshly ground black pepper.

Place pork chops in a large nonstick skillet with a cover. Sear over high heat, about 4 minutes per side. Cover pan and cook 4 minutes more on each side.

Remove chops and salt lightly. Reheat reduced cider and drizzle over pork chops. Serve immediately.

Serves 4

THICK PORK CHOPS WITH SWEET VINEGAR PEPPERS

Sweet red salad peppers and their vinegary brine make a mouthwatering foil for pork. Sauté the chops slowly for optimum moistness.

    12 ounces sweet salad peppers in brine, about 1 cup
    4 thick rib pork chops, about 9 ounces each
    3½ tablespoons extra-virgin olive oil

Drain sweet peppers, saving any brine.

Season pork chops on both sides with salt and freshly ground black pepper. Heat 1 tablespoon olive oil in a very large nonstick skillet. Cook pork chops over medium heat for about 8 minutes on one side and 6 minutes on the other, or until desired doneness. Transfer chops to a warm platter and cover with aluminum foil.

Add remaining olive oil to the pan, and scrape up any browned bits. Add sweet peppers and cook over high heat for 3 to 4 minutes, until soft, adding 1 tablespoon of reserved brine and any accumulated juices from pork. Add salt and pepper to taste. Immediately pour peppers and sauce over pork chops and serve.

Serves 4

SLOW-COOKED HOISIN PORK WITH SCALLIONS

Thick chocolatey-looking Chinese hoisin sauce is one of the few great convenience foods I use with abandon. It turns humble pork shoulder into a sexy, yielding dish. Serve this with Wasabi-Whipped Potatoes (page 51) and sautéed snow peas.

    6-pound boned pork shoulder
    ½ cup hoisin sauce
    2 bunches scallions

Preheat oven to 300°F.

Using a sharp thin-bladed knife, trim pork well, removing skin if any, and leaving a little fat on top. Roll pork tightly, fat side out, and, using kitchen string, tie it in 2-inch intervals.

Heat a very large heavy flameproof casserole with a cover until very hot. Add pork, fatty side down, and brown for a few minutes over high heat. Turn pork and brown on all sides, about 10 minutes total.

Remove from heat. With pork still in casserole, spread hoisin sauce over pork. Trim scallions, removing all roots. Cut on the bias into 1-inch lengths, using both white and green parts. Scatter scallions over pork and add 1 teaspoon black peppercorns. Cover casserole and bake for 3½ hours, or until pork is very tender.

Remove from oven and transfer pork and scallions to a cutting board. Using a large spoon, remove as much fat as possible from cooking liquid and place casserole on stovetop. Reduce liquid over high heat until very thick and syrupy, adding salt and freshly ground black pepper to taste.

Sprinkle pork lightly with salt and cut into thick slices, being sure to remove string. Scatter with baked scallions and pour hot pan sauce over top.

Serves 6

POT ROAST OF PORK WITH SMOKED PAPRIKA AND ONIONS

Smoked paprika is a trendy new spice available in specialty food stores and many supermarkets. Its flavor and bouquet are most intriguing.

    6-pound boned pork shoulder
    ¼ cup smoked paprika
    3 pounds yellow onions

Using a sharp thin-bladed knife, remove skin from pork, if any, and trim well, leaving a very thin layer of fat. Discard skin but save 2 ounces (about ¼ cup) of the fat. Roll pork tightly, fat side out, and using kitchen string, tie it in 2-inch intervals. Melt reserved fat in a very large heavy flameproof casserole with a cover. Brown pork over high heat on all sides, about 10 minutes total, and transfer pork to a cutting board. Season with 1 tablespoon smoked paprika and 1 tablespoon salt.

Peel onions and cut them in half. Cut into very thin slices through the root end. Add onions to hot fat with a large pinch of salt. Cook over medium-high heat, stirring often, until onions are soft and very dark brown (it's okay if they burn a little). This will take about 25 minutes.

Add remaining paprika and ⅓ cup water to onions and scrape up browned bits on bottom of casserole. Place pork on top of onions, and season with salt and freshly ground black pepper. Cover casserole and cook over low heat for 3 hours, turning once or twice during cooking. Transfer pork to cutting board and thinly slice. Be sure to remove string. Using a large spoon, skim as much fat as possible from onions. Add salt and pepper to taste and return sliced pork to pot. Cook, covered, over very low heat for 30 minutes, or until pork is very tender. Transfer pork to a warm platter and cover with onions and pan juices.

Serves 6

"IRISH BACON" AND CABBAGE

Corned beef is never served in Ireland on Saint Patrick's Day. What is traditional is a pork butt or shoulder brined for 24 hours before cooking. Simply boiled with garlic and green cabbage, the meat is incredibly rich and moist. Its only other accompaniment should be some very spicy mustard—imported Colman's is best.

  7-pound trimmed pork shoulder or Boston butt, bone in
  3 or 4 very large heads garlic, about 8 ounces
  1 large head green cabbage, about 3 pounds

Using a sharp thin-bladed knife, trim pork of almost all its fat. Place pork in a very large pot with a cover. Dissolve 3 cups kosher salt in 1 gallon water and pour brine over pork, adding more water if needed to cover. Cover pot and refrigerate for 24 hours.

When ready to cook, bring pork and brine to a boil. Boil for 10 minutes and drain. Add fresh water to pot to cover pork, and bring to a rapid boil. Cut garlic heads in half through the equator and add to pot with ½ tablespoon black peppercorns. Cover pot and cook over medium-low heat for 3 hours (approximately 25 minutes per pound), or until pork is very tender. Transfer pork to a cutting board. Cover with aluminum foil or plastic wrap to keep warm.

Most of the garlic will have dissolved into sauce. Remove any peels. Cut cabbage into 6 wedges and add to broth. Bring to a boil and cook until cabbage is soft, about 20 minutes. Remove cabbage and garlic with a slotted spoon and place on a warm platter. Lightly sprinkle vegetables with kosher salt. Cut pork into thick slices and place alongside cabbage. Ladle hot broth over pork before serving.

Serves 6 or more

EIGHTEEN-HOUR ROAST PORK WITH FENNEL SEEDS AND GARLIC

This amazingly aromatic pork is marinated, then cooked at a very low temperature. Put it in the oven around midnight and it will be ready for dinner tomorrow.

> 9-pound whole pork shoulder, skin on
> 3 or 4 very large heads garlic, about 8 ounces, peeled
> 6 tablespoons fennel seeds

Make deep slits across top of pork, about 1 inch apart, being sure to cut through the fat to the flesh.

Put garlic in bowl of a food processor and process until minced. Add 2 tablespoons kosher salt and 1 tablespoon ground black pepper, and process briefly. Fill slits in pork shoulder with garlic mixture, and then spread mixture all over the surface of the pork.

Using a spice grinder, electric coffee grinder, or mortar and pestle, coarsely grind fennel seeds. Pack onto surface of pork. Wrap pork in a large piece of aluminum foil. Refrigerate for 6 to 12 hours.

Preheat oven to 450°F.

Unwrap pork and place on a rack in a roasting pan. Roast for 30 minutes. Reduce oven temperature to 250°F and cook for 18 hours, basting with pan juices from time to time. When roast is done, the skin should crackle and pork should be very soft and moist. Remove from oven. Transfer to cutting board and carve into thick slices.

Serves 8 or more

STICKY SPARE RIBS

To serve as hors d'oeuvres, have your butcher cut the ribs into three pieces, sawing across the bones.

> 1 scant cup unsulphured molasses
> 1 cup balsamic vinegar, plus more for drizzling
> 3 pounds pork spare ribs in racks, trimmed

In a medium saucepan, combine molasses, vinegar, 2 teaspoons salt, and freshly ground black pepper. Bring just to a boil, whisking constantly with a wire whisk. Remove from heat and let cool.

Place ribs in a large bowl and toss with molasses mixture. Cover and refrigerate for 4 to 6 hours.

Preheat oven to 350°F.

Place ribs in a single layer on a broiler pan, meaty side up. Cover with aluminum foil and bake for 30 minutes. Uncover and bake for 1 hour or longer, until ribs are tender. Turn several times during baking. Remove pan from oven and place ribs on a cutting board. Cut between ribs. Place on a warm platter and sprinkle with more vinegar if desired.

Serves 4

BARBECUED PORK PULL

Mouthwatering and puckery, this begs for an icy beer and some freshly made white bread to mop up the sauce.

6-pound pork shoulder, bone in, skin removed
1½ cups cider vinegar, plus more for serving
1 cup ketchup

Preheat oven to 300°F.

Choose a heavy flameproof casserole with a cover, large enough to easily accommodate the pork. Sear the pork over medium-high heat, fat side down, then turn and brown on all sides, about 10 minutes total.

In a small saucepan, mix vinegar, ketchup, 2 cups water, 2 teaspoons salt, and lots of coarsely ground black pepper, and bring to a boil. Pour mixture over the roast and cover casserole.

Bake for 35 minutes per pound (about 3½ hours), basting occasionally with drippings. Turn once every hour. The meat should be very soft when done.

Transfer pork to a cutting board. Remove meat from the bone. Chop or shred pork as desired. Pour some of the pan juices over meat until moist. Season with additional vinegar, salt, and pepper. If necessary, quickly reheat before serving.

Serves 6

CINNAMON-SUGAR GLAZED HAM

A very merry main course for the holidays.

10-pound ready-to-cook ham, shank portion
1 cup coarse-grain mustard
1 cup cinnamon-sugar (page 242)

Preheat oven to 325°F.

Place ham in a shallow roasting pan and add ⅛-inch water to pan. Cover ham with aluminum foil and bake for 2 hours and 15 minutes. Remove ham from oven and increase oven temperature to 450°F. Pour most of fat from pan. Using a sharp knife, remove rind from ham, except for area around shank bone, and most of the fat. Score remaining fat by cutting diagonal slashes in a diamond pattern. Cover surface thickly with mustard, then heavily coat with cinnamon-sugar, patting down if necessary. Add freshly ground black pepper.

Return ham to oven and bake for 25 minutes, or until sugar melts and hardens. It will become a bit crackly. Present ham on a large platter. Carve and serve while still hot.

Serves 12

CRACKLING PORK SHOULDER WITH FRESH THYME

An unusual baking method, with the temperature rising incrementally, ensures that this roast has a crackling crust and a meltingly moist interior.

5½- to 6-pound pork shoulder, bone in
2 large bunches fresh thyme
8 large cloves garlic, peeled

Preheat oven to 350°F.

Using a sharp thin-bladed knife, remove skin, if any, and trim most of fat from pork. Chop fat into very small pieces to get ⅓ cup.

Remove enough leaves from thyme to get ⅓ packed cup. Set aside any remaining thyme branches.

Press 2 cloves garlic through a garlic press and rub all over pork. Mince remaining garlic and chop with reserved thyme leaves, pork fat, and 1 teaspoon kosher salt to make a paste. Make holes ¼-inch wide and 1-inch deep all over pork and fill with garlic-thyme mixture. Also insert mixture around the bone. The idea is to infuse the flesh with as much flavor as possible.

Put remaining thyme branches in bottom of a roasting pan or large shallow casserole. Place pork shoulder on top.

Roast for 45 minutes, then turn up heat to 400°F and roast 25 minutes longer. Turn up heat again to 450°F and roast for an additional 25 minutes, or until a meat thermometer reads 145°F. Transfer pork to a cutting board and let rest for 10 minutes before carving.

Serves 6

CUMIN-RUBBED PORK SHOULDER WITH APRICOTS

This flavor combination is also suitable for boned leg of lamb.

⅓ cup ground cumin
12 ounces good-quality large dried apricots
4½-pound boned pork shoulder

Preheat oven to 400°F.

Put cumin and 2½ teaspoons kosher salt in a small skillet over medium heat. Cook for 1 to 2 minutes, stirring frequently, until the aroma rises. Remove from heat and let cool.

Place apricots in a bowl, and pour boiling water over them to cover. Let sit for 15 minutes to plump. Drain thoroughly.

Lay the boned shoulder flat on a work surface. Trim most of the fat, then sprinkle with half the cumin mixture and some black pepper.

Place drained apricots in a long, overlapping row, down the center of pork. Roll pork tightly around the apricot filling, jelly-roll style. Using kitchen string, tie the roast at 1-inch intervals.

Rub rolled pork with remaining cumin mixture. Coat a large shallow roasting pan with nonstick cooking spray. Place roast in pan and cook for about 1 hour and 20 minutes, or until a meat thermometer reads 145°F.

Remove roast from oven and transfer to a cutting board. Add 1 cup boiling water to pan juices, scraping up any browned bits, and pass through a fine-mesh sieve into a saucepan. Cook over high heat until syrupy, adding salt and freshly ground black pepper to taste. Carve pork and serve with hot pan juices.

Serves 8

PAN-SEARED SAUSAGES WITH OVEN-DRIED GRAPES

The union of grapes and sausages is traditional in the Umbria region of Italy. Here the grapes are used two ways: as a counterpoint to the coarsely textured sausage and as a base for the wine-glazed sauce.

2½ pounds seedless grapes (half red, half green)
8 large sweet Italian sausages (or hot if you like)
1 cup dry red wine

Preheat oven to 275°F. Wash grapes and remove stems. Place 1 cup of each color on a rimmed baking sheet. Bake for 1 hour and 30 minutes, shaking pan often, until grapes shrivel and caramelize. This can be done in advance.

Place 1 cup of each color uncooked grapes in a food processor and process thoroughly. Pour contents through a coarse-mesh sieve, pressing to extract juice. You should have 1 cup grape juice.

Prick sausages all over with a fork. Place in a very large nonstick skillet and cook over medium-high heat until browned all over and almost cooked through. Add grape juice and remaining uncooked grapes. Cook until grapes have softened but not collapsed. Using a slotted spoon, transfer sausages and grapes to a platter. Keep warm.

Raise heat to high and add wine. Cook until sauce has thickened substantially, about 5 minutes, and pour over sausages and grapes. Scatter roasted grapes on top. Serve hot.

Serves 4

SPICED LAMB WITH GINGER AND MINT

A good dish for Easter dinner. The vivid flavors marry nicely with such spring vegetables as asparagus, artichokes, and peas.

> 6-inch piece fresh ginger, about 5 ounces
> 2 large bunches fresh mint
> 4½-pound leg of lamb (butt half), bone in

Peel ginger using a small sharp knife. Cut into large chunks and place in bowl of a food processor. Wash mint and dry well. Wrap one bunch in plastic wrap and refrigerate for later use. Remove leaves from remaining mint and add to ginger. Add 1 teaspoon kosher salt and ½ teaspoon cracked black pepper. Process until a coarse paste forms. Do not overprocess, or it will be watery.

Rub ginger-mint mixture all over lamb. Pack it tightly on top and sides of lamb to form a thick layer. Place in a large plastic bag and secure tightly. Refrigerate for 8 hours.

Preheat oven to 375°F. Allow lamb to sit at room temperature for 30 minutes before cooking.

Using a sharp knife, score top of lamb lightly with lines 1 inch apart. Place lamb in a heavy shallow roasting pan and roast for about 1 hour and 20 minutes (18 minutes per pound), or until a meat thermometer reads 145°F for medium-rare. (You may need to drain fat halfway through cooking.)

Transfer lamb to a cutting board. Let rest for 5 minutes, then carve as desired. Serve immediately and garnish with reserved mint sprigs.

Serves 6

BOMBAY LAMB WITH YOGURT AND LIME

This is especially good when cooked over coals, but it's satisfying when broiled, too.

> 3 pounds butterflied leg of lamb
> 1 cup plain yogurt
> 3 large limes

Put lamb and yogurt in a large nonreactive bowl or shallow casserole. Grate rind of 2 limes then cut limes in half and squeeze to get ¼ cup juice. Add zest and juice to bowl with 1 teaspoon kosher salt and lots of coarsely cracked black pepper. Mix well so that lamb is thoroughly coated in marinade.

Cover and refrigerate for 8 hours, turning one or twice.

Preheat broiler or light a grill. Remove lamb from marinade. Place lamb in a broiler pan or directly on your grill. Broil or grill lamb for 6 to 8 minutes on each side, until a meat thermometer reads 130°F for rare, 140°F for medium-rare.

Transfer lamb to a cutting board and let it rest for 5 minutes. Sprinkle generously with salt and pepper. Slice thinly and serve with wedges of remaining lime.

Serves 4

FIVE-HOUR LEG OF LAMB WITH FORTY CLOVES OF GARLIC

Through slow-cooking, the wine permeates the meat with heady vapors while the lamb's sinewy muscle is transformed to spoon-tender richness. Copious cloves of garlic perfume the meat and thicken the sauce.

5½-pound boned leg of lamb, rolled and tied
1 bottle (750 milliliters) Côtes du Rhône, or other sturdy dry red wine
40 very large cloves garlic

Place lamb in a very large heavy flameproof casserole with a cover. Pour all but ½ cup wine over lamb. Using the bottom of a saucepan or heavy chef's knife, gently crush all but 1 garlic clove and remove skins. Place peeled cloves in pot. Cover and refrigerate for 8 hours.

Preheat oven to 300°F.

Place casserole on stovetop. Uncover and add 1 teaspoon whole black peppercorns. Bring to a boil, removing some of the foam on top. Cover pot and put in the oven. Cook for 1 hour. Turn lamb over and cook 4 hours longer, or until spoon-tender, turning once or twice during cooking.

Remove lamb from pot and place on a cutting board. Skim as much fat as possible from pan juices. Add remaining wine and 1 clove garlic, peeled and pushed through a garlic press, to pot. Over high heat, reduce liquid by half. Add a generous amount of salt and freshly ground black pepper. Slice lamb and add to pot. Let lamb absorb juices. Reheat gently before serving.

Serves 6

RACK OF LAMB WITH PESTO CRUMBS

8-rib rack of lamb, trimmed, flap removed, bones exposed
½ cup prepared pesto
¾ cup breadcrumbs made from fresh white bread

Preheat the oven to 375°F.

Season lamb with salt and freshly ground black pepper. Spread the pesto over the surface of the meat. Coat the meat thoroughly with breadcrumbs, packing them down lightly with your hands. Cover the exposed bones with aluminum foil and place lamb, breadcrumb side up, on a baking sheet.

Roast lamb for 15 minutes, then remove foil and bake 20 minutes longer. Remove lamb from oven, let it rest for 5 minutes, then dust lightly with salt. Slice into thick double chops or single chops. Serve immediately.

Serves 2

ROAST LAMB SHOULDER WITH GRUYÈRE AND ROSEMARY

I first encountered aïado, *a stuffed and rolled shoulder of lamb, at the restaurant La Mère Besson in the south of France. Instead of Swiss Gruyère, you can try the less familiar French cheese called Comté, or Gruyère de Comté.*

6-pound lamb shoulder, bones removed and reserved
2 large bunches fresh rosemary
8 ounces Gruyère or Comté cheese

Put lamb bones in a medium pot with 2 cups water, 1 large sprig rosemary, ½ teaspoon whole black peppercorns, and ¼ teaspoon salt. Bring to a boil. Reduce heat and simmer for 30 minutes, removing any foam from the top. Discard bones (or reserve meat from bones for another use) and pour liquid through a fine-mesh sieve into a clean saucepan. Reduce until you have 1 cup.

Meanwhile, preheat oven to 375°F.

Unroll lamb, boned side up, on a clean work surface. Rub salt and freshly ground black pepper into the meat.

Grate cheese on the large holes of a box grater. Scatter evenly on lamb. Coarsely chop 2 tablespoons rosemary and scatter on cheese. Roll lamb tightly, jelly-roll style, and tie with kitchen string at 2-inch intervals. Distribute remaining rosemary branches in center of a heavy shallow roasting pan. Place lamb on rosemary and season with salt and freshly ground black pepper.

Roast lamb until a meat thermometer reads 140°F for medium-rare. This should take approximately 1 hour and 10 minutes, but use a meat thermometer to ensure desired doneness. Transfer lamb and rosemary branches to a platter and let rest for 10 minutes.

Add reserved broth to pan juices, scraping up browned bits. Pour through a fine-mesh sieve into a clean saucepan and cook over high heat for 2 minutes. Add salt and pepper to taste. Slice lamb, removing string, and serve with pan juices.

Serves 6

OVEN-BRAISED LAMB STEW WITH CUMIN AND TOMATO

For a slightly more exotic flavor profile, substitute ras el-hanout *for the cumin. This intriguing Moroccan spice blend includes cinnamon, cloves, ginger, cardamom, caraway, and nutmeg. It's available in Middle Eastern food stores.*

¼ cup ground cumin or ras el-hanout
2 pounds very ripe tomatoes
3 pounds lamb stew meat on the bone, cut into 2½-inch pieces

Preheat oven to 350°F.

In a small bowl, mix cumin, 2 teaspoons salt, and ¼ teaspoon freshly ground white pepper. Rub seasoning into each piece of lamb, covering lightly but completely. Set aside.

Cut all but 1 tomato in half and scoop out the seeds. Cut tomatoes into ½-inch pieces and place in bottom of a large flameproof casserole with a cover. Place lamb pieces on top of chopped tomatoes in 1 layer. Cover casserole and bake for approximately 2 hours, or until lamb is fork-tender. Check several times during cooking, adding a little water if necessary, so that tomatoes don't stick.

Remove casserole from oven. Using a slotted spoon, transfer lamb to a large platter. Place casserole on stovetop. Add remaining tomato, seeded and cut into ¼-inch dice. Add up to ½ cup water if needed, and salt, pepper, or more cumin to taste. Cook over high heat for a few minutes, until syrupy. Spoon sauce over lamb and serve.

Serves 4

LAMB CHOPS WITH GOAT CHEESE AND LAVENDER

Lavender, which has a special affinity for lamb and goat cheese, is one of my husband's favorite herbs; we grow it year-round in our kitchen window box. Served with Watercress Sauté with Garlic Chips (page 63), this makes an elegant but speedy dinner for company.

8 large thick rib lamb chops, about 5 ounces each
6 ounces fresh goat cheese
1 bunch fresh lavender

Ask your butcher to french the lamb chops, that is, cut all the meat from the bones up to the eye of the chops. The long exposed bones make an elegant presentation.

Preheat oven to 375°F.

In a small bowl, mix goat cheese and 2 tablespoons finely chopped lavender leaves. Season both sides of lamb chops well with salt and freshly ground black pepper. Heat a large nonstick skillet until hot and sear chops 1 minute on each side until browned, leaving meat very rare inside.

Transfer chops to a shallow roasting pan. Pack about 1½ tablespoons cheese mixture on top of each lamb chop to cover meat completely. Place chops in oven for 8 minutes, or until desired doneness. If you wish, brown the cheese under the broiler for 30 seconds before serving immediately. Garnish with fresh lavender sprigs.

Serves 4

LAMB CHOPS PROVENÇAL

These yummy shoulder chops—a much less expensive cut than rib chops—were inspired by a trip to the south of France. They are made with herbes de Provence, a mixture that traditionally includes rosemary, thyme, marjoram, and lavender; it's available in most supermarkets. Blackened lemons provide a great look and more intense flavor.

> 4 large lemons
> 4 thick shoulder lamb chops on the bone, about 10 ounces each
> ¼ cup herbes de Provence

Preheat broiler.

Cut 2 lemons into 4 wedges each. Place in a pie tin. Put under broiler for 8 minutes, or until lemons blacken. Set aside.

Tie a string around the circumference of each chop and pull tightly to make a nice round, compact shape. Place lamb chops in a shallow casserole. Grate rind of 2 remaining lemons to get 2 tablespoons zest. Set aside. Cut lemons in half and squeeze ½ lemon over both sides of each chop. Let sit for 20 minutes. Pat chops very dry and season with salt and freshly ground black pepper.

Preheat oven to 375°F.

Place herbes de Provence in a small bowl. Add lemon zest, 2 teaspoons kosher salt, and freshly ground black pepper. Mix well. Pack as much of the mixture as needed on 1 side of each lamb chop to cover completely. Place chops, herb side up, on a rimmed baking sheet. Bake for 15 minutes. Carefully turn over and bake for 5 minutes longer, or until desired doneness. Remove chops from oven and, using a spatula, turn herb side up. Remove string. Serve with blackened lemons.

Serves 4

SHISH KEBABS WITH ONIONS AND POMEGRANATE MOLASSES

Marinating lamb in grated onion tenderizes, softens, and flavors the meat. Pomegranate molasses, a syrupy reduction of pomegranate juice, is available in Middle Eastern food stores.

> 2 pounds boneless leg of lamb
> 4 medium onions
> 4 tablespoons pomegranate molasses

Cut lamb into 20 to 24 pieces, about 1½ inches square. Do not trim fat. Place lamb in a large bowl. Peel 2 onions and cut them in half. Grate them on the large holes of a box grater so that you have ½ cup grated onions and onion juice. Mix lamb with grated onions and juice, and add 2 tablespoons pomegranate molasses and freshly ground black pepper. Mix well and cover. Refrigerate overnight or a minimum of 8 hours.

When it's almost serving time, preheat broiler or light a charcoal grill. Peel remaining onions and cut in half through the stem end. Separate onion layers and cut them into 1-inch pieces. On each of 4 10- or 12-inch metal skewers, alternate pieces of onion and lamb. Each skewer should have 5 or 6 pieces of lamb. Sprinkle lamb with kosher salt and pepper. Place on broiler pan or directly on grill and cook for 3 minutes on each side, or until medium rare, or to desired doneness.

Drizzle each kebab with ½ tablespoon pomegranate molasses and serve hot.

Serves 4

LAMB SHANKS, ALSATIAN-STYLE

This recipe is inspired by the Alsatian dish called baeckeoffe, *or "baker's oven"—generally a mutton stew sealed in an earthenware pot and cooked very slowly. Be sure to follow the directions carefully; you want the shanks to bathe, not drown, in the winey onion sauce. A crisp potato cake (page 52) is a terrific accompaniment.*

> 2 large lamb shanks, 1½ pounds each
> 1½ pounds yellow onions
> 2 cups dry Riesling

Preheat broiler.

Season lamb shanks with salt and freshly ground black pepper. Place them on a broiler pan and broil them about 8 inches away from heat source until browned on all sides, about 3 minutes total. Remove from broiler and preheat oven to 350°F.

Peel onions and slice them in half through the root end, then crosswise into ¼-inch-thick slices. Place onions in a heavy shallow flameproof casserole with a secure cover. (An enamel Le Creuset casserole is perfect.)

Place lamb shanks on onions. Cover and bake for 1 hour. Turn shanks and add 1½ cups wine. Cover and bake 1 hour longer.

Using a slotted spoon, transfer shanks to a warm platter. Place casserole on stovetop. Add remaining ½ cup wine, and salt and pepper to taste. Cook over medium-high heat for about 2 minutes, scraping up any browned bits and stirring constantly. Pour onions and reduced pan juices over shanks and serve.

Serves 2

BRAISED VEAL WITH LEEKS AND RIESLING

A many-splendored thing, here leeks function as flavoring agent, vegetable, sauce base, and garnish. The Riesling wine vaporizes into a delicate sauce.

> 2 pounds rump roast of veal or boneless veal shoulder, rolled and tied
> 6 large fat leeks
> 1½ cups dry Riesling

Preheat oven to 350°F.

Rub salt and freshly ground black pepper onto the surface of veal.

Cut off dark green parts of leeks and set aside for later. Cut white part of the leeks into thin slices and wash well. Place in bottom of a large heavy casserole.

In a large nonstick skillet, sear veal quickly until browned on all sides. Place veal on top of leeks. Add ¼ cup wine to pan, bring to a boil, and scrape up any browned bits. Pour pan liquid over veal and add remaining wine. Cover and bake for 1 hour. Reduce heat to 300°F and cook 1 hour and 15 minutes longer, or until very tender.

Meanwhile, finely julienne dark green parts of leeks and boil in salted water for several minutes, or until just tender. Drain and set aside.

Transfer veal to a cutting board and let it rest while you make sauce. Process half of the leeks that veal was cooked with in a blender, adding enough pan juices to make a thick, smooth sauce; add water only if necessary. Pass sauce through a coarse-mesh sieve. Add salt and pepper to taste.

Slice veal and serve it on top of a mound of remaining braised leeks. Cover with sauce and the julienned leeks, briefly reheated in boiling water if necessary.

Serves 4 or more

GRILLED VEAL CHOPS WITH FRESH BASIL-LEMON SAUCE

You'll get great satisfaction from making this fresh herb sauce—a felicitous match with veal.

> 4 veal rib chops, 1 inch thick
> ½ cup lemon olive oil (page 228)
> 2 large bunches fresh basil

Preheat oven to 350°F.

Drizzle veal chops with 2 tablespoons lemon olive oil and coat thoroughly. Let sit at room temperature while you prepare the fresh basil oil.

Wash basil and pat dry. Remove leaves from 1½ bunches. Bring a medium saucepan of salted water to a boil. Boil leaves for 1 minute, then plunge them into ice water. Drain and gently squeeze water from basil. Place blanched basil in a blender. Add 6 tablespoons lemon oil and puree until very smooth. Add salt to taste.

Season chops with salt and freshly ground black pepper. Heat remaining oil in a large cast-iron skillet or nonstick skillet until hot. Sear the veal chops on both sides until golden brown, about 5 minutes total. Place on a rimmed baking sheet and bake for 15 minutes, or until desired doneness (rare and juicy is best).

Remove chops from oven. Sprinkle with more salt and pepper, and drizzle with fresh basil oil. Garnish with fresh basil leaves.

Serves 4

VEAL LOIN CHOPS WITH BROWN BUTTER AND SAGE

Butter, browned until nutty, and sage is a classic pairing that lends itself beautifully to juicy veal chops. A little sage goes a long way, so don't overdo it. Serve with Very Lemony Mashed Potatoes (page 48).

4 veal loin chops, ¾ inch thick
3 tablespoons unsalted butter
1 large bunch fresh sage

Season veal chops with salt and freshly ground black pepper. In a nonstick skillet large enough to hold chops in 1 layer, heat butter until it's golden brown. Add chops and cook until browned on 1 side, about 4 minutes.

Place 3 sage leaves on uncooked side of each chop and turn chops over. Cook over high heat for 3 to 4 minutes, until browned. Season lightly with salt and coarsely ground black pepper, and garnish with a few fresh sage leaves.

Serves 4

SUN-DRIED TOMATO MEATLOAF

This flavorful riff on everyone's favorite comfort food—without the eggs, breadcrumbs, or added fat—underscores the principle that less is truly more. It's the ice cubes that keep this meatloaf moist and juicy.

1 cup sun-dried tomatoes in olive oil
1 packed cup finely chopped yellow onion
1½ pounds ground sirloin

Preheat oven to 350°F.

Drain oil from sun-dried tomatoes and set aside. Finely dice tomatoes and set aside.

In a large nonstick skillet, combine reserved tomato oil and onions and cook slowly until onions are soft and golden, about 10 minutes.

In a large bowl, combine meat, diced tomatoes, cooked onion with all the pan juices, 1 teaspoon salt, and freshly ground black pepper. Mix together ¼ cup cold water and 3 slightly crushed ice cubes and add to meat. Mix thoroughly. Shape into an 8 by 4¼-inch loaf.

Place meatloaf on a rimmed baking sheet or shallow roasting pan. Bake for 35 to 40 minutes, until firm. Remove from oven and let rest for 5 minutes before serving.

Serves 4

BALSAMIC-GLAZED STUFFED BURGERS

You may never want to eat a burger any other way. These can be prepped early in the day and pan-seared right before serving. Serve as is, or on a big toasted Kaiser roll.

2¼ pounds ground beef, preferably chuck
5 ounces Boursin cheese
1 cup balsamic vinegar

Divide meat into 8 portions. Flatten each portion into a patty that is 4½ inches in diameter. Cut cheese into 4 portions, and crumble it. Scatter cheese in center of 4 patties. Sprinkle with coarsely ground black pepper. Top with a plain patty and press edges together to form one big burger. Make sure edges are sealed well. Wrap each in aluminum foil and refrigerate until ready to cook.

Meanwhile, put vinegar in a small saucepan and bring to a boil. Lower heat to medium-high and cook until reduced to ⅓ cup, about 15 minutes. Set aside.

When ready to serve, season burgers with salt and pepper. Heat a very large nonstick skillet until hot. Put burgers in pan and cook on each side for 5 minutes, or until the outside is browned and slightly crisp and the center is a bit soft to the touch. These are best medium-rare. Quickly heat reduced vinegar and pour 1 generous tablespoon over each patty. Serve immediately.

Serves 4

CHOPPED SKILLET STEAK WITH SCALLIONS AND SOY

This is an adaptation of one of James Beard's favorite recipes. Try it with Double-Baked Cheese Potatoes (page 51).

3 pounds ground beef round
2 bunches scallions
5 tablespoons soy sauce

Place chopped meat in a large bowl. Finely chop enough scallions, using both white and green parts, to get ½ cup. Mix scallions, 3 tablespoons soy sauce, and a generous grinding of black pepper into meat. Form mixture into a large cake, approximately 10 inches in diameter and 1½ inches thick.

Heat a heavy cast-iron skillet until hot and sprinkle lightly with salt. Place meat in the pan and cook over high heat for 6 to 9 minutes. Using 2 spatulas, carefully turn meat over and cook for 6 to 8 minutes. Each side should be rather charred and crisp on the outside, but still rare in the center.

When finished, turn out onto a large plate. Sprinkle with remaining 2 tablespoons soy sauce. Thinly slice 2 scallions on the bias and scatter on top. Cut meat into wedges.

Serves 6

SMOTHERED POT ROAST

This simple preparation requires no browning, sautéing, or really much attention at all. Your kitchen will smell wonderful for hours, as the beef and onions surrender their juices.

  4 pound rump or chuck roast
  2 pounds red onions
  1 cup dry vermouth

Preheat oven to 275°F.

Season roast with salt and freshly ground black pepper. Peel onions and cut in half through the stem end. Place cut side down on a cutting board and thinly slice onions across the width. Put the onions in a large flameproof casserole with a cover (an enamel Le Creuset is very good for this) and place meat on top. Cover casserole and cook for 3½ to 4 hours, until meat is very soft but not falling apart. Remove from oven and transfer meat to a cutting board.

Place casserole with onions on stovetop. Add vermouth and bring to a boil. Cook over high heat for 5 minutes. Add salt and pepper to taste. Cut meat across the grain into thin slices and place in onion gravy. Cover pot and heat gently for 10 minutes, or until meat has soaked in some of the juices.

Serves 6 or more

SIZZLING STEAK PICANTE WITH LIME

Few dishes are easier or more flavor-packed. Chili paste with garlic, borrowed from the Chinese pantry, is available in most supermarkets and all Asian food stores. When teamed with sizzling beef and fresh lime, it smacks of the American Southwest.

    3 tablespoons chili paste with garlic
    4 thick shell or rib-eye steaks, about 12 ounces each
    3 large limes

Cut 4 large pieces of aluminum foil. Rub ½ tablespoon chili paste to coat all surfaces of steaks. Place steaks on foil. Grate rind of ½ lime onto each and sprinkle each with 1 teaspoon lime juice. Wrap foil into tightly sealed packages and refrigerate steaks for 4 to 6 hours.

Heat 2 large cast-iron grill pans or nonstick skillets until very hot. Place steaks in hot pans and cook over high heat for 5 minutes. Turn over and cook 4 minutes longer, or until desired doneness. When steaks are just about finished, squeeze juice of remaining lime into pans and let it sizzle. Sprinkle with kosher salt and serve immediately.

Serves 4

SLOW-COOKED BEEF SHANK, MARSALA-TOMATO SAUCE

This cut of meat also is known as beef soup meat shank. At my supermarket, I have bought it with the marrow bone, which is easily removed with a small sharp knife.

    3 pounds beef shank or shin meat, cut into 2½-inch pieces
    2½ cups dry Marsala
    3 14½-ounce cans stewed tomatoes with herbs, about 5½ cups

Place meat in a shallow casserole in 1 layer. Pour 1 cup Marsala over meat and marinate for 1 hour at room temperature.

Meanwhile, drain tomatoes in a large coarse-mesh sieve, pressing down hard to release all the juices. You will have about 2¼ cups tomato liquid. Set aside for later.

Drain meat. Season with salt and freshly ground black pepper. Place meat in 1 layer in a large flameproof casserole or pot with a cover. Spread drained tomatoes on top of meat. Add 1 cup Marsala. Bring to a boil. Lower heat, cover, and simmer for 3 hours.

Meanwhile, put tomato liquid and remaining ½ cup Marsala in a small saucepan and reduce to get ¾ cup sauce. Keep warm.

When meat is tender, transfer to a platter. Raise heat under casserole and cook liquid until thick and syrupy, adding salt and pepper to taste. Pour sauce over meat and drizzle with Marsala-tomato reduction. Serve immediately, or the next day.

Serves 6

WINE-DARK SHORT RIBS

Have the butcher cut the short ribs between the bones into four large pieces. This is known as long cut to differentiate it from flanken, which is short ribs cut through the bones.

4 large meaty short ribs, about 3½ pounds
½ cup plus 2 tablespoons hoisin sauce
2 cups full-bodied red Zinfandel

Place ribs, ½ cup hoisin sauce, and 1 cup Zinfandel in a large nonreactive bowl. Cover and refrigerate for 6 to 8 hours or overnight. Remove ribs from marinade and set aside.

Bring marinade to a boil with 3 cups water in a heavy pot large enough to hold short ribs in 1 layer. Add ribs and ½ teaspoon black peppercorns. Cover and cook slowly over low heat for 2½ hours, turning several times during cooking.

Meanwhile, place remaining 1 cup Zinfandel and 2 tablespoons hoisin sauce in a small nonreactive saucepan. Cook slowly over low heat until reduced to ½ cup. Set aside.

When tender, remove short ribs with a slotted spoon. Increase heat to high and reduce cooking liquid until thick and syrupy. Whisk in enough of the reserved wine-hoisin reduction until you have a well-balanced sauce. Add salt to taste. Pour sauce over hot ribs and serve immediately.

Serves 4

DOUBLE-GARLIC SKIRT STEAK WITH SALSA VERDE

Sometimes, aggressive flavors are a virtue. Here, garlic—both roasted and raw—does double duty, adding complexity and tenderness to skirt steak (a cut I adore).

2 very large heads garlic, plus 4 large cloves
2 1-pound skirt steaks
2 cups prepared medium-hot salsa verde

Preheat oven to 400°F.

Wrap 2 heads of garlic loosely in aluminum foil. Bake in a pie tin for 1 hour. Remove from oven and let cool.

Place skirt steaks in a large bowl and add 1½ cups salsa verde. Cut roasted garlic heads in half through the equator and squeeze the soft garlic pulp into the bowl. Slice raw garlic cloves lengthwise into paper-thin slices. Add to bowl and mix thoroughly. Cover and refrigerate for a minimum of 6 hours or overnight.

Heat 1 very large or 2 smaller nonstick skillets. Cut each steak into 2 portions. Place in hot pans and cook over high heat for 3 to 5 minutes on each side, until desired doneness. You want the steak blackened and caramelized on the outside and rare inside. Sprinkle with kosher salt and pepper. Cut on the bias into ¼-inch-thick slices. Serve with remaining salsa verde.

Serves 4

RIB STEAK WITH GORGONZOLA

This sinful trio of macho ingredients will end up pleasing everyone. Rib steaks have great flavor and are always tender. It is worth buying a bottle of grappa to explore its unique flavor and its affinity for Gorgonzola.

> 4 thick rib steaks, bone in, about 14 to 16 ounces each
> ¾ pound creamy Italian Gorgonzola cheese
> 3 or more tablespoons grappa or gin

Preheat oven to 450°F.

Season steaks with salt and freshly ground black pepper. Using 2 large nonstick skillets, sear steaks on each side over very high heat, about 3 minutes. Place steaks on rimmed baking sheets and finish cooking in hot oven until desired doneness, approximately 5 minutes for rare.

Cut rind off cheese with a sharp knife and cut cheese into small cubes. Place in a heavy medium saucepan with 3 tablespoons grappa. Heat slowly, stirring constantly until cheese melts. Continue to cook for several minutes, until sauce is thick. Taste and add a little more grappa, if desired. Or add a little water instead.

Plate the steaks and pour the cheese sauce over them. Serve immediately.

Serves 4

FLORENTINE STEAK

This classic recipe from Tuscany is known as bistecca fiorentina. *In Italy, the very best version is made with a special breed of cattle known as Chianina. The best Florentine steak I ever had was at the three-star Michelin restaurant La Tenda Rossa in Cerbaia, south of Florence. Use long bushy rosemary branches to "paint" the steak with oil during and after cooking.*

> 1½-inch-thick porterhouse steak, about 1¾ pounds
> ⅓ cup extra-virgin olive oil, plus more for drizzling
> 1 bunch fresh rosemary

Place steak in a large casserole. Pour olive oil over the top. Crush about 2 tablespoons rosemary needles and sprinkle over meat. Crack 1 tablespoon black peppercorns and scatter on top. Let sit at room temperature for 2 hours, or longer in the refrigerator.

Preheat grill until very hot. Place the steak on the hottest part and grill about 5 to 6 minutes on each side or until still very rare. Transfer to area of grill that is less hot and continue to cook until desired doneness.

Transfer to a cutting board. Cut meat from the bone, and then slice meat into ½-inch-thick slices on a slight bias. Drizzle with fresh olive oil and any accumulated juices from the board. Sprinkle with kosher salt and cracked black pepper. Garnish with chopped rosemary. Serve slices from both sides of the bone to each guest.

Serves 2 or more

PAN-SEARED SIRLOIN, OYSTER SAUCE REDUCTION

A twist on the classic Carpetbag steak, which is a grilled sirloin stuffed with fried oysters, this version uses a staple of the Chinese kitchen as its secret ingredient. The flavors mingle and then resound.

4 New York strip steaks, 12 ounces each
3½ tablespoons unsalted butter, chilled
3 tablespoons Chinese oyster sauce

On a clean kitchen towel, crack 4 teaspoons white peppercorns with the bottom of a saucepan, with the flat side of a cleaver, or with a chef's knife. Lightly salt both sides of the steak. Press the cracked peppercorns into the top of each steak, pounding lightly with your fist.

Melt ½ tablespoon butter in a very large nonstick skillet. Cook the steaks over high heat on each side for 3 to 4 minutes, until the surface is caramelized and the interior of the steaks is rare to medium-rare. Remove the steaks and place on a cutting board. Lightly cover with aluminum foil.

Add the oyster sauce to the pan. Bring to a boil. Remove from the heat and whisk in the remaining butter, cut into small pieces. The sauce will get creamy. Cut the steaks thickly on the bias, or leave them whole. Drizzle the sauce over each steak and serve immediately.

Serves 4

FLANK STEAK *LA TAGLIATA*

Tagliata *means "sliced" in Italian. I love the look of thick charred slices of rare steak topped with a thicket of julienned arugula. And I love the meat juices mingling with the garlicky oil and lots of kosher salt.*

2 pounds flank steak
½ cup garlic olive oil (page 228)
2 bunches fresh arugula

Place steak in a shallow casserole and pour ¼ cup garlic oil over top. Sprinkle with kosher salt and freshly ground black pepper and let marinate for 1 hour.

Meanwhile, wash arugula and dry well. Cut into julienned strips, about ¼ inch wide. Cover and refrigerate until ready to use.

Light a charcoal grill and when hot, cook steak for 5 to 6 minutes on one side, then turn over and cook 5 minutes longer or until desired doneness. You can also do this in a large grill pan and finish the steak in a very hot oven for about 10 minutes, or until desired doneness.

Slice steak on the bias into ½-inch-thick slices, making sure to save all juices from the meat. Mound arugula on sliced steak. Drizzle with remaining garlic oil and any accumulated juices from steak. Sprinkle with kosher salt and serve immediately.

Serves 4

SALT-AND-PEPPER PRIME RIB WITH HORSERADISH SAUCE

Primal and succulent, prime rib is a showstopper that most of us don't make at home any more. Serve hot with cold horseradish sauce, best made from fresh horseradish you grate yourself.

3-rib prime rib roast, about 5½ pounds, trimmed well, chine bone removed
5-inch piece fresh horseradish
8 ounces crème fraîche

Preheat oven to 300°F.

Make sure roast is at room temperature. Mix together 3 tablespoons kosher salt and 1 teaspoon each coarsely ground black pepper and white pepper. Rub well into fat on top and sides of roast. Place in a shallow roasting pan, fatty side up, and roast for 1 hour and 50 minutes (about 20 minutes per pound), or until rare.

Meanwhile, peel horseradish using a small sharp knife. Grate on the fine holes of a box grater to get ⅓ cup. Mix crème fraîche and horseradish in a small bowl, adding salt to taste. Cover and refrigerate until ready to use.

Fifteen minutes before roast is finished, increase oven temperature to 450°F. The roast is done when a meat thermometer reads between 125°F and 130°F. Place roast on a cutting board and let sit, loosely covered with aluminum foil, for 15 minutes. Carve meat as desired. Serve with accumulated pan juices and horseradish sauce.

Serves 6

BONELESS RIB ROAST WITH THYME-MUSTARD JUS

A boneless prime rib beef roast is a superb cut for entertaining. Here fresh thyme adds a subtle perfume to the pan juices, and serves as a pretty garnish.

½ cup good-quality honey-Dijon mustard
1 bunch fresh thyme
3½- to 4-pound boneless prime rib beef roast, fat trimmed

Place mustard in a small bowl. Remove 2½ teaspoons thyme leaves and stir into mustard. Place beef in a large heavy roasting pan. Coat beef with mustard mixture. Cover and let stand for 1½ hours at room temperature, or refrigerate for 12 hours or overnight.

Preheat oven to 375°F. Scrape mustard from beef and reserve. Cook beef for 1 hour, then brush reserved marinade over beef. Roast until a meat thermometer reads between 125°F and 130°F for rare, about 10 minutes longer. Transfer beef to a cutting board. Tent with aluminum foil to keep warm.

Pour pan juices into a glass measuring cup. Spoon fat off top of juices and return juices to pan. Place pan over medium-high heat. Add 1 cup water. Boil until juices are reduced to ½ cup, scraping up any browned bits. Strain through a fine-mesh sieve and add 1 teaspoon fresh thyme leaves, and salt and pepper to taste.

Cut beef into ½-inch-thick slices. Sprinkle with kosher salt and pepper. Serve with reduced pan juices.

Serves 6

RIB-EYE ROAST, GRAVLAX STYLE

One of my favorite roasts, this is cured like fresh salmon for gravlax. The roast is buried in a mixture of fresh dill, sugar, kosher salt, and pepper, and allowed to marinate for 24 hours.

3½-pound boneless rib-eye roast, tied
2 large bunches fresh dill
3 tablespoons sugar

Pat beef dry with paper towels. Wash dill and dry well. Chop enough leaves to yield 1 tightly packed cup. Save remaining dill for garnish.

Stir together sugar, ¼ cup kosher salt, and 1 teaspoon coarsely ground black pepper. Coat all sides of meat with this mixture, rubbing it into the surface of the roast. Pat chopped dill on top, bottom, and sides of roast. Wrap tightly in plastic wrap and place in a small roasting pan. Weight meat down with a baking sheet topped with several heavy cans or a tea kettle filled with water. Refrigerate for 24 hours.

Remove roast from plastic wrap and let sit at room temperature for 30 minutes. Preheat oven to 400°F.

Scrape off and discard all the dill and spice mixture from roast. Cook meat in a shallow heavy roasting pan for 1 hour and 15 minutes, or until a meat thermometer reads between 125°F and 130°F for rare.

Transfer roast to a cutting board and let rest for 10 minutes. Carve into ½-inch slices and garnish with remaining dill.

Serves 8

CÔTES DE BOEUF PATRICIA WELLS

This fabulous cut of meat is one of France's favorites and Patricia Wells' method is fool-proof. It is a single, thick prime rib of beef roasted at a high temperature.

2 large bunches fresh thyme
1 prime rib of beef, about 2 pounds
2 large cloves garlic

Preheat oven to 500°F.

Place 12 ounces (about 1½ cups) coarse sea salt in a mound on a rimmed baking sheet. Place 1 bunch thyme on salt. Trim the beef of any excess fat. Place the beef, fat side up, so that the bone is sitting in the salt. Use the salt to "anchor" the bone. Place in the lower portion of the oven and roast until the skin is crackling and brown, and the meat begins to exude fat and juices, about 22 minutes. A meat thermometer should read 125°F to 130°F for rare.

Remove from oven. Place the beef on a rack set over a pan or a platter to collect drippings. Cut garlic in half and rub meat on all sides with flat side of garlic. Sprinkle beef with 1 tablespoon thyme leaves plucked from second bunch. Loosely tent with aluminum foil and let rest in a warm place for 15 minutes. Cut the meat away from the bone, and slice into thick diagonal slices. Serve with the accumulated juices that have been briefly warmed. Sprinkle with sea salt and pass the peppermill.

Serves 2

TOURNEDOS *BALSAMICO*

Tournedos are thick round slices taken from the heart of a fillet of beef. There are many recipes for tournedos in the classic French repertoire, but this one is thoroughly modern and swings toward Italian.

4 1-inch-thick beef tenderloin fillets, about 10 ounces each
⅓ cup extra-virgin olive oil, plus more for drizzling
⅓ cup balsamic vinegar

Place meat in a shallow casserole. Pour olive oil over top and drizzle with 2 tablespoons vinegar. Marinate for 1 hour, turning tournedos several times.

Remove tournedos from marinade. Sprinkle with salt on both sides. On one side of each fillet, press 2 teaspoons very coarsely ground black pepper.

Coat a cast-iron grill pan or large nonstick skillet very lightly with olive oil. Heat pan until very hot and cook tournedos for about 3 to 4 minutes on each side, until medium-rare.

Meanwhile, place remaining vinegar in a small saucepan and cook over medium heat until reduced to ¼ cup. When tournedos are done, transfer to warm plates. Drizzle each with a little reduced vinegar and a sprinkling of kosher salt.

Serves 4

BAY-SMOKED CHÂTEAUBRIAND WITH TRUFFLE-ROASTED SALT

This is a glorious dish for company. Bay leaves, slightly bitter when fresh, sweeten as they dry and gently perfume the beef. Instead of the truffle oil, you may serve the châteaubriand with a Marsala reduction: reduce dry or sweet Marsala until syrupy and mix with pan drippings.

2¾ pounds "trimmed weight" fillet of beef, tied in 1½-inch intervals
2 or 3 tablespoons white truffle oil
18 fresh California bay leaves

Preheat oven to 400°F.

Coat the beef with 1 tablespoon truffle oil, using your hands. Grind black pepper all over the fillet.

In the center of a heavy shallow roasting pan, scatter 15 of the bay leaves. Place the beef on top. Tuck the remaining bay leaves on top of the beef, under the butcher's string. Roast for 35 minutes, or until a meat thermometer reads between 125°F and 130°F for rare. (Cook longer if you prefer medium-rare). Transfer to a cutting board and cover with an aluminum foil tent. Let rest 10 minutes.

Mix 2 tablespoons coarse French sea salt with ½ teaspoon truffle oil. Place in a small nonstick skillet and toast over medium heat, stirring constantly. Remove when salt begins to brown. Cool on a paper towel.

Carve meat into ½-inch-thick slices. Drizzle each slice with a little truffle oil and serve little mounds of truffle-roasted salt with the meat.

Serves 6 or more

pasta
and grains

I've been struck in recent years by how restaurant chefs, and magazines that follow their creative antics, have popularized the idea that "more is better" when it comes to pasta and grains. The result is ingredient-laden recipes like Risotto of Sweet Corn, Clams, Shrimp, Smoked Sausage, Goat Cheese, Tarragon, and Cream or Linguine Tossed with Tomatoes, Pepperoni, Mushrooms, Zucchini, Basil, and Mint in a Veal Reduction.

I'd rather have carbs with clarity. So my pasta and grain recipes celebrate just a few intense flavors and textures—and every ingredient serves a specific gastronomic purpose. These are the ultimate comfort foods: meltingly soft, moist (or saucy), perfumed dishes that are spectacularly unfussy and direct in their flavors. My favorite of these recipes comes from childhood. I still beg my mother to cook her soul-satisfying Hungarian Cabbage and Noodles (page 194) whenever I visit. Another soothing and surprising pasta recipe was discovered by my teacher Giuliano Bugialli in an 1841 Italian cookbook. Macaroni and Tomatoes (page 194) is made with uncooked pasta that is soaked in olive oil then slow-baked with tomatoes.

A luxurious emergency meal, Michael's Squid Ink Pasta (page 193), was named for my husband, whose idea of comfort was to gobble down a three-portion test recipe before I had a chance to see whether it belonged in this book! Black linguine is now a staple in our kitchen.

In truth, the rice section alone could be expanded into a book. The recipes feature Arborio, basmati, jasmine, brown and domestic Carolina rices, but I could name a dozen more varieties from faraway cultural enclaves that are beginning to appear in supermarkets. Each has its own characteristics, and I encourage you to experiment with all of them.

Although traditionally grouped with rice, wild rice is no such thing. It actually is the seed of a native American grass that happens to look like dark rice, and it's cooked in a similar manner. My Wild Rice with Five-Hour Onions (page 202) serves twelve; it's the perfect accompaniment to a holiday turkey or roast ribs of beef.

Bulgur is similarly misunderstood. It's not an individual grain, but kernels of wheat that are steamed, dried, and then cracked. And you may be surprised to learn that couscous is not a grain. Technically, it is pasta that is formed into tiny pearls, once made by rolling a paste of semolina flour between the thumb and forefinger.

Sadly, what restaurant chefs never make anymore are simple dishes like *Riso al Burro* (page 198), fat grains of boiled Arborio rice tossed with sweet butter and freshly grated Parmigiano-Reggiano. It doesn't get more comforting than that, unless, of course, you try a bowl of Normandy Oats with Cider Syrup (page 204), or *Mamaliga* (cooked cornmeal) topped with butter and cheese (page 207).

FIRST-COURSE PASTAS

GARLIC-AND-OIL SPAGHETTI

    4 medium cloves garlic
    6 tablespoons extra-virgin olive oil
    8 ounces spaghetti

Peel garlic and finely chop it. In a small skillet, combine garlic and olive oil, and cook garlic over low heat until it is golden brown. Do not let it get darker or it will taste bitter.

Bring a large pot of salted water to a boil. Add spaghetti and cook until al dente, about 12 minutes. Drain well, reserving ⅓ cup cooking water.

Put reserved cooking water, garlic and oil, and well-drained pasta in a large, heated bowl. Toss gently and season with salt and freshly ground black pepper. Serve immediately.

Serves 4

TORTELLINI WITH FRESH SAGE BUTTER

You also can use this sauce with small ravioli or crescent-shaped agnolotti filled with pumpkin, cheese, or meat.

    3 bunches fresh sage
    1 pound good-quality tortellini
    7 tablespoons unsalted butter

Wash sage and dry well. Remove 6 leaves and cut into very fine julienne. Coarsely chop enough sage to get ½ packed cup.

Bring a large pot of salted water to a boil. Add tortellini and cook until al dente, about 8 minutes.

Melt 6 tablespoons butter in a large nonstick skillet. Add chopped sage, a pinch of salt, and freshly ground black pepper. Cook over medium heat until butter just begins to brown and bubble; the sage should get crispy.

Drain tortellini in a colander, saving ¼ cup cooking water. Immediately put pasta in a large warm bowl, adding remaining butter. Toss with melted butter-sage mixture and add enough cooking water to make a smooth sauce. Add salt and pepper to taste and sprinkle with julienned sage. Divide immediately among warm pasta bowls.

Serves 4

FETTUCCINE ALFREDO

The true fettuccine Alfredo hails from Rome, where it was invented almost one hundred years ago. It seems that the secret to this famous three-ingredient dish is great-quality ingredients and perfect timing. The original was made with rich egg pasta, sweet butter, and young Parmigiano-Reggiano. That's it. No cream, parsley, or even pepper.

1½ pounds fresh fettuccine
2 sticks (½ pound) unsalted butter, at room temperature
1¾ cups freshly grated young Parmigiano-Reggiano, about 6 ounces

Fill a large ceramic bowl with boiling water. Let it sit to warm the bowl.

Bring a large pot of salted water to a boil. Add fettuccine and cook until al dente, about 5 minutes. Carefully pour water out of bowl and dry it. Slice butter and put it in hot bowl to melt.

Drain pasta in a colander, saving ½ cup cooking water. Quickly add pasta to bowl, with some of its cooking water still clinging to it, and sprinkle with grated cheese. Add ¼ cup of the cooking water and, using a large serving fork and spoon, toss for a minute or two to thoroughly blend the ingredients. Add a little more cooking liquid if needed. Serve immediately in warmed pasta bowls.

Serves 6 or more

FARFALLE WITH BROCCOLI, BROCCOLI-BUTTER SAUCE

This has become one of my signature dishes and a good example of using one ingredient—broccoli—in two distinct ways. It can be made with many different varieties of pasta, from orecchiette to ziti.

1 very large head broccoli, or two smaller ones
4 tablespoons unsalted butter, chilled
8 ounces farfalle pasta

Cut broccoli into small florets, leaving ½ inch of small stems attached. Set aside. Using a vegetable peeler, peel the thick stalks. Cut into 1-inch pieces.

Place chopped stalks in a medium saucepan with 1¼ cups salted water. Bring to a boil, lower heat to medium, and cook, covered, for 25 minutes. When very soft, transfer stalks and cooking liquid to a blender. Puree until very smooth. Cut butter into small pieces, add to puree, and process, adding a little water, if necessary, to make a smooth sauce. Add salt and freshly ground black pepper to taste and transfer to a clean saucepan.

Meanwhile, bring a large pot of salted water to a boil. Add farfalle and cook for 10 minutes. Add the broccoli florets and cook another 3 to 4 minutes, until broccoli is tender and bright green and pasta is cooked through. Drain pasta and broccoli in a colander, then transfer to a large warm bowl or individual pasta bowls. Reheat sauce gently, and pour it over the pasta and broccoli.

Serves 4

PENNE WITH ASPARAGUS TIPS, GORGONZOLA SAUCE

Thin spears of fresh asparagus are used as a crunchy accompaniment to the pasta and as the base for a sophisticated cheese sauce.

 1 pound medium asparagus, about 24 spears
 8 ounces penne pasta
 8 ounces imported creamy Gorgonzola cheese

Using a light touch, peel asparagus stalks with a vegetable peeler. Cut off asparagus tips, 3 inches from the top, and set aside. Remove woody bottoms from stalks, about ½ inch, and discard them.

Cut stalks into ¼-inch pieces. Place in a small saucepan with 1¾ cups water and ¼ teaspoon salt. Bring to a boil. Lower heat to medium and cook for 13 to 14 minutes, until asparagus pieces are soft but still retain their shape.

Transfer asparagus and cooking liquid to a blender. Remove rind from cheese and cut cheese into small pieces. Add to blender. Process on high very carefully, since contents are very hot (see Note). When sauce is very, very smooth, return it to saucepan. Add salt and freshly ground black pepper to taste. Reheat sauce over low heat for a few minutes, until creamy and thick.

Bring a large pot of salted water to a boil. Add penne and cook for 10 minutes. Add reserved asparagus tips and cook 3 to 4 minutes longer, until just tender and still bright green. Drain pasta and asparagus well in a colander. Transfer to a large warm bowl or individual pasta bowls, and top with sauce that has been gently reheated. Dust with coarsely ground black pepper. Serve immediately.

Note: I remove the centerpiece from the blender's cap and hold a kitchen towel over the top. The idea is to let some of the steam escape.

Serves 4

BUCATINI *CACIO E PEPE*

Bucatini, long strands of pasta with a hole through the middle, is the traditional pasta for this dish, although spaghetti can be substituted. The title simply means "with cheese and pepper." Lots of it.

 1 pound bucatini pasta
 3 tablespoons extra-virgin olive oil, plus more for drizzling
 1½ cups freshly grated imported Pecorino Romano, about 6 ounces

Smash 1 tablespoon whole black peppercorns with flat side of a chef's knife, then chop until coarsely ground. This also can be done using a mortar and pestle.

Bring a large pot of salted water to a boil. Add bucatini and cook until al dente, 12 to 14 minutes. Drain pasta in a colander, saving ½ cup cooking liquid.

Return hot pasta, with some of its water still clinging to it, to the pot. Add 3 tablespoons olive oil and the coarsely ground black pepper. Add 1 cup of cheese and enough of the reserved cooking liquid to coat pasta, tossing thoroughly. Add salt to taste and reheat gently. Transfer to warm bowls, sprinkle with remaining cheese, and drizzle with more oil.

Serves 4 or more

SPINACH LINGUINE WITH TOMATOES AND SARDINES

Fresh pasta is best for this dish, but dried spinach linguine tastes good, too. If you're using dried pasta, cook it longer, about twelve minutes, or until al dente.

> 28-ounce can plum tomatoes with thick puree
> 3¾-ounce can boneless, skinless sardines packed in oil
> 9 ounces fresh spinach linguine, fresh or dried

Place tomatoes and sardines and their oil in a 4-quart pot with a cover. Add ¼ teaspoon whole black peppercorns and a large pinch of salt. Bring to a boil. Lower heat, cover pot, and simmer for 30 minutes, stirring frequently with a wooden spoon to break up sardines. Uncover pot and cook another 30 minutes over low heat. Mixture should be rather thick and chunky.

Bring a large pot of salted water to a boil. Add linguine and cook for 3 to 4 minutes, or until just tender. Drain pasta thoroughly in a colander. Reheat sauce and pour over hot pasta. Serve immediately.

Serves 4

MICHAEL'S SQUID INK PASTA

I created this quite by accident and my husband loved it.

> 6 ounces tomato paste seasoned with garlic
> 7 tablespoons unsalted butter
> 8 ounces squid ink linguine, fresh or dried

Put tomato paste in a small heavy saucepan and add ¼ cup water. Heat gently. Cut butter into pieces and add to tomato mixture. Stir sauce with a wooden spoon over low heat until butter is incorporated. Season with salt and freshly ground black pepper to taste.

Bring a large pot of salted water to a boil. Add linguine and cook until tender, about 6 minutes for fresh linguine and 12 minutes for dried. Be careful not to overcook. Drain immediately in a colander, saving a few tablespoons cooking water. Reheat sauce, whisking a little of the cooking water into it. Serve sauce atop hot pasta.

Serves 4

HUNGARIAN CABBAGE AND NOODLES

This was my favorite comfort dish growing up, courtesy of my beautiful Hungarian mother. The goal is to squeeze the water from the cabbage after it's salted, and then melt the cabbage into dark golden strands.

> 1 very large head green cabbage, about 3 pounds
> 8 tablespoons unsalted butter
> 12 ounces medium-wide egg noodles

Wash cabbage and pat dry. With a sharp knife, shred cabbage into ¼-inch-wide slices. Place in a colander and sprinkle generously with kosher salt to coat. Cover with a small plate and put a heavy object on top to weight it down. Put the colander in a pan to collect any liquid, or set it in the sink. Let sit for 3 to 4 hours. Then press down hard and squeeze cabbage with your fists to extract as much water as possible.

In a very large nonstick skillet, melt butter and add shredded cabbage. Cook over medium heat, stirring frequently, for 30 to 40 minutes, until cabbage is a deep golden brown. It will shrink considerably. Lower heat, if necessary, so cabbage does not burn.

Cook noodles in a large pot of boiling water, until just tender, about 15 minutes. Drain noodles thoroughly and place in a warm bowl. Add hot cabbage and toss so the noodles are completely integrated with cabbage. Add lots of freshly ground black pepper and serve immediately.

Serves 4

MACARONI AND TOMATOES

Rediscovered in an Italian cookbook from 1841 by Italian cooking authority Giuliano Bugialli, this pasta hails from Naples and employs an interesting technique. Dried pasta is soaked in olive oil before cooking.

> 8 ounces dried cavatelli or fusilli pasta
> 6 tablespoons extra-virgin olive oil, plus more for brushing casserole
> 28-ounce can imported plum tomatoes with thick puree

In a medium bowl, mix cavatelli and olive oil. Let pasta soak in the oil for 20 minutes.

Preheat oven to 400°F.

Add tomatoes and their puree to pasta and oil. Add 1 teaspoon kosher salt and freshly ground black pepper to taste, and mix well.

Transfer pasta to a shallow casserole brushed with a little olive oil. Bake for 45 minutes, stirring several times during baking to prevent pasta from sticking to casserole. Serve immediately.

Serves 4

WARM SALAD OF PASTA AND CHICKPEAS

Use dried, not canned, chickpeas for the best results.

> 8 ounces dried chickpeas
> 8 ounces penne or orecchiette pasta
> ½ cup garlic olive oil (page 228)

Soak chickpeas overnight or use this quick-soak method: In a large saucepan, cover beans with 2 inches water, bring to a boil, and boil for 2 minutes. Remove from heat, cover, and let sit for 1 hour. Drain well.

Put soaked chickpeas in a medium pot with water to cover by 2 inches. Bring to a boil. Lower heat and simmer for 1 hour and 45 minutes, or longer, until chickpeas are tender.

When chickpeas are tender, add more water, if necessary, so that chickpeas are still covered by 2 inches. Add kosher salt to taste. Bring to a boil again and add penne, stirring frequently with a wooden spoon. Cook until al dente, about 15 minutes.

Drain in a colander, leaving pasta a little wet. Put pasta and chickpeas in a warm bowl. Toss with garlic oil, 1½ teaspoons coarsely ground black pepper, and salt to taste. Serve hot or at room temperature.

Serves 4

TUBETTI WITH ZUCCHINI

> ¾ pound small zucchini
> 2 cups chicken broth
> 8 ounces tubetti pasta

Wash zucchini and trim ends. Cut zucchini in half through the diameter. Then slice lengthwise into ⅛-inch-thick slices. Meticulously cut slices into ⅛-inch cubes. You should have 2 heaping cups.

Put chicken broth in a small saucepan. Cook over medium-high heat until broth is reduced to ½ cup.

Bring a medium pot of salted water to a boil and add tubetti. Cook for 8 minutes, add diced zucchini, and cook 4 minutes longer. Drain in a coarse-mesh sieve.

Toss pasta with hot reduced broth. Add freshly ground black pepper.

Serves 4

FETTUCCINE WITH BASIL-GARLIC SAUCE

The essential ingredient in this thick herb sauce is garlic olive oil that has been frozen. This technique emulsifies the sauce so that each strand of pasta gets color- and flavor-coated.

> 5 tablespoons garlic olive oil (page 228)
> 2 large bunches fresh basil
> 12 ounces fettuccine, preferably imported Italian

Place garlic olive oil in a small dish and freeze for several hours, until frozen solid.

Wash basil and dry thoroughly. Coarsely chop enough basil to get 4 packed cups. Bring a medium saucepan of salted water to a boil. Add basil and boil for 2½ minutes. Drain immediately and put in a blender with frozen garlic oil and 4 to 5 tablespoons water.

Process until thick and creamy. You should have about 1 cup. Add salt and freshly ground black pepper to taste. This can be made ahead and refrigerated until ready to use. Bring to room temperature before stirring into cooked pasta.

Bring a large pot of salted water to a boil. Add fettuccine and bring to a boil again. Lower heat a bit and cook until al dente, 12 to 14 minutes. Drain in a colander, shaking off any excess water. Place in a large warm bowl and add as much basil puree as needed to coat pasta. Add salt and pepper to taste. Reheat gently, if necessary.

Serves 6

TOASTED ORZO AND RICE

> 4 tablespoons unsalted butter
> 1 cup orzo
> 1 cup extra-long-grain rice

Put 1½ tablespoons butter in a 4-quart pot with a cover. Add orzo and cook over medium heat, stirring often, until orzo turns golden brown. This will take about 2 minutes.

Add rice and cook for 1 minute, stirring constantly. Add 2 cups boiling water and ¼ teaspoon salt, and cover pot. Lower heat and simmer for 15 minutes. Do not remove cover.

Remove from heat and let sit for 20 minutes. The steam will continue to cook the orzo and rice. Remove cover, fluff with a fork, and add remaining butter. Season with salt and freshly ground black pepper. Serve immediately.

Serves 6

GREEK-STYLE ORZO

For the best results, go shopping at a food store that specializes in Greek products. Greek orzo is longer than the Italian brands you normally find, and the right cheese is essential to this dish. Kasseri is a sheep's milk cheese that melts beautifully into the pasta. This dish is a great accompaniment to lamb.

12 ounces orzo pasta
5 tablespoons unsalted butter, chilled
6 ounces Kasseri cheese, shredded, about 1½ packed cups

Bring a large pot of salted water to a boil. Add orzo and cook until tender, 10 to 12 minutes. Immediately drain in a colander and put in a warm bowl.

Add butter, cut into small pieces, and stir to coat orzo. Mix well and add cheese. Stir until incorporated. Add salt and freshly ground black pepper to taste. Serve immediately.

Serves 6

MINTED COUSCOUS WITH CURRY OIL

Couscous is not a grain, but a pasta. Here it is mixed with a new staple in my kitchen, Thai-style curry oil, now available in supermarkets and Asian food stores. Heat releases its flavor and also the essential oils in the fresh mint.

2 tablespoons Thai curry oil
1 cup couscous
1 small bunch fresh mint

Put 1¾ cups water in a 4-quart pot with a cover. Add 1 tablespoon curry oil and ½ teaspoon kosher salt, and bring to a boil.

Slowly stir in couscous, and cook over high heat for 1 minute, until couscous begins to thicken. Lower heat and cook 1 minute longer. Cover pot and remove from heat. Let sit for 5 minutes.

Meanwhile, finely chop or julienne enough mint to yield ¼ cup. Reserve the rest of the mint.

Fluff couscous with a fork, breaking up any small clumps. Transfer to a warm bowl. Add chopped mint and remaining curry oil, stirring with a fork. Add salt and freshly ground black pepper to taste. Garnish with fresh mint sprigs.

Serves 4

COUSCOUS WITH GRILLED SCALLIONS

   2 bunches scallions
   3 tablespoons unsalted butter
   1½ cups couscous

Trim roots from scallions. Finely chop 1 bunch of scallions, both white and green parts. You should have about 1 cup. Melt 2 tablespoons butter in a medium pot with a cover, and add chopped scallions. Cook over medium heat until scallions are soft and translucent. Do not let them brown.

Add couscous and stir over medium heat for 1 minute. Add 3 cups boiling water and stir over low heat for 3 minutes. Remove from heat, cover, and let stand for 5 minutes, until water is absorbed.

Meanwhile, melt remaining butter in a small saucepan. Lightly brush remaining bunch of scallions with butter. Heat a cast-iron grill pan until very hot. Add scallions and cook, turning several times, until they begin to soften and grill marks are emblazoned on the greens. This will take several minutes.

Remove cover from couscous mixture. Fluff with a fork, and add salt and freshly ground black pepper to taste. Place on a warm platter, or pack into timbales and turn out on individual plates. Top with grilled scallions.

Serves 5 or 6

RISO AL BURRO

In this simple Italian recipe, Arborio rice, generally used for making risotto, is instead fast-boiled, then stirred with browned butter and freshly grated cheese. In Italy, this is generally served as a primi piatti, *or first course, but I think it's more appropriate as a side dish.*

   1½ cups Arborio rice
   3 tablespoons unsalted butter
   1 cup freshly grated Parmigiano-Reggiano

In a 4-quart pot with a cover, bring salted water to a boil, as though you were making pasta. Add rice and bring to a boil again. Lower heat and cover pot. Cook for 16 minutes, or until rice is tender. Drain rice well in a colander, shaking off any excess water.

Put butter in a large nonstick skillet and cook over medium-high heat until butter melts and turns a nutty brown color. Do not let it burn. Add rice and stir until rice is coated with butter. Add ¾ cup cheese and stir. Add salt and freshly ground black pepper to taste. Reheat gently. Sprinkle remaining cheese on top.

Serves 4 or more

BASMATI RICE WITH TANGERINES

This fragrant dish will become one your favorite accompaniments when tangerines are in season. Other times, oranges may be substituted.

5 tangerines
1½ tablespoons roasted peanut oil
1 cup basmati rice

Cut 1 tangerine in half and squeeze to get ¼ cup juice. Set aside.

Remove rind from remaining tangerines. Using a small sharp knife, remove as much white pith from rind as possible. Finely mince enough of the rind to get 3 teaspoons. Cut in between the membranes of each tangerine to release segments. You should have ½ cup tangerine segments. Squeeze remaining membranes to extract several more tablespoons juice.

In a medium pot with a cover, heat 1 tablespoon peanut oil. Add rice and cook over medium heat for a few minutes, stirring frequently, until rice begins to take on a little color and smells nutty. Add 2 teaspoons minced tangerine rind, tangerine juice, 1¾ cups water, and 1 teaspoon salt.

Cover pot and cook for 20 to 25 minutes until liquid is absorbed. Add tangerine segments and cook for 30 seconds, to warm gently. Add salt and freshly ground black pepper to taste. Fluff with a large fork and transfer to a warm bowl. Drizzle with remaining oil and scatter with remaining minced rind. Serve immediately.

Serves 4

AROMATIC GINGER RICE

This is a simple way to add interest to ordinary rice. Fresh ginger is grated and squeezed to extract its spicy aromatic juice.

5-inch piece fresh ginger
1 cup long-grain rice
2 tablespoons unsalted butter

Peel ginger and finely mince enough to get 1 heaping tablespoon. Grate remaining ginger on the large holes of a box grater. Place grated ginger in a paper towel and squeeze ginger very hard over a small dish. You should get about 1 tablespoon juice.

Bring 2¼ cups water and ½ teaspoon salt to a boil in a medium pot with a cover. Add rice and minced ginger. Cover pot, lower heat, and simmer for 20 minutes, or until water is evaporated.

Melt butter in a small saucepan and add ginger juice. Drain rice well in a colander and then transfer rice to a warm bowl. Toss with butter mixture, and add salt and freshly ground white pepper to taste.

Serves 4

RICE PILAF BAKED IN LAVASH

This unusual pilaf is adapted from a lovely book called Through the Kitchen Window: Women Explore the Intimate Meanings of Food and Cooking *edited by Arlene Voski Avakian. In this recipe, lavash, a soft, thin Armenian flat bread, crisps as it bakes and becomes an edible "bowl" for the rice.*

    1½ cups basmati rice
    6 tablespoons unsalted butter
    1 or 2 large lavash breads

Soak rice in a bowl of salted water in refrigerator for 12 hours or overnight.

Preheat oven to 350°F.

Drain rice and rinse repeatedly in a bowl until water is clear. Drain again. Bring 2 cups water to a boil in a medium pot. Add rice and cook for 10 minutes, stirring often. The center of the rice should still be hard. Drain rice in a colander. Stir in a large pinch of salt and freshly ground black pepper.

Spread 1 tablespoon butter on bottom of a shallow 9 by 11-inch casserole large enough to hold the rice in a thick layer. Melt remaining butter. Place a thin layer of lavash in casserole so that bread covers bottom and comes up the sides. Add rice and pour melted butter over top.

Cover casserole tightly and bake for 45 minutes. Remove from oven. Serve rice with some of the crisped lavash bread.

Serves 6

JASMINE RICE WITH COCONUT MILK

Fragrant rice becomes more so in its milky coconut-infused bath. Crushed pistachios, a suggestion from my food-journalist friend Erica Marcus, add flavor, crunch, and color.

    1 cup jasmine rice
    1 cup coconut milk
    ⅓ cup pistachio nuts

Put rice, coconut milk, 1 cup water, and 1 teaspoon salt in a 4-quart pot with a cover. Bring to a boil, stirring once. Reduce heat, cover pot, and simmer for 20 minutes. Remove from heat and let stand, covered, for 5 to 10 minutes.

Meanwhile, put nuts in a nonstick skillet and cook until lightly toasted and aromatic. Chop nuts very fine.

Remove cover from rice and fluff with a fork. Add salt and freshly ground white pepper to taste. Stir in most of the nuts, saving some to use as a garnish.

Serves 4

PERSIAN RICE WITH SAFFRON BROTH

Threads of golden saffron tint and flavor the basmati rice, and the steaming technique creates a highly desirable bottom crust. The accompanying liquid fools the eye; it looks like a vat of melted butter.

½ teaspoon saffron threads
1½ cups basmati rice
3 tablespoons unsalted butter

Put 2 quarts water, saffron, and 1½ tablespoons kosher salt in a 4-quart pot with a cover. Bring to a boil. Add rice and boil for 10 minutes. Drain rice in a colander, reserving the saffron cooking liquid.

Rinse out the pot and dry. Melt 2 tablespoons butter in pot and add cooked rice.

Cover pot with a clean kitchen towel, then fit the lid over the towel. Fold edges of towel over lid to cover. Cook over very low heat for 35 to 40 minutes, until a nice crust forms at the bottom.

Meanwhile, bring reserved saffron liquid to a boil and cook over medium heat for 5 minutes. Add 1 tablespoon butter and freshly ground white pepper. Keep warm.

Turn hot rice out onto a warm platter, so that the crisp crust is on top. Serve hot saffron broth in a separate sauceboat or pitcher to pour over rice as desired. Serve immediately.

Serves 6

BROWN RICE WITH SUN-DRIED CHERRIES

This fragrant, nubby side dish just begs for a juicy grilled venison chop or roasted turkey leg.

1 cup long-grain brown rice
½ cup unsweetened sun-dried cherries
2 tablespoons lemon olive oil (page 228)

Put 2 cups water, ½ teaspoon salt, and rice in a medium saucepan with a cover. Bring to a boil. Lower heat, cover, and simmer for 15 minutes. Add sun-dried cherries, stir, and cover again. Continue to cook over low heat for 20 to 25 minutes, or until water is absorbed and rice is tender, but not too soft.

Remove from heat and let sit for 5 minutes. Fluff rice with a fork. Add lemon oil; season with salt and freshly ground black pepper to taste.

Serves 4

WILD RICE WITH FIVE-HOUR ONIONS

This is a superb side dish for a holiday crowd that can easily be reheated. The recipe also can be halved; just put the whole onions in a smaller covered casserole.

12 medium yellow onions, about 3 pounds, plus 1 cup finely diced onion
10 tablespoons unsalted butter
1 pound wild rice

Preheat oven to 275°F.

Peel whole onions and place them in a heavy casserole just large enough to fit onions comfortably. Thinly slice 8 tablespoons butter and scatter over onions. Cover casserole and bake for 5 hours. Onions will be golden and give off lots of juice. Set aside.

One hour before serving time, wash rice and drain in a colander. Melt remaining butter in a 4-quart pot with a cover. Add rice and diced onion. Stir with a wooden spoon for 5 minutes, or until rice is a bit crisp. Slowly add 2 quarts cold water. Bring to a boil. Add 2 teaspoons salt and freshly ground black pepper.

Lower heat to medium, cover, and cook for 55 minutes. Uncover pot, increase heat to high, and cook for about 10 minutes, or until rice is tender. Add salt and pepper to taste. If necessary, drain in a colander to remove excess liquid. Transfer to a large warm platter or bowl.

Reheat onions gently. Using a slotted spoon, place onions on rice. Pour onion juices over rice and serve. This dish can be reheated easily in the oven.

Serves 12

COOKED BULGUR WITH TOASTED PINE NUTS

Bulgur, or cracked wheat, is often soaked in hot water, not cooked. In this recipe, the bulgur is cooked, for a plumper, moister texture.

2 cups coarse bulgur wheat
1 bunch fresh cilantro
½ cup pine nuts

In a 4-quart pot, bring 7 cups water and 1 teaspoon salt to a boil. Add bulgur, stirring constantly. Reduce heat to medium. Cook for 15 minutes, stirring frequently, until bulgur is tender.

Meanwhile, wash cilantro and dry well. Julienne enough leaves so that you have ½ cup. Put pine nuts in a small nonstick skillet and cook over low heat for several minutes, shaking pan constantly, until nuts are just golden. Be careful not to burn them.

Drain bulgur in a colander. Place in a warm bowl. Add salt and freshly ground black pepper to taste. Toss with pine nuts and most of the julienned cilantro. Scatter remaining cilantro on top.

Serves 6

CRACKED WHEAT AND CARAMELIZED ONIONS

2 large yellow onions
3 tablespoons olive oil, plus more for drizzling if desired
1 cup coarse bulgur wheat, about 8 ounces

Peel onions. Cut 1 onion into ¼-inch dice. Reserve remaining onion.

In a large nonstick skillet, heat 2 tablespoons olive oil. Add diced onion and cook over medium-high heat for 20 minutes, or until dark brown, soft, and caramelized.

Meanwhile, put bulgur in a medium bowl and cover with 2½ cups boiling water. Cover bowl and let bulgur sit until soft, about 20 minutes. Drain excess water, if necessary.

Add drained bulgur to cooked onions in skillet and cook for 10 minutes, until bulgur and onions are incorporated and bulgur is soft, fluffy, and rather dry.

Meanwhile, cut remaining onion in half through the root end and slice very thin. Heat remaining olive oil in a small nonstick skillet and add onion slices. Cook over medium-high heat until onion becomes almost blackened, adding a little water if necessary. This will take about 10 minutes.

When ready to serve, reheat bulgur and garnish with blackened onions. Add salt and freshly ground black pepper to taste, and drizzle with a little more olive oil, if desired.

Serves 4

PEARL BARLEY WITH WILD MUSHROOMS AND DATES

Pearl barley gets slightly viscous when it cooks, making it taste like it's already buttered! Earthy wild mushrooms—your choice of dried porcini, morels, or shiitakes—and bits of sweet dates complete this unexpected trio.

1¼ ounces dried porcini, morels, or shiitakes
1 packed cup pearl barley
4 ounces pitted dates

Place mushrooms in a fine-mesh strainer and shake to remove any pieces of sand or dirt.

Transfer mushrooms to a 4-quart pot with a cover. Add 6 cups water and 1 teaspoon salt. Bring to a rapid boil. Add barley and bring to a boil again. Cover pot and reduce heat to low. Cook for 50 minutes.

Meanwhile, cut dates into ¼-inch dice, and set aside.

When barley is tender, but not too soft, drain barley and mushrooms in a colander, saving some of the cooking liquid to moisten barley if necessary. Put hot barley and mushrooms in a warm bowl and add dates. Toss well, adding salt and freshly ground black pepper to taste, and a little cooking liquid if necessary. Serve hot.

Serves 4 or more

NORMANDY OATS WITH CIDER SYRUP

This grain dish is meant for breakfast. Topped with soft whipped cream, it's sweet and satisfying.

2½ cups apple cider
3 cups old-fashioned rolled oats
⅔ cup heavy cream

Put apple cider in a small saucepan and bring to a boil. Lower heat to medium and cook for 30 minutes, whisking often, until cider is reduced to ½ cup. Set syrup aside.

Bring 5¼ cups water and ¼ teaspoon salt to a boil in a large heavy saucepan. Add oats and cook over medium heat for 5 minutes, stirring frequently. Add 2 tablespoons heavy cream. Cook for a minute or so more, until oatmeal reaches desired consistency.

Meanwhile, in a medium bowl, whip remaining cream with a wire whisk until soft peaks form. Divide hot oatmeal among flat soup plates. Top with whipped cream and drizzle with cider syrup. Serve hot.

Serves 6

OVEN-BAKED POLENTA WITH ROSEMARY

The beauty of this particular polenta preparation is that you only need to stand and stir it for five minutes, instead of the more typical thirty-five minutes. The result is molten and creamy, but it does firm up after a while. Another option: allow the polenta to firm up completely, then cut it into large squares and heat them in the oven.

1¾ cups stone-ground yellow cornmeal
3½ tablespoons unsalted butter
1 scant tablespoon finely minced fresh rosemary, plus more for garnish

Preheat oven to 375°F.

Put 7 cups water and 1½ teaspoons salt in a 4-quart pot. Bring to a rapid boil, then lower heat to medium. Slowly add cornmeal in a steady stream, whisking constantly with a wire whisk. Bring just to a boil, then cook over high heat for 5 minutes, stirring constantly.

Stir in 2½ tablespoons butter and minced rosemary. Season with salt and freshly ground black pepper. Pour mixture into a shallow buttered casserole. Cover tightly with a piece of buttered aluminum foil (buttered side down) and bake for 1 hour. Uncover and sprinkle with a little chopped rosemary if desired. Serve immediately.

Serves 6

POLENTA TART WITH ROASTED TOMATOES AND SMOKED MOZZARELLA

This savory tart makes a nifty side dish, or a main course for your favorite vegetarian. The slow-roasted tomatoes can be prepared earlier in the day.

12 large plum tomatoes
8 ounces smoked mozzarella
1 cup stone-ground yellow cornmeal

Preheat oven to 275°F.

Wash tomatoes and cut in half lengthwise. Sprinkle cut sides lightly with salt. Line a rimmed baking sheet with parchment paper or aluminum foil and bake tomatoes, cut side down, for 1 hour. Carefully turn them over with a spatula and bake 1 hour longer. Turn again and bake 30 minutes longer. Remove from oven.

Meanwhile, shred cheese on large holes of a box grater. In a medium pot, bring $3\frac{1}{2}$ cups water and 1 teaspoon salt to a boil. Slowly add cornmeal, whisking with a wire whisk until completely integrated, about 10 minutes. Stir in one third of the cheese. Continue to cook over medium heat for 10 minutes, stirring constantly with a wooden spoon, until polenta is very thick but still creamy. Add salt and freshly ground black pepper to taste.

Raise oven temperature to 375°F.

Using nonstick cooking spray, coat an $8\frac{1}{2}$-inch tart pan with a removable bottom. Pour polenta into pan, smoothing the top. Arrange roasted tomatoes, cut side down, on top of polenta in an attractive pattern. Sprinkle with remaining cheese. Bake for 8 to 10 minutes. Place under broiler briefly, until golden. Serve warm, cut into wedges.

Serves 6

CHEESE POLENTA *L'ULTIMO*

The name of this dish, "the ultimate," is how I feel about its mac-and-cheese taste and ultra-creamy texture. Be sure to use authentic farmhouse Cheshire cheese or Caerphilly from England, or a top-quality cheddar from a good producer.

   6 ounces good-quality cheddar cheese
   3 medium cloves garlic
   1½ cups fine yellow or white cornmeal

Grate cheese on the large holes of a box grater and set aside.

Put 6½ cups water and ½ tablespoon salt in a 4-quart pot. Peel garlic, push it through a garlic press, and add to the water. Bring water to a rapid boil, then lower heat to medium. Add cornmeal in a slow, steady stream, whisking constantly to make sure polenta has no lumps. Continue to cook, stirring constantly with a wooden spoon, for 20 minutes.

Add cheese and continue to cook and stir for 10 to 15 minutes, or until polenta is very thick and begins to pull away from sides of pot. When polenta is thick and creamy, add salt and freshly ground black pepper to taste. Serve immediately.

Serves 6

TOMATO POLENTA

The flavors of tomato and butter are immensely comforting to me, so this dish is something I whip up on wistful days. Nice as a starter or a side dish, it's also good all by itself, or all by yourself.

   1½ cups tomato juice
   4 tablespoons unsalted butter, chilled
   1 cup stone-ground yellow cornmeal

In a small saucepan, bring ½ cup tomato juice to a boil. Lower heat and simmer until tomato juice is reduced to ¼ cup. Whisk in 1 tablespoon butter, turn off the heat, and stir until creamy. Set aside.

In a heavy medium pot, bring 2¾ cups water and remaining tomato juice to a boil. Lower heat to medium. Slowly add cornmeal, letting it slip through your fingers. Stir constantly with a wooden spoon, making sure no lumps form. Stir until thick, but still runny and creamy, about 15 minutes.

Cut remaining butter into small pieces and add bit by bit, stirring constantly. Cook another 4 to 5 minutes, or until polenta pulls away from sides of pot. Add a pinch of salt and freshly ground black pepper to taste. Quickly spoon into a large warm bowl and drizzle reduced tomato juice over the top, reheating first if necessary. Serve immediately.

Serves 4

MAMALIGA

Mamaliga *is the great national dish of Romania, a kind of cornmeal porridge that appears at practically every meal. When served with butter and salty cheese it becomes Jewish soul food, and is also terrific for breakfast on a chilly morning. It is traditionally prepared with Bryndza (sometimes spelled Brinza) cheese—a creamy, salty sheep's milk cheese from Romania—but mild feta can be substituted.*

2 cups stone-ground yellow cornmeal
6 tablespoons unsalted butter
6 ounces Bryndza cheese or mild feta

Bring 8 cups water plus ½ tablespoon salt to a boil in a medium pot. Slowly add cornmeal, letting it slip through your fingers; stir constantly with a wire whisk.

Reduce heat to medium-low and continue to whisk for 5 minutes. Add 2 tablespoons butter. Continue to cook for 20 to 25 minutes. The porridge is finished when it is very thick and smooth and begins to come away from the sides of the pot.

Melt remaining butter in a small saucepan over low heat. Do not let the butter brown.

Transfer porridge to individual dishes or to a casserole. Thinly slice or crumble cheese on top of cornmeal, and drizzle melted butter on top. Serve immediately.

Serves 6

eggs
and cheese

In the time it takes to toast two slices of bread, you also can scramble two eggs. But fewer and fewer people cook their own breakfasts these days. They're too rushed, so they make do with "deskfast"—a calorie-laden cinnamon bun or muffin that's wolfed down with coffee while their computers boot up.

How ironic, because eggs used to be called nature's perfect food. In addition to their nutritive value, eggs bind disparate ingredients and flavors together, which is why they're the "glue" of omelets, quiches, frittatas, flans, and soufflés.

Eggs are delicate things, and their worst enemy is overcooking; too much heat for too long tends to rubberize them and alter their flavor. This is true even of hard-boiled eggs, so I urge you to be gentle when preparing the following recipes.

Modernity has its costs. My husband recalls the lost pleasures of double-yolk eggs, which he hasn't seen in a decade, and "unborn" eggs that occasionally were found in chickens purchased at live poultry markets, few of which exist anymore. My late mother-in-law used to remind me that, before the age of supermarkets and plastic packaging, there were stores called dairies that sold primarily eggs, butter, and cheese.

Eggs, butter, and cheese, alone or in combination, are the basis for this chapter. Included you'll find a classic fondue recipe (remember where you put your fondue pot?). It's great fun and brings people together in a common enterprise, much like toasting marshmallows over a campfire. Brillat-Savarin's Fondue, on the other hand, is more egg than cheese, but it still engenders communal dunking. In the dessert chapter, on page 268, you will find more cheeses that, in combination with fruit, can be served as either a dessert or light meal.

Never be caught without a dozen eggs in your refrigerator; I always use extra-large. They come in handy for numerous dishes and occasions: a spontaneous frittata or soufflé for an unexpected guest, weekday morning meals, gracious weekend brunches served with special breads, or casual suppers accompanied by a simple salad). Eggs can easily become a snack or dessert; a yielding omelet filled with chunky preserves is something I adore any time of day.

And, of course, there are those fantasy egg dishes that need no recipes and are reserved for breakfast-in-bed. These include buttered bread fingers (or *mouillettes*) dipped in the yolks of runny soft-boiled eggs that have been sprinkled with kosher salt; soft scrambled eggs topped with osetra caviar; eggs fried in olive oil and showered with white truffles; or a thick slice of just-baked brioche slathered with mayonnaise and a warm sliced egg.

JALAPEÑO-CHEDDAR FRITTATA

The pickling juice from the jalapeños reacts with the eggs to give them a custardy texture. Choose an artisanal English or Vermont cheddar for the best results.

    12 ounces sharp yellow cheddar cheese
    ½ cup sliced pickled jalapeños from a jar, 3 tablespoons liquid reserved
    12 extra-large eggs

Preheat oven to 350°F.

Grate cheese on the large holes of a box grater and set aside.

Pat jalapeño slices dry with a paper towel. Using nonstick cooking spray, spray a 10-inch springform pan with a removable bottom. Scatter jalapeños evenly on the bottom of the pan. Sprinkle evenly with cheese.

Put eggs, ½ teaspoon salt, and ⅛ pinch of white pepper in the bowl of an electric mixer. Mix on medium-high speed for 4 minutes, or until very light. Add reserved jalapeño liquid and mix briefly.

Pour eggs over cheese in pan. Place pan on a rimmed baking sheet and bake for 20 to 25 minutes until just firm. Let cool several minutes before removing from pan. Cut into wedges and serve immediately.

Serves 6

FRITTATA WITH PANCETTA AND MINT

    1 large bunch fresh mint
    4 ounces pancetta, cut into ¼-inch-thick slices
    10 extra-large eggs

Wash mint and dry thoroughly. Pick off enough leaves to get ½ packed cup. Set aside.

Cut pancetta into ¼-inch dice. Put in a 10-inch ovenproof nonstick skillet and cook over low heat for 8 minutes, or until fat is rendered and pancetta begins to get crisp, but not brown.

Meanwhile, in bowl of an electric mixer, put eggs, 3 tablespoons cold water, ¼ teaspoon salt, and freshly ground black pepper. Beat well.

Pour beaten eggs into hot pan with pancetta. Add reserved mint leaves. Stir briefly with a wooden spoon over low heat, and then let eggs cook slowly, without stirring. After 1 minute, cover pan and cook eggs until almost firm, about 7 minutes. Meanwhile, preheat broiler.

Place frittata under broiler for 30 seconds to 1 minute, until just firm. Cut into wedges and serve immediately.

Serves 4

ITALIAN RICE FRITTATA

With a simple salad of arugula, splashed with red wine vinegar and good olive oil, this frittata becomes a special meal. I love the texture of the soft egg pancake and the slightly chewy grains of Arborio rice within.

½ cup Arborio rice
2 tablespoons unsalted butter
4 extra-large eggs

Put rice in a large saucepan with a large pinch of salt and water to cover by several inches. Bring to a rapid boil, lower heat, and cover pan. Cook for 15 minutes or longer, until rice is just tender. Drain immediately in a coarse-mesh strainer.

Melt butter in a 9-inch nonstick skillet. Add rice and spread it to cover bottom of pan. Beat eggs very well with a wire whisk and pour over rice. Cook over very low heat until eggs begin to set. Sprinkle with salt and a liberal amount of coarsely ground black pepper. Cover pan and cook about 6 minutes longer, or until the top of the eggs are set. Do not overcook: the frittata should be light and fluffy. Serve immediately.

Serves 2 or more

SCRAMBLED EGGS, HOLLANDAISE STYLE

These eggs are made with the same ingredients as an authentic hollandaise sauce. The method is also the same; the eggs are slowly stirred in the top of a double boiler.

16 extra-large eggs
10 tablespoons unsalted butter
2 large lemons

Using a large wire whisk, beat eggs until light and fluffy. Season with ½ teaspoon salt and freshly ground white pepper.

Butter a large metal bowl (one that will fit over a pot of water to create a double boiler) with 2 tablespoons butter.

Grate rinds of lemons to get 1½ teaspoons zest. Cut lemons in half and squeeze to get 2½ tablespoons lemon juice. Set aside.

Place the buttered bowl over a pot of simmering water. You do not want the bottom of the bowl to touch the water. Add eggs and stir, using a flexible rubber spatula. Cut remaining butter into small pieces and periodically add to egg mixture, stirring constantly and scraping sides of bowl. The eggs will eventually begin to thicken. After 5 minutes, add lemon zest and juice, and any remaining butter. Continue to cook until eggs meld into a smooth, thick, saucelike consistency, about 15 minutes. Add salt and white pepper to taste. Serve hot.

Serves 6

GLAZED APPLE FRITTATA

Follow this recipe carefully and you'll be rewarded with a voluptuous sweet pancake studded with translucent apples. Use Fuji apples from Washington State—they are sweet, firm, and juicy. Serve with thickly sliced bacon or your favorite sausages.

> 6 large Fuji or Golden Delicious apples
> 1 cup confectioners' sugar
> 7 extra-large eggs

Preheat oven to 300°F.

Peel and core the apples. Cut each into 8 wedges. Choose a baking dish that is large enough to hold apples in a single layer, and spray it with nonstick cooking spray. Arrange apples in the dish. Sprinkle with all but 3 tablespoons of the confectioners' sugar. Add ⅓ cup water. Bake apples for 45 minutes, stirring several times during baking.

Spray a 9½-inch springform pan with cooking spray and, using a slotted spoon, transfer apples to pan. Spread evenly to make 1 thick layer. Let cool. Save 3 tablespoons pan juices from baked apples. If there is more juice than that, cook it over high heat until it's reduced to 3 tablespoons.

Increase oven temperature to 350°F.

Beat eggs in the bowl of an electric mixer until thick, about 5 minutes at high speed. Add reduced pan juices and a pinch of salt. Beat again and pour mixture over apples. Bake for 25 minutes or until frittata is set.

Remove frittata from oven. Let cool for 5 minutes and turn over onto a large flat plate.

Serve warm or at room temperature, cut into wedges. Using a sifter or sieve, dust with remaining confectioners' sugar.

Serves 6

SCRAMBLED EGGS AND LEEKS

A more distinctive version of eggs and onions, these are sweeter and more colorful.

> 3 large leeks
> 4 tablespoons butter
> 12 extra-large eggs

Cut white and light green parts from leeks. Set aside dark green parts. Cut enough of the white and light green leeks into ¼-inch pieces to get 2 cups. Wash thoroughly in a colander and pat dry.

Melt 1½ tablespoons butter in a small nonstick skillet with a cover. Add diced leeks and cook over medium heat for 5 minutes. Cover pan and cook 5 minutes longer, or until leeks are soft but not brown. Meanwhile, wash and julienne ½ cup dark green leeks and boil for 2 minutes in a small saucepan. Drain and pat dry.

Beat eggs thoroughly in the bowl of an electric mixer, adding salt and freshly ground black pepper.

Melt remaining butter in a 12-inch nonstick skillet. Add eggs and begin to cook over medium heat until eggs just begin to set, stirring frequently with a flexible rubber spatula. Add cooked diced leeks and blanched dark green leeks. Stirring constantly, continue to cook eggs until desired doneness is achieved. Serve immediately.

Serves 4 or more

EGGPLANT-FETA FLAN

This tastes like smoky baba ghanoush suspended in a feta soufflé. It's lovely direct from the oven or cooled to room temperature. Serve with slow-roasted tomatoes (page 61) and grilled pita bread for Sunday brunch.

2 large eggplants, 1¼ pounds each
5 extra-large eggs
10 ounces plain or flavored feta cheese

Preheat oven to 450°F.

Over an open gas fire or on an aluminum foil-lined baking sheet under the broiler, char whole eggplants until skin is blackened, a few minutes on each side. Use tongs to turn them carefully. You will begin to detect a smoky fragrance. Then bake eggplants in the preheated oven for 50 minutes. Remove from oven and let cool.

Reduce oven temperature to 350°F.

Cut eggplants in half lengthwise and remove all the flesh using a spoon. Place flesh in a colander and let drain for 10 minutes.

In bowl of an electric mixer, beat eggs until light. Add eggplant pulp and blend thoroughly. Add 8 ounces crumbled feta cheese, ¼ teaspoon salt, and lots of freshly ground black pepper. Beat well to incorporate cheese.

Put mixture in an 8-cup soufflé dish. Create a water bath by placing the filled soufflé dish in a deep baking pan large enough to accommodate the dish. Fill baking pan with boiling water almost up to the top of the dish. Bake for 45 minutes. Remove from oven and preheat broiler.

Carefully lift dish from water bath. Very thinly slice remaining cheese and place on top of flan. Broil for 30 seconds, or until cheese begins to melt. Serve immediately or at room temperature.

Serves 6

POACHED EGGS WITH LIME HOLLANDAISE

12 tablespoons unsalted butter
3 limes
11 extra-large eggs

Melt butter in a small heavy saucepan. Let stand for 10 minutes and skim white foam from the surface using a large spoon. When the whey has separated and sunk to the bottom, carefully pour off clear yellow liquid into a small bowl. You should have approximately ½ cup clarified butter. This can be prepared ahead of time and rewarmed.

Grate the zest of the limes and cut them in half. Squeeze to get ¼ cup juice. Set aside.

Separate 3 eggs and discard the whites (or save them for another use). In the top of a double boiler over a pot of simmering water, whisk the yolks and 1 tablespoon water until very fluffy. Slowly add warm clarified butter, whisking constantly to incorporate butter; this will take about 4 minutes. Add the lime zest and 3 or more tablespoons of lime juice, whisking vigorously. Add salt and freshly ground white pepper to taste. Keep warm.

In a very large nonstick skillet, add water to the depth of 1 inch. Add 1 teaspoon salt and bring to a boil, then lower to a simmer. Break remaining eggs, one at a time, and slip into the simmering water. Cook eggs until whites are firm and yolks reach desired doneness. Remove poached eggs with a slotted spoon and drain on paper towels.

Warm as many plates as needed. Place 1 or 2 eggs on each plate and top each egg with 2 tablespoons warm lime hollandaise. Serve immediately, with a thin slice or wedge of remaining lime.

Serves 4 or 8

HAM 'N EGGS WITH RED-EYE GRAVY

2 large ham steaks with bone, about 10 ounces each
½ cup or more freshly brewed black coffee
4 extra-large eggs

Trim fat from ham steaks. Cut fat into small dice and set aside.

Heat 2 large nonstick or cast-iron skillets. Place ham steaks in hot skillets and brown well, about 2 minutes on each side. Press down hard with a spatula to keep ham from curling. Put ham on a warm platter and cut each steak in half.

Deglaze pans with coffee, scraping up browned bits. Cook over high heat until sauce reduces a little and pour over ham. Cover with aluminum foil to keep warm.

In one of the skillets, melt reserved ham fat. Add the eggs and quickly fry to desired firmness. Serve 1 egg atop each piece of ham. Pass the pepper mill.

Serves 4

PARMESAN-CRUSTED ASPARAGUS WITH EGGS

1¾ pounds medium asparagus
3 ounces freshly grated Parmigiano-Reggiano
8 extra-large eggs

Preheat broiler.

Snap off woody bottoms from asparagus and discard. With a sharp knife, trim stalks to equal length. Peel stalks with a vegetable peeler, using a light touch.

Bring a medium pot of salted water to a boil. Add asparagus and cook, uncovered, over medium heat for 6 to 7 minutes, or until just tender and bright green. Drain and refresh asparagus under cold water. Pat dry.

Place asparagus on a large ovenproof platter in one layer. Sprinkle with cheese and place under broiler until cheese turns golden and begins to crisp. Remove from broiler and put platter in oven to keep warm.

Bring 1 inch of salted water to a boil in a very large nonstick skillet. Break eggs, one at a time, and poach until desired doneness. Remove asparagus from oven and top with poached eggs. Sprinkle with kosher salt and coarsely ground black pepper.

Serves 4

EGGS FONTINA RANCHERO

Here, eggs are poached directly in a spicy sauce.

6 ounces fontina cheese, preferably imported
1¾ cups medium-hot salsa verde with tomatillos
6 extra-large eggs

Preheat broiler.

Remove rind from cheese and grate cheese on the large holes of a box grater.

Pour salsa verde into a heavy 10-inch nonstick skillet with a cover. Bring to a boil, then lower heat to a simmer. Carefully break eggs directly into salsa: place 1 in the center and the others in a circle. Season with freshly ground black pepper and a pinch of salt.

Mound cheese over each egg. Cover pan and cook over medium heat for 6 to 8 minutes, or until whites are just set.

Put under broiler for 1 to 2 minutes, until yolks are cooked as you like. (It tastes great if the yolks are a little runny.) Serve immediately.

Serves 2 or 3

BAKED EGGS *SPLENDIDO*

Depending upon my mood, I sometimes make this with fresh cilantro instead of basil.

  2 cups tomato juice
  1 large bunch fresh basil
  4 extra-large eggs

Put tomato juice in a small saucepan. Bring to a boil. Lower heat to medium and cook until reduced to 1 cup, about 20 minutes.

Put reduced tomato juice in a 9-inch nonstick skillet. Bring to a boil, then lower heat. Meanwhile, pluck basil leaves, pile them in a stack, and roll them up like a cigar. Then, holding them firmly, cut crosswise into $1/16$-inch strips. The resulting shreds are called chiffonade. Continue to do this until you have a scant $1/2$ cup. Reserve the rest of the basil.

Sprinkle basil over reduced juice and carefully break eggs into sauce. Let cook over medium-low heat until whites just begin to set, about 2 minutes.

Cover pan and cook until desired doneness. It's best to leave the yolks a little runny. Garnish with fresh basil sprigs and serve immediately.

Serves 2

PUFFY MAPLE PANCAKE

It is astonishing how this pancake puffs up and holds its shape. I love the synergy of sweet and salty, so I sprinkle a bit of salt on the warm syrup that anoints this pancake cloud.

  4 extra-large eggs
  6 tablespoons maple syrup
  1 tablespoon unsalted butter

Preheat oven to 400°F.

Separate egg yolks from egg whites. In a medium bowl, whisk together yolks, 2 tablespoons maple syrup, and freshly ground black pepper until thick.

Beat egg whites and $1/4$ teaspoon salt in the bowl of an electric mixer until they look like thick whipped cream with firm peaks. Fold whites into yolks.

Melt butter in an ovenproof 10-inch nonstick skillet over medium-high heat. Add the egg mixture to pan and reduce heat to low. Cook for 2 minutes, until eggs are just set. Shake the pan to check; it should only jiggle a little.

Place skillet in oven. Cook for 5 to 6 minutes, until puffy and golden in color. Be careful not to overcook or the pancake will fall and be dry. Warm the remaining syrup in a small pan and drizzle on pancake. Serve immediately.

Serves 2 or more

GOAT CHEESE OMELET CRÊPE

My wonderful assistant, Kate Merker, a Yale grad and Culinary Institute of America student, grew up eating ultrathin crêpelike omelets that were folded in thirds and hung over the plate. Tender and more delicate than traditional omelets, these are dedicated to her.

5 extra-large eggs
4 ounces fresh goat cheese with herbs, at room temperature
1½ tablespoons unsalted butter

Beat eggs in bowl of an electric mixer with 2 ounces of goat cheese until smooth. Add salt and freshly ground black pepper.

Melt ¾ tablespoon butter in a very large nonstick skillet and add half the egg mixture. Cook over medium-low heat until eggs begin to set but are still runny. Crumble 1 ounce cheese in a line down the center of eggs.

While eggs are still soft, flip 1 side of eggs over cheese using a spatula, and then fold the other side over the flap to lay flat. You will end up with a long omelet. Cook about 1½ minutes and flip the entire omelet over. It should be a light golden brown. Cook another 30 seconds and slip onto a plate.

Repeat with remaining egg mixture, keeping first omelet warm in the oven, or make omelets in 2 pans.

Serves 2

STAR ANISE TEA EGGS

A bowl of these marblized eggs make a fun, unexpected morning meal. Serve with rice cakes and whole oranges.

12 extra-large eggs
6 tablespoons loose black tea leaves
4 whole star anise

Place eggs in a large saucepan with water to cover. Bring to a boil, lower heat, and cook for 10 minutes, or until eggs are hard-boiled. Chill under cold running water.

Tap each egg lightly on a flat surface to make a web of small cracks all over the shell. Return eggs to saucepan. Add tea, star anise broken into pieces, and 2 tablespoons salt. Cover with cold water.

Bring to a boil. Reduce to a simmer and cook, with cover askew, for about 2 hours. Let eggs cool in liquid and peel them before serving.

Serves 6

BUTTERMILK-GRITS SOUFFLÉ

This is actually a fallen soufflé with a dense, creamy center. Yellow stone-ground cornmeal can be substituted for the grits.

1 cup quick-cooking grits
1½ cups buttermilk
4 extra-large eggs

Preheat oven to 375°F.

Bring 2 cups water and 1 teaspoon salt to a boil in a medium pot. Slowly add grits, stirring constantly. Lower heat to a simmer and cook for 5 minutes, stirring constantly, until grits are thick and smooth. Remove from heat. Add 1 cup buttermilk and stir until very smooth.

Separate egg yolks from egg whites. Add yolks to grits, and stir until ingredients are thoroughly incorporated. Add freshly ground black pepper and stir. Beat egg whites with a pinch of salt in bowl of electric mixer until stiff.

Fold whites into grits mixture. Spray a 2-quart soufflé dish with nonstick cooking spray. Carefully pour grits mixture into dish.

Bake for 40 to 45 minutes, until golden brown and puffy. Serve hot directly from the soufflé dish. Using a cake knife, cut into large wedges. Pour 2 tablespoons buttermilk over each portion and sprinkle with coarsely ground black pepper.

Serves 4

MARMALADE SOUFFLÉ

I suppose this could be a dessert, but it is also a wonderful morning treat with a pot of Earl Grey tea.

½ cup sugar
1 scant cup bitter orange marmalade
6 extra-large egg whites

Preheat oven to 400°F.

Prepare a 5- or 6-cup soufflé dish with a collar: Fold a 1½-foot length of aluminum foil in half lengthwise and wrap it around the soufflé dish so that it forms a 4-inch-high foil collar above the rim. You can either tie the foil with kitchen string or fold its 2 ends together to hold it in place.

Spray the inside of soufflé dish and foil with nonstick cooking spray. Sprinkle bottom of dish with 2 teaspoons sugar.

Melt marmalade in a small saucepan with 2 tablespoons water. Keep warm.

Place egg whites and a pinch of salt in bowl of an electric mixer. Beat on high until they begin to thicken. Continue to beat, adding the sugar slowly. Beat until glossy and stiff, so the mixture looks like marshmallow fluff.

Transfer warm marmalade to a large bowl and, using a rubber spatula, fold one-fourth of egg whites into jam. Then add remaining whites, folding gently. Spoon mixture into prepared dish and bake for 18 to 20 minutes, until top is golden and soufflé looks firm. Remove collar and serve immediately.

Serves 4 or more

EGGS AND ASPARAGUS GEORGES BLANC

This dish was inspired by three-star Burgundian chef Georges Blanc. It was his idea to treat simple asparagus stalks in different ways in the same dish; it was my idea to fold them into soft-scrambled eggs sauced with nutty beurre noisette.

1 pound medium-thick asparagus
10 extra-large eggs
7 tablespoons unsalted butter

Cut top 2 inches of asparagus tips off stalks. Cut tips into fine julienne strips. Blanch in salted boiling water for 1 minute. Drain under cold running water and pat dry.

Cut woody bottoms from stalks with a sharp knife and discard. Using a vegetable peeler, scrape stalks until you have reached the pale interior (there should be no dark green left).

Cut white stalks into ¼-inch pieces. Boil in salted water until tender, about 6 minutes. Drain in a colander under cold running water.

Break eggs into a large bowl and beat well with a wire whisk. Using 1 tablespoon butter, butter a stainless-steel bowl set atop a pot of simmering water. Add eggs and cook over medium-low heat so that water is just below a boil, stirring constantly with a wooden spoon. You want the eggs to be creamy, almost like a sauce. Lower heat if eggs thicken too quickly. Gradually add 3 tablespoons butter, cut in small pieces. Add cooked asparagus stalks and continue cooking for about 5 minutes. Add salt and freshly ground black pepper to taste.

Meanwhile, melt remaining butter in a small nonstick skillet over medium-high heat, about 1 minute, until butter turns brown. To serve, put hot eggs in center of a large plate. Surround with blanched asparagus tips (warmed briefly in boiling water) and pour hot browned butter over eggs.

Serves 4

SOUFFLÉD RICOTTA TERRINE

This addictive soufflé is highly versatile. You may serve it warm or at room temperature, but chilled it tastes like cheesecake, only lighter. Serve with a simple fruit salad.

> 2 15-ounce containers whole-milk ricotta cheese
> 6 extra-large eggs
> ⅔ cup vanilla-sugar (page 242)

Preheat oven to 350°F.

Place ricotta cheese in a fine-mesh sieve over a bowl. Let drain for 20 minutes to release any liquid.

Beat eggs lightly in bowl of an electric mixer. Add drained ricotta and sugar, and blend well. Beat on medium speed for 1 minute, until very smooth.

Spray a 2-quart glass loaf pan with nonstick cooking spray. Pour in ricotta mixture.

Bake for 60 to 70 minutes, until golden brown and puffy. Remove from oven, let cool slightly before serving, then cut into thick slices. This is also delicious at room temperature.

Serves 6

BRILLAT-SAVARIN'S FONDUE

Unlike any fondue you've had before. This version, offered by the revered gastronome Anthelme Brillat-Savarin in The Physiology of Taste, *is somewhere between molten cheese sauce and soft-scrambled eggs. Spoon over toast or dunk slices of baguette in it.*

> 6 extra-large eggs
> 6 ounces aged Gruyère cheese
> 4½ tablespoons unsalted butter

Break eggs into a bowl and whisk with a wire whisk until yolks and whites are thoroughly incorporated. Add ¼ teaspoon salt and freshly ground black pepper. Cut cheese and 4 tablespoons butter into small pieces and stir into eggs.

Grease a 10-inch nonstick skillet with remaining butter. Pour mixture into pan and cook over medium heat, stirring slowly and constantly with a wooden spoon until eggs are thick, soft, and smooth, about 10 minutes. Add a good amount of pepper, one of the characteristics of this time-honored dish, and serve it on a warm platter.

Serves 4

WINE AND CHEESE FONDUE

La fondue, *as the Swiss call their beloved dish, is a party in itself. Quality is critical here. Use Appenzeller cheese for a piquant taste or real Swiss Gruyère for a nutty, more mild flavor. This is a great mid-morning meal or prelude to a splendid brunch. Dunk wedges of sweet pears and slices of wonderful bread, like raisin-walnut, into the fondue.*

1½ pounds Appenzeller or aged Gruyère cheese
3 tablespoons all-purpose flour
1½ cups Chardonnay

Using a sharp knife, remove rind from cheese. Grate cheese on the large holes of a box grater. Mix with 1½ tablespoons flour.

Place floured cheese in a small heavy saucepan or fondue pot. Add wine and ½ teaspoon salt, and bring just to a boil. Lower heat to medium and stir vigorously with a wooden spoon until cheese is completely melted, about 5 minutes. Add remaining flour, stirring constantly. Cook for about 2 minutes, until floury taste is gone.

The result should be a thick, creamy sauce. If it's too thick, add a little wine that has been warmed. Fondue can be reheated: Place 1 or 2 tablespoons water in a heavy saucepan and add the hardened fondue. Cover and cook over very low heat until creamy and hot.

Serves 6

MORNING QUESADILLAS WITH CHEESE

You can make fancy breakfast cheese quesadillas by sandwiching large flour tortillas with two more ingredients:

- jalapeño jack cheese and crisp bacon
- smoked salmon and herbed goat cheese
- cream cheese and pepper jelly
- Canadian bacon and dill Havarti cheese
- prosciutto and Bel Paese cheese

Place quesadilla flat in a large, hot, nonstick skillet, and toast on both sides over medium-high heat until tortillas are golden and cheese has softened. Serve immediately or keep warm in a 300°F oven. Cut into wedges to serve.

condiments, sauces, and dressings

Not many years ago, when most Americans heard "condiments," they thought ketchup, mayonnaise, mustard, and, if they were brave, Tabasco Sauce.

No longer. Today, there's more shelf space in your supermarket devoted to salsa alone than to yesterday's condiments combined. And then there are the myriad incendiary flavorings from hot-climate countries brought to our country by wave after wave of immigrants.

Now, I often find that food is the medium and condiments are the message. I actually know people who are wishy-washy about sushi but love it as a conveyance for wasabi paste and pickled ginger. These are the same people who shovel red pepper flakes onto their pizza slices and think palate-scorching Szechuan noodles are bowls of fun.

For the rest of us, the real purpose of condiments is to complement a dish's intrinsic qualities. They make innocuous foods taste zippy, temper something sweet with something bitter, or soothe a sharp flavor with a mellow one.

It's all about what I call ISR, or Instant Salivary Response.

Just saying the names of such sensory agitators as ginger, all kinds of chilies, horseradish, cinnamon, peppercorns, or the many vinegars, triggers a craving that starts our salivary juices flowing. What would we do without chutneys, relishes, hoisin sauce, salsas, flavored oils, and mustards? You can buy these condiments by the armload, but there's greater satisfaction in making your own—and homemade versions taste fresher than anything you can purchase.

Sauces are quite another thing; because we associate their preparation with great French chefs, we're intimidated to try our hand at them. Nonsense, I say! Some of the classic sauces are composed of only three ingredients (how convenient), so in this chapter I've concentrated on basic techniques, occasionally tweaking their balance of flavors. Included in this list is hollandaise, which you can modify by using fresh lime juice, or should you hanker for Sauce Maltaise, blood oranges when in season; beurre meunière, a lemon-parsley butter that's fabulous with simply cooked fish or steamed potatoes; and beurre blanc, a snappy white butter sauce that used to terrify even restaurant chefs, but which is truly a cinch to make.

Or try the following condiments, guaranteed to enliven any dish: Rosemary Mayonnaise dolloped on char-grilled swordfish; Pickled Pink Onions atop a juicy rare steak; Orange-Rum Cream Cheese on a toasted bagel; Apple-and-Cranberry Salsa in a turkey sandwich, and Lemon Vinaigrette splashed on bitter greens. All will trigger ISR almost immediately.

FLAVORED OILS

Garlic Olive Oil 228

Lemon Olive Oil 228

WARM SAUCES

Classic Hollandaise 228

Beurre Blanc 229

Beurre Meunière 229

Creamy Mustard Sauce 230

FLAVORED MAYONNAISES

Rosemary Mayonnaise 230

Sun-Dried Tomato Mayonnaise 230

Anchovy-Lemon Mayonnaise 231

COLD SAUCES, DRESSINGS, AND CONDIMENTS

Classic Vinaigrette 231

Lemon Vinaigrette 231

Raspberry-Dijon Vinaigrette 232

Asian-Style Vinaigrette 232

Roasted Beet Vinaigrette 232

Last-Minute "French" Dressing 233

Homemade Mayonnaise 233

Red Wine Apple Sauce 233

Black Olive Paste 234

Swedish Mustard Sauce 234

Spicy Cocktail Sauce 234

Yellow Tomato Salsa 235

Yogurt Tahina 235

Sun-Dried Cherry and Cranberry Compote 235

Apple-and-Cranberry Salsa 236

Pickled Pink Onions 236

Onion and Sumac Salad 236

Pickled Greens 237

Onion Marmalade 237

FLAVORED CREAM CHEESES

Honey-Walnut Cream Cheese 238

Maple-Raisin Cream Cheese 238

Orange-Rum Cream Cheese 238

Strawberry-Cheesecake Cream Cheese 239

"Chocolate" Cream Cheese 239

FLAVORED OILS

GARLIC OLIVE OIL

1 cup extra-virgin olive oil
8 large cloves garlic
¼ teaspoon crushed red pepper flakes

Put olive oil in a small saucepan. Peel garlic and add to oil with red pepper flakes. Cook over medium heat until small bubbles form at the surface, then continue cooking over very low heat for 5 minutes.

Remove from heat and add a large pinch of kosher salt. Let sit for 2½ hours. Strain through a fine-mesh sieve into a clean jar. Cover and refrigerate. Keeps for 2 weeks.

Makes 1 cup

LEMON OLIVE OIL

1 cup mild olive oil
2 lemons
1 fresh or dried California bay leaf

Place olive oil in a small saucepan. Using a vegetable peeler, peel all the lemon rind into strips, being sure to remove any white pith. Add to oil with bay leaf. Cook over medium heat for 2 minutes, or until tiny bubbles just begin to appear. Simmer for 5 minutes, stirring often.

Remove from heat, add a pinch of kosher salt, and stir. Let sit for 2 hours. Strain through a fine-mesh sieve into a clean jar. Cover and refrigerate. Keeps for 2 weeks.

Makes 1 cup

WARM SAUCES

CLASSIC HOLLANDAISE

Small amounts of ethereal hollandaise sauce won't make you feel guilty. In fact, you'll feel good when you've mastered the art.

2 sticks (½ pound) unsalted butter
3 large egg yolks
1 large lemon

Clarify butter by heating it in a small heavy saucepan until it just melts. Do not cook butter. Remove from heat and let melted butter stand for 10 minutes. Skim white foam from surface using a large spoon. When the whey has separated and sunk to the bottom, carefully pour off clear yellow liquid into a bowl or measuring cup. You should have approximately ⅔ cup clarified butter. This can be prepared ahead of time and rewarmed.

Put yolks and 1 tablespoon water in the top of a double boiler or in a stainless steel bowl over a pot of simmering water. Using a wire whisk, whisk yolks until very fluffy. Add warm clarified butter very slowly, whisking constantly to incorporate it, until sauce is fluffy and thick, about 5 minutes. Cut lemon in half and squeeze to get 2 tablespoons juice. Whisk into sauce. Add salt and freshly ground white pepper to taste. If sauce is too thick, you can add up to 1 tablespoon water. Serve warm.

Makes 1 cup

BEURRE BLANC

Also known as white butter sauce, this is wonderful on fish or steamed vegetables.

3 tablespoons white wine vinegar
2 tablespoons minced shallots
14 tablespoons unsalted butter, chilled

Put vinegar and shallots in a small heavy saucepan. Cook over medium-high heat until liquid has almost evaporated and shallots are moist, about 2 minutes. Remove from heat and add 1 tablespoon water.

Place saucepan over low heat and slowly add butter, bit by bit, whisking constantly with a wire whisk. Remove from heat from time to time so that sauce thickens but doesn't separate. When all the butter has been added, whisk sauce for a few minutes so that it is creamy and thick. Add salt and freshly ground white pepper to taste.

Makes 1 cup

BEURRE MEUNIÈRE

8 tablespoons unsalted butter
2½ teaspoons fresh lemon juice
2 tablespoons finely minced fresh parsley

In a small heavy skillet, melt butter over medium heat. Cook it for several minutes, stirring occasionally, until butter turns nut brown. Be careful not to let it burn.

Remove pan from heat and stir in 2 teaspoons lemon juice, parsley, freshly ground white pepper, and salt to taste. Mixture should be foamy. Add remaining lemon juice and serve immediately.

Makes about ⅓ cup

CREAMY MUSTARD SAUCE

This is made in the style of a beurre blanc; small bits of cold butter are whisked into a reduced acid, in this case dry white wine.

¾ cup dry white wine
7 tablespoons unsalted butter, chilled
1 tablespoon good-quality Dijon mustard

Place wine in a small heavy saucepan. Cook over medium-high heat until wine is reduced to 2 tablespoons.

Remove from heat. Cut butter into small pieces and, over very low heat, add 6 tablespoons butter, bit by bit, whisking constantly with a wire whisk. Sauce will begin to thicken. Add mustard and continue whisking. Add remaining tablespoon butter and a pinch of freshly ground white pepper, and continue whisking until sauce is smooth, creamy, and thick.

Serve immediately or let cool. The sauce can be reheated in a small saucepan over very low heat.

Makes ¾ cup

FLAVORED MAYONNAISES

ROSEMARY MAYONNAISE

2 teaspoons distilled white vinegar
2 tablespoons minced fresh rosemary
1 cup mayonnaise

Place vinegar and rosemary in a small bowl. Let sit for 5 minutes. Stir in mayonnaise. Add a pinch of freshly ground white pepper and stir to combine. Transfer to clean jar. Cover and refrigerate. Keeps for several weeks.

Makes 1 cup

SUN-DRIED TOMATO MAYONNAISE

1 cup light mayonnaise
¼ cup sun-dried tomatoes packed in oil
1 small clove garlic

Put mayonnaise in bowl of a food processor. Drain tomatoes, reserving oil, and chop coarsely. Add to processor with garlic, peeled and pushed through a garlic press. Add 2 teaspoons reserved oil and freshly ground black pepper. Process until smooth. Transfer to a clean jar. Cover and refrigerate. Keeps for several weeks.

Makes about 1 cup

ANCHOVY-LEMON MAYONNAISE

1 cup light mayonnaise
2-ounce can rolled anchovies with capers packed in oil
1 lemon

Put mayonnaise and drained anchovies with capers in bowl of a food processor. Grate rind of lemon and add zest to processor with 1½ tablespoons of the lemon juice. Process until smooth. Add freshly ground black pepper. Transfer to a clean jar. Cover and refrigerate. Keeps for several weeks.

Makes about 1 cup

COLD SAUCES, DRESSINGS, AND CONDIMENTS

CLASSIC VINAIGRETTE

1 medium clove garlic
¼ cup red wine vinegar or sherry vinegar
¾ scant cup extra-virgin olive oil

Peel garlic and smash it with the side of a chef's knife. Add ¼ teaspoon kosher salt and finely mince with the garlic until a fine paste forms. Put in a small nonreactive bowl, add vinegar, and using a wire whisk, slowly whisk in olive oil until vinaigrette emulsifies. Add salt and freshly ground black pepper to taste.

Makes 1 cup

LEMON VINAIGRETTE

2 large shallots
2 lemons, preferably Meyer lemons
1 cup extra-virgin olive oil

Peel shallots and finely mince to get 1 packed tablespoon. Place in a small nonreactive bowl. Grate peel of 1 lemon to get ½ teaspoon zest. Add to shallots. Cut lemons in half and squeeze to get ¼ cup juice. Pour over shallots and let sit for 20 minutes. Using a wire whisk, slowly whisk in olive oil until vinaigrette emulsifies. Add salt and freshly ground black pepper to taste.

Makes about 1¼ cups

RASPBERRY-DIJON VINAIGRETTE

2½ tablespoons good-quality Dijon mustard
3 tablespoons raspberry vinegar
1 scant cup mild olive oil

In a medium nonreactive bowl, whisk together mustard and vinegar. Using a wire whisk, slowly whisk in olive oil until vinaigrette emulsifies. Add 1 to 2 tablespoons cold water, and whisk in salt and freshly ground black pepper to taste.

Makes about 1 cup

ASIAN-STYLE VINAIGRETTE

I adore this simple piquant dressing over steamed bok choy, snow peas, or asparagus. You also can drizzle it over bitter greens or slices of ripe avocado.

2 tablespoons white balsamic vinegar
7 tablespoons roasted peanut oil
1 teaspoon soy sauce

Put vinegar in a small nonreactive bowl. Using a wire whisk, slowly whisk in peanut oil until vinaigrette emulsifies, about 1 minute. Whisk in soy sauce. Add salt and freshly ground black pepper to taste.

Makes about ½ cup

ROASTED BEET VINAIGRETTE

Magenta-hued and addictive, try this sauce on grilled vegetables, tossed with spinach, drizzled over grilled swordfish. Let me count the ways.

2 medium beets, about 8 ounces
3 to 4 tablespoons balsamic vinegar
⅓ cup walnut oil

Preheat oven to 400°F.

Scrub beets. Wrap them in a large square of aluminum foil and seal tightly to make a pouch. Place in a pie tin. Bake for 1 hour and 30 minutes, or until tender when pierced with a knife. Unwrap and peel beets, saving any juices.

While still warm, cut beets into small pieces and place in bowl of a food processor with vinegar. Process until very smooth. Transfer to a medium bowl. Slowly whisk in walnut oil. Season with salt and freshly ground black pepper.

Makes about 1 cup

LAST-MINUTE "FRENCH" DRESSING

I invented this totally by accident, discovering a macho, steakhouse-style dressing perfect for thickly sliced tomatoes and onions or for sturdy greens.

⅔ cup ketchup
¼ cup good-quality Dijon mustard
2 tablespoons honey

Using a wire whisk, whisk ketchup and mustard together in a small bowl. Add honey and 2 table-spoons cold water. Continue whisking until ingredients are well blended. Cover and refrigerate.

Makes about 1 cup

HOMEMADE MAYONNAISE

Just in case you run out of the jarred stuff, here is the easiest way to make your own.

1 extra-large egg yolk
½ to ¾ cup mild olive oil
½ lemon

Put egg yolk in a medium bowl. Add a pinch of salt. Using a wire whisk, begin adding the olive oil in a slow trickle, whisking constantly until mixture emulsifies. (You might not need all the olive oil.) Add lemon juice to taste, whisking continuously until a very creamy and firm mayonnaise forms. Continue whisking until mayonnaise is thick, smooth, and a bit glossy. Add salt and a pinch of freshly ground white pepper to taste. Add a little more lemon juice, if desired. Transfer to a jar. Cover and refrigerate. Can be kept for up to 1 week.

Makes about ⅔ cup

RED WINE APPLE SAUCE

Try with roasted turkey, duck, or pork chops; with blintzes or crêpes.

6 large tart apples, about 2½ pounds
2 tablespoons cinnamon-sugar (see page 242)
⅔ cup sweet red wine, such as Banyuls

Peel and core apples. Cut them into large pieces. Put the apples, cinnamon-sugar, and wine into a medium pot with a cover. Add freshly ground black pepper and a pinch of salt. Bring to a boil, lower heat, cover, and cook for 15 minutes. Uncover and simmer 10 minutes longer, or until most of the liquid has evaporated.

Lightly mash apple mixture with a potato masher, leaving some chunks of apple. Cover and refrigerate. This improves with age.

Makes about 3 cups

BLACK OLIVE PASTE

This Provençal-style olive paste has found a permanent place in America's condiment cabinet. Its lusty, assertive taste adds titillation to a variety of foods, from a basket of crudités to a leg of lamb.

2 cups pitted oil-cured black olives
2-ounce can rolled anchovies with capers packed in oil
¼ cup or more extra-virgin or garlic olive oil (see page 228)

Put olives and drained anchovies with capers in the bowl of a food processor or blender. With machine on, slowly add olive oil until smooth. Add more oil, if necessary, to make a smooth paste. Add a liberal amount of freshly ground black pepper.

Makes about 1½ cups

SWEDISH MUSTARD SAUCE

This is the perfect accompaniment to Gravlax (page 308), smoked salmon, herring, or shrimp. Or you can drizzle it on a ham sandwich.

3 tablespoons sugar
2 tablespoons distilled white vinegar
⅓ cup good-quality Dijon mustard, preferably French

Put sugar and vinegar in a small nonreactive bowl and stir until sugar dissolves. Using a wire whisk, whisk in the mustard until thoroughly blended. Cover and refrigerate. After 1 day, sauce will thicken and be ready to use.

Makes about ½ cup

SPICY COCKTAIL SAUCE

Fresher tasting and better than any cocktail sauce you can buy.

1 cup ketchup
4-inch piece fresh horseradish
1 lemon

Put ketchup in a small nonreactive bowl. Peel horseradish and grate it on the small holes of a box grater to yield ⅓ packed cup. Add to ketchup and stir until thoroughly mixed. Grate rind of lemon to get ½ teaspoon zest. Cut lemon in half and squeeze to get 2 tablespoons juice. Add zest and 1½ to 2 tablespoons lemon juice to taste. If you like it hotter, add more horseradish. Cover and refrigerate. Lasts several weeks.

Makes about 1 cup

YELLOW TOMATO SALSA

3 large ripe yellow tomatoes
1 clove garlic
1 small bunch fresh basil

Wash tomatoes and core them. Cut as meticulously as you can into ¼-inch cubes. Place in a medium nonreactive bowl. Peel garlic and push through a garlic press. Add to tomatoes. Wash basil and dry well. Very finely chop enough to get ⅓ cup. Toss with tomatoes along with coarse sea salt and freshly ground black pepper to taste. Marinate at room temperature for 30 minutes before serving.

Serves 4

YOGURT TAHINA

This is delicious spooned over freshly steamed vegetables, chilled cucumbers, or tomatoes.

1 cup plain yogurt
3 tablespoons tahina (sesame paste)
1 small clove garlic

Put yogurt in a small bowl. Using a wire whisk, whisk in tahina until thoroughly blended. Peel garlic and push it through a garlic press. Add garlic; season with salt and freshly ground white pepper to taste. Cover and refrigerate.

Makes about 1 cup

SUN-DRIED CHERRY AND CRANBERRY COMPOTE

This is my favorite cranberry sauce. For a mouthwatering cranberry relish, you can grind up the uncooked ingredients in a food processor. Or serve both versions with a holiday turkey, pork roast, or duck.

¾ cup packed dark brown sugar
12 ounces fresh cranberries, about 3 cups
4 ounces unsweetened dried cherries, about ¾ cup

In a heavy medium saucepan, put 1 cup water, brown sugar, a pinch of salt, and freshly ground black pepper to taste. Bring to a boil. Add cranberries and cherries, and return to a boil. Reduce heat to medium and cook for 10 minutes, or until cranberries have popped and sauce has thickened. If it's too thick, you can add a little water; remember that cranberries will thicken further as they cool because of their high pectin content. Let cool, then cover, and refrigerate until cold.

Makes about 2¼ cups

APPLE-AND-CRANBERRY SALSA

Great on a turkey sandwich.

> 4 large McIntosh apples, about 1½ pounds
> ½ cup fresh cranberries
> ¼ cup light brown sugar

Peel and core apples. Cut into ½-inch pieces. Place in bowl of a food processor with cranberries, brown sugar, and a pinch of kosher salt. Pulse until mixture is the texture of salsa, with tiny discernible pieces. Refrigerate until cold.

Serves 4

PICKLED PINK ONIONS

These pretty onions make a very enticing add-on. Toss with chilled shrimp, tuck into sandwiches, or serve atop salads or grilled fish, poultry, pork, or burgers.

> 1 pound medium red onions
> 1 cup tarragon vinegar
> ½ cup sugar

Peel onions and slice them into ¼-inch-thick rings. Put in a large jar. In a small saucepan, combine vinegar, sugar, 1 cup water, and ½ teaspoon each kosher salt and whole black peppercorns. Bring to a boil and stir until sugar dissolves. Let cool, then pour liquid over onions. Cover jar and refrigerate for 1 day before serving. Lasts up to 1 week.

Makes about 3 cups

ONION AND SUMAC SALAD

Ubiquitous in the eastern Mediterranean region, this sprightly condiment is served with grilled foods and is dynamite on almost any sandwich. Sour-salty ground sumac is available in Middle Eastern food stores.

> 3 medium onions
> 2 tablespoons ground sumac
> 2 tablespoons extra-virgin olive oil

Peel onions and cut them in half through the stem end. Place cut side down on a cutting board and cut across the width into very thin slices. Place onion slices in a medium bowl. Sprinkle sumac over onions and drizzle with olive oil. Toss with 1 teaspoon salt and freshly ground black pepper to taste. Let marinate for 4 hours, stirring occasionally.

Serves 4 or more

PICKLED GREENS

An unusual preparation of bitter greens that winds up sweet and sassy. Serve alongside Barbecued Pork Pull (page 165) or Crispy Fried Chicken (page 139).

1 pound mustard greens, collard greens, or kale
⅔ cup sugar
½ cup apple cider vinegar

Thoroughly wash and dry greens. Coarsely chop them, including stems. In a large pot, combine 2 cups water, sugar, vinegar, 1½ tablespoons kosher salt, and 1 teaspoon whole black peppercorns. Bring to a boil, lower heat, and cook for 5 minutes, or until sugar dissolves. Add greens. Bring to a boil again and boil for 2 minutes.

Remove from heat and let cool in liquid. Pack greens in a clean jar, adding the brine to cover. Tightly screw on lid. Refrigerate for 2 days before using. Best used within 1 week.

Makes 1 quart

ONION MARMALADE

The idea of slowly cooking onions until they melt into a savory jam has created the caramelization craze. Adding balsamic vinegar balances the sweetness with acidity. You can spread this versatile marmalade on bread, mix it into pasta, or grace a veal chop or pizza with it.

2 pounds medium yellow onions
3 tablespoons extra-virgin olive oil
3 tablespoons balsamic vinegar

Peel onions and cut them in half through the stem end. Place cut side down on a cutting board and slice very thin.

Heat olive oil in a large nonstick skillet. Add onions to hot oil and cook over medium-high heat for 25 minutes, stirring frequently, until onions are soft and brown. Add 2½ tablespoons vinegar, 2 tablespoons water, salt, and freshly ground black pepper to taste. Lower heat to a simmer and cook 30 minutes longer, adding a little water to help scrape up browned bits in bottom of pan. When onions are very dark brown and soft, add remaining vinegar and more salt and pepper if necessary. Remove from heat. Cover and refrigerate. Lasts up to 1 week. Let come to room temperature before using.

Makes about 2 cups

FLAVORED CREAM CHEESES

Dress up a basket of breakfast breads or even simple toast with this array of flavorful, colorful, and lightly sweetened cream cheeses. The sweet cream cheeses make great tea sandwiches and are nice with an afternoon scone.

HONEY-WALNUT CREAM CHEESE

½ cup coarsely chopped walnuts
8 ounces cream cheese
3 tablespoons wildflower honey

Put walnuts in a small nonstick skillet and heat for 1 to 2 minutes over medium heat, stirring often, until toasted. Let cool.

Place cream cheese and honey in bowl of an electric mixer. Beat just until smooth. Add nuts and mix well. Cover and refrigerate.

Makes 1¼ cups

MAPLE-RAISIN CREAM CHEESE

8 ounces cream cheese
3 tablespoons pure maple syrup
⅓ heaping cup raisins

Place all ingredients in bowl of a food processor. Process briefly until all ingredients are incorporated. Do not overprocess. Cover and refrigerate.

Makes about 1¼ cups

ORANGE-RUM CREAM CHEESE

8 ounces cream cheese
¼ cup orange marmalade
½ teaspoon rum extract

Place all ingredients in the bowl of a food processor. Process briefly until just blended.

Do not overprocess. Cover and refrigerate.

Makes 1 heaping cup

STRAWBERRY-CHEESECAKE CREAM CHEESE

This is named for what it tastes like. Lovely for tea time on a slice of toasted brioche.

- 8 ounces cream cheese
- 3 tablespoons strawberry preserves
- ¼ cup confectioners' sugar

Put all ingredients in bowl of an electric mixer. Beat just until smooth. Cover and refrigerate.

Makes 1 heaping cup

"CHOCOLATE" CREAM CHEESE

Serve with a basket of freshly baked croissants. Nutella is a jarred hazelnut spread made with cocoa, now available in most supermarkets.

- 8 ounces cream cheese
- ⅓ cup Nutella
- 1 tablespoon confectioners' sugar

Put all ingredients in bowl of an electric mixer. Beat until ingredients are thoroughly incorporated. Do not overmix. Cover and refrigerate.

Makes 1 heaping cup

desserts

It takes some sorcery to make soulful, satisfying desserts with just three ingredients, but, as they say, the proof of the pudding is in the eating. Here are more than sixty examples. Some are homey and comforting, many are modern and sleek, others luxuriously rich. All are meant to intrigue.

You'll discover half a dozen wonderful three-ingredient cakes you may not want to live without. It sounds improbable but you can fashion a fabulous tea cake from walnuts, two eggs, and some maple syrup. White Chocolate Gâteau (page 248) will have you nibbling all day long. And you'll be hard-pressed to select which of the eleven cookies is your favorite.

The truth is this: You don't need a shelf full of products, your grandmother's instincts, or a pastry chef's technique to satisfy your sweet tooth. These recipes are so easy, you can entertain without breaking a sweat.

When it comes to fruit desserts, a light touch reveals nature's most sensual flavors. Even though the availability of fruits from other countries widens, you have no doubt experienced the pure pleasure of a local peach, a succulent fig, or the perfume of a perfectly ripe melon. In some cases, just adding a little sugar can elevate the inherent sweetness of the fruit, or transform it into an icy sorbet. Add a little salt and some things taste even sweeter.

These days, sophisticated combinations of fresh fruit and cheese are considered sleek alternatives to dessert, especially when matched with singular wines that harmonize with their virtues. You'll find Slow-Baked Pears with Stilton and Warm Honey Syrup (page 266) and fourteen more "recipe ideas."

For 100 more three-ingredient treats, please refer to my earlier book, *Desserts 1-2-3*. For scores of desserts that are specifically fat free, low fat, and low cal, see *Healthy 1-2-3*; several desserts in this chapter (marked with an asterisk) have less than one gram of fat.

Two ingredients indispensable to dessert making are cinnamon-sugar and vanilla-sugar. They can be purchased ready made, but it is more economical, and satisfying, to prepare your own.

CINNAMON-SUGAR

2 cups granulated sugar

3 tablespoons good-quality ground cinnamon

Place sugar in a small bowl. Stir in cinnamon and mix thoroughly. Transfer to a jar or container with a tight-fitting cover. Lasts indefinitely.

Makes 2 cups

VANILLA-SUGAR

4 cups granulated sugar

2 long vanilla beans

Put sugar in a medium bowl. Place vanilla beans on a cutting board and cut beans in half lengthwise. With the tip of a small knife, scrape out the seeds and add them to the sugar, using your fingers to incorporate them. Transfer to a jar or container with a tight-fitting cover. Stick halved vanilla beans deep into the sugar and cover tightly. Lasts indefinitely.

Makes 4 cups

★ LESS THAN 1 GRAM OF FAT

CAKES AND TARTS

DARK MOIST CHOCOLATE CAKE

If Original Sin were a cake, this would be it.

> 16 ounces good-quality semisweet chocolate
> 10 tablespoons unsalted butter
> 5 extra-large eggs

Preheat oven to 375°F.

Line the bottom of an 8½-inch springform pan with parchment paper or aluminum foil. Coat inside of pan with nonstick cooking spray.

Chop chocolate into pieces. Cut butter into small chunks. Place chocolate and butter in a double boiler or in a large metal bowl over simmering water, making sure bowl doesn't touch water. Melt, stirring frequently, until smooth. Remove from heat.

Whisk eggs and a pinch of salt in bowl of an electric mixer, until mixture triples in volume, about 8 minutes. Fold chocolate mixture into egg mixture with a flexible rubber spatula until completely incorporated.

Pour mixture into prepared pan. Bake for 20 minutes. The center will still be a little soft. Remove from oven. Let cool at least 30 minutes before cutting. The center will sink a little as it cools. You can refrigerate the cake for up to 2 days (let sit at room temperature for 1 hour before serving).

Serves 8

CHOCOLATE TRUFFLE TORTE

Pure gourmandise. This is the time to use a great chocolate like Scharffen Berger, Michel Cluizel, Callebaut, or Valrhona.

> ½ cup crème de framboise (raspberry liqueur)
> 2 cups heavy cream
> 1½ pounds good-quality semisweet chocolate

Put framboise in a small saucepan and cook over medium heat until reduced to ¼ cup. Let cool. At the same time, let 1½ cups cream come to room temperature.

Chop chocolate into small chunks and melt in a double boiler or a large metal bowl over simmering water. Stir until melted. (Be sure not to let the chocolate get too hot or it will seize up.) Remove from the heat. Stir in 2 tablespoons of reduced framboise. Let mixture cool a few minutes, then put in bowl of an electric mixer with the room-temperature heavy cream. Whip until the ingredients are just incorporated.

Line the bottom of a 9- to 9½-inch springform pan with parchment paper. Coat the inside of pan with nonstick cooking spray. Pour chocolate mixture into pan and smooth the top. Tap pan on a flat surface to remove air bubbles. Cover with aluminum foil and refrigerate 8 hours or more.

Before serving, run the blade of a sharp knife around the edge of the cake to loosen it. Remove from pan. Cut cake with a knife that has been warmed in hot water, then dried.

Whip remaining cream with an electric mixer or wire whisk until it thickens slightly. Add remaining reduced framboise and continue beating until thick. Serve with cake.

Serves 12 or more

CHOCOLATE MERINGUE LAYER CAKE

Airy crisp disks of chocolate meringue are frosted with a thick chocolate paste made in the style of zabaglione: egg yolks are beaten and cooked in a double boiler, then tempered with gobs of melted chocolate.

    5 extra-large eggs
    1 cup sugar
    12 ounces good-quality bittersweet chocolate

Preheat oven to 275°F.

Separate eggs. Put 4 whites (save extra white for another use) in bowl of an electric mixer. Add a pinch of salt and beat until whites begin to stiffen. Slowly add sugar, beating until whites are very stiff and glossy.

Chop 3 ounces chocolate and place in a small heavy saucepan. Melt over very low heat. Let cool for 2 minutes, then fold into beaten egg whites, mixing gently.

Line the bottom of 3 9-inch pie pans with parchment paper. Evenly divide chocolate–egg white mixture among pans. Using a flexible rubber spatula, spread into thin layers, about ½ inch thick. Bake for 60 to 70 minutes, until layers are dry and crisp. Remove from oven and let cool.

Chop 6 ounces of the remaining chocolate into small pieces. Place in a small heavy saucepan and melt over very low heat. Keep warm.

Put egg yolks in the top of a double boiler over, but not touching, simmering water. Add 2 tablespoons water to yolks and beat for several minutes with a wire whisk, cooking yolks slightly and increasing their volume. Working quickly, add the melted chocolate to beaten yolks and fold in gently. Set filling aside.

Carefully remove 1 meringue layer from pan, peel off the parchment, and place on a cake plate; spread with one third of the filling. Repeat with remaining layers. Finish the last layer by smoothing the remaining icing with a dull, thin-bladed knife. Let cool.

Grate remaining chocolate on the large holes of a box grater and sprinkle over cake. Best served the same day it is made.

Serves 8

ULTRALIGHT CHOCOLATE CAKE

Slightly moussy and deeply satisfying—at under 200 calories a slice!

>   8 ounces good-quality semisweet chocolate
>   8 large eggs
>   6 tablespoons confectioners' sugar

Preheat oven to 350°F. Lightly coat the inside of an 8½-inch springform pan with nonstick cooking spray. Line the bottom of the pan with parchment paper.

Melt chocolate in a double boiler or in a large metal bowl over simmering water, stirring it until smooth. Remove from heat but keep chocolate warm over the water.

Separate egg whites from yolks. Allow both to come to room temperature. Place yolks in bowl of an electric mixer and beat until thick, about 4 minutes. Fold melted chocolate into beaten yolks with a flexible rubber spatula until completely incorporated.

Using clean beaters and a clean bowl, beat egg whites with 4 tablespoons confectioners' sugar and a pinch of salt until they hold stiff peaks. Using a clean spatula, fold one quarter of the whites into the chocolate mixture to lighten it, then fold in remaining whites and blend thoroughly.

Pour batter into prepared pan and bake in the middle of oven for 25 to 30 minutes, until cake is almost set but still trembles slightly in the center. If you cook beyond this stage, the center won't be mousselike. Let cake cool on a rack (it will settle as it cools) and refrigerate (still in the pan), covered, for at least 6 hours.

Let cake stand at room temperature for 30 minutes before serving. Dust with remaining confectioners' sugar.

Serves 10

PECAN SPONGE CAKE

"Big flavor, light texture," says my husband who generally does not eat cake.

>   6 ounces pecans
>   ¾ cup sugar
>   5 large eggs

Preheat oven to 350°F.

Spread pecans out on a rimmed baking sheet and bake for 10 minutes, or until nuts are toasted. Remove from oven and let cool completely.

Place cooled nuts in bowl of a food processor with 2 tablespoons sugar. Process until very finely ground, like flour. Do not overprocess or nuts will become nut butter.

Line the bottom of a 10-inch springform pan with parchment paper. Coat interior of pan with nonstick cooking spray.

Separate egg whites from yolks, then allow both to come to room temperature.

In bowl of electric mixer, beat whites and a pinch of salt on medium speed until frothy. Add 2 tablespoons sugar and increase speed to high. Beat whites until stiff; they should look like shaving cream.

Using cleaned beaters and another bowl, combine egg yolks and 2 tablespoons water. Beat on medium speed, gradually adding remaining sugar. Increase speed to medium-high and continue beating until yolk mixture is very thick and pale yellow, like mayonnaise, about 4 minutes. Using a flexible rubber spatula, stir in nuts until just combined. Gently fold beaten whites into batter, deflating whites as little as possible.

Pour batter into prepared pan and smooth top with spatula. Bake for 45 minutes, or until golden brown and firm; an inserted wooden skewer should come out clean. (Do not open oven door during baking.) Transfer to a rack and run a small sharp knife between sides of pan and cake. Let cool completely. Cake will settle as it cools.

Serves 8 or more

MAPLE-WALNUT SQUARES

You can serve this special moist cake with a scoop of Maple Snow, a sorbet made with one of the cake's ingredients. Combine three-quarters cup maple syrup with one and one-eighth cups water; freeze in an ice cream maker.

> 8 ounces walnut pieces
> 2 extra-large eggs, at room temperature
> ½ cup plus 2 tablespoons pure maple syrup

Preheat oven to 350°F.

Place walnuts on a rimmed baking sheet and bake for 10 minutes, or until nuts are lightly browned, shaking pan once or twice. Remove from oven and let cool completely. Place nuts in the bowl of a food processor and process until finely ground, like flour. Set aside.

Pour boiling water into bowl of an electric mixer, then pour it out and dry the bowl thoroughly. (This warms the bowl so that when you whip the eggs, they increase dramatically in volume.) Place eggs, ½ cup maple syrup, and a pinch of salt in warmed bowl. Beat on maximum speed for 8 minutes, or until mixture is very thick and quadrupled in volume.

Using a flexible rubber spatula, gently fold ground nuts into egg mixture. Line the bottom of an 8-inch-square glass baking dish with parchment paper. Pour batter into pan.

Bake for 45 minutes or a few minutes longer, until cake is firm. Using a pastry brush, brush top of cake with remaining maple syrup. Let cake cool in pan and cut into 9 squares.

Serves 9

WHITE CHOCOLATE GÂTEAU

I adore this flat, custardy cake that is baked in a pie tin. The texture, which is hard to describe, is somewhere between a sponge cake and a flan. It changes dramatically when warm, room temperature, or chilled, but is delicious at every stage.

> 8 ounces good-quality white chocolate
> 5 tablespoons unsalted butter
> 3 large eggs

Preheat oven to 375°F.

Chop chocolate into small chunks. Cut butter in small pieces. Put chocolate and butter in a double boiler or a large metal bowl over simmering water. Melt chocolate and butter together, stirring constantly until smooth. Remove from heat but keep chocolate mixture warm over the water.

Put eggs and a pinch of salt in bowl of an electric mixer. Beat for 6 minutes, or until mixture is very thick and has tripled in volume. Fold warm chocolate mixture into beaten eggs with a flexible rubber spatula. Mix gently until thoroughly incorporated.

Spray an 8-inch pie tin with nonstick cooking spray. Transfer batter to pan and smooth top with a spatula. Bake for 18 minutes, or until cake is set but still a little soft in the center. Remove from oven. Let cool for at least 20 minutes before serving, or serve at room temperature or chilled.

Serves 6

VANILLA TEA RING

This delicate cake levitates, then magically holds its shape.

> 6 extra-large eggs
> 1¼ cups vanilla-sugar (page 242)
> 1⅓ cups self-rising cake flour

Preheat oven to 350°F.

Separate egg whites from yolks. Place 4 yolks (save 2 for another use) in bowl of an electric mixer and begin to beat, adding 2 tablespoons water. Beat on medium-high, gradually adding 1 cup vanilla-sugar, until mixture is thick and pale yellow, about 6 minutes. Using a flexible rubber spatula, fold in flour. Mixture should be stiff.

In a separate bowl, using an electric mixer, beat egg whites with a pinch of salt until they begin to thicken. Add remaining vanilla-sugar and beat until stiff and glossy. Using a flexible rubber spatula, fold beaten whites into flour mixture, blending gently but thoroughly.

Spray a 10-inch bundt pan with nonstick cooking spray. Pour batter into pan and bake for 35 minutes, until golden and firm; an inserted wooden skewer should come out clean. Transfer to a rack and cool cake in pan. Run a small knife between edges of cake and pan. Invert onto a plate.

Serves 8

PUITS D'AMOUR

Named after the 1843 comic opera Le Puits d'Amour, *these are puff pastry "wells of love" dusted with confectioners' sugar and filled with thick raspberry jam or red currant jelly.*

2 sheets frozen puff pastry, about 16 ounces
½ cup confectioners' sugar
¾ cup best-quality seedless raspberry jam or red currant jelly

Preheat oven to 425°F.

Thaw puff pastry until pliable but still very cold. Roll out each sheet with a rolling pin until it is ½ inch longer and wider. With a 2½-inch round cookie cutter, cut 12 circles from each sheet to make a total of 24. Prick each circle in several places with a fork.

Cut out centers of 12 circles with a 1¼-inch cookie cutter and discard. Brush resulting rings with a little water. Using a spatula, invert rings on top of uncut circles. Be careful not to handle sides of cut dough, as pastry will puff unevenly or be lopsided if it is handled too much. Place circles on a large baking sheet. Bake for 15 minutes, or until puffed and golden brown. Let cool.

Using a fine-mesh sieve or flour sifter, dust with confectioners' sugar, so that the tops of the pastry rings are thickly covered. Very carefully spoon about 1 tablespoon jelly or jam into the center of each ring. These are best eaten the day they are made.

Makes 12

FRENCH APPLE TARTS

You'll feel like a professional baker after you tackle these pretty tarts.

1 sheet frozen puff pastry, about 8 ounces
½ cup good-quality apricot jam
3 large McIntosh or Fuji apples

Preheat oven to 375°F.

Thaw puff pastry until pliable but still very cold. Cut the dough in half lengthwise, then across into thirds to get 6 rectangles. Using the tines of a fork, prick a ¼-inch-wide border on each side of pastry, then prick the center portion thoroughly with the fork.

Heat jam with 1 tablespoon water in a small saucepan over low heat until melted. Keep warm.

Peel, core, and seed apples. Slice them into very thin wedges. Arrange slices in an overlapping pattern on top of each piece of pastry, leaving the borders clear. Using a pastry brush, brush apple slices with melted jam.

Spray a rimmed baking sheet with nonstick cooking spray. Place tarts on pan and bake for 22 to 25 minutes, until edges are golden brown and puffy. Remove tarts from oven and brush apples and sides of pastry with melted jam. Let cool a bit. Serve warm or at room temperature.

Makes 6

COOKIES

TWICE-BAKED OATCAKES

Terrific with cheese and fruit, a glass of port, or a cup of tea.

2¾ cups old-fashioned rolled oats
8 tablespoons unsalted butter
½ cup sweetened condensed milk

Preheat oven to 325°F.

Put oatmeal in bowl of a food processor and process until it is the consistency of flour. Transfer to bowl of an electric mixer. Cut all but ½ tablespoon butter into small pieces, and add to mixer with condensed milk and a pinch of salt. Mix until well combined but sticky.

Lightly butter an 8-inch pie tin or tart pan with the remaining butter. Spread oatmeal mixture into pan, being sure to fill in all the spaces and smooth the top. Bake for 25 to 30 minutes, until golden. Remove from oven and reduce oven temperature to 275°F.

Cut oatcake into 16 thin wedges and place on a baking sheet. Bake for 12 minutes or until lightly browned. Let cool. These cookies keep well in a covered tin.

Makes 16

CINNAMON SHORTBREAD

You'll love making these. They look just like the expensive imports, right down to the decorative little marks made with the tines of a fork.

8 tablespoons unsalted butter, at room temperature
2 cups self-rising cake flour
½ cup plus 1 teaspoon cinnamon-sugar (page 242)

Preheat oven to 325°F.

Cut butter into small pieces. Place flour in bowl of an electric mixer and add ½ cup cinnamon-sugar. Process briefly. Add butter and continue to mix on medium speed until small clumps begin to form. Add 1 tablespoon cold water and continue to mix until the dough comes together in a smooth ball.

Place dough in an ungreased 9-inch pie pan. Press down firmly to make a uniform layer. Using a butter knife, smooth the top. Sprinkle remaining cinnamon-sugar on top. Score dough into 16 wedges and then, using a fork, prick each wedge 3 times near and parallel to the outer rim.

Bake for 40 minutes, or until dark beige and firm to the touch. Remove from oven. While still warm, cut into wedges with a small, sharp knife. Let cool completely. Store in a tightly covered tin.

Makes 16

MAYOR KOCH'S MERINGUES

When I was twenty-four and the chef to New York's Mayor Ed Koch at Gracie Mansion, I satisfied his sweet tooth with these.

3 extra-large egg whites
14 tablespoons sugar
1¼ cups miniature chocolate chips

Preheat oven to 375°F.

Line baking sheet with parchment paper.

In bowl of an electric mixer, beat egg whites until frothy. Add a pinch of salt and slowly add sugar. Beat for several minutes, until very stiff and glossy. The mixture should look like marshmallow fluff. Gently fold in chocolate chips and drop onto baking sheet by heaping tablespoons, mounding meringue so it is at least 1 inch high.

Place in oven on middle rack and turn off oven immediately. Leave door closed for 12 hours. Remove from oven and let cool. These can be stored in a tightly-covered tin.

Makes about 28

HUNGARIAN NUT COOKIES

I adore these intensely flavored, light-as-a-feather cookies. I always have the ingredients on hand so I can make them for drop-in guests, or when I need something comforting to nibble. Walnuts can be substituted.

2 cups hazelnuts, lightly toasted
2 extra-large egg whites
1 packed cup dark brown sugar

Preheat oven to 350°F.

In bowl of a food processor, pulse nuts until coarsely chopped. Set aside.

Place egg whites in bowl of an electric mixer with a pinch of salt. Beat until they just begin to stiffen. Add brown sugar and beat until stiff peaks form; mixture should be very thick and glossy—almost taffylike. Carefully fold in chopped nuts with a flexible rubber spatula.

Line a baking sheet with parchment paper. Drop heaping tablespoons of batter onto parchment. Bake for about 22 minutes, or until cookies are dark beige and firm.

Remove from oven and let cookies cool on baking sheet. Remove with a spatula and store in a tightly covered tin.

Makes 24

CHICKPEA FLOUR COOKIES

Perfect for anyone on a gluten-free diet, these alluring cookies can be made with roasted or plain chickpea flour, available in Middle Eastern and health food stores. They also are delectable made with all-purpose flour, but roasted chickpea flour imparts the most distinctive flavor.

2 sticks (½ pound) unsalted butter, at room temperature
1½ cups confectioners' sugar
2 cups roasted or plain chickpea flour, plus more for dusting

In bowl of an electric mixer, beat butter until light and fluffy. Add 1 cup confectioners' sugar and mix thoroughly. Stir in chickpea flour and add a pinch of salt. Continue to mix until dough forms a smooth ball. Wrap in plastic wrap and refrigerate for 30 minutes.

Preheat oven to 300°F.

Sprinkle pastry board lightly with chickpea flour. Using a rolling pin, roll chilled dough out to ¼-inch thickness. Using a cookie cutter—round, square, numbers, or ones with fluted edges—cut out desired shapes. You can also cut out rounds and remove a little circle, bagel-like, from the center.

Place cookies on an ungreased rimmed baking sheet. Bake for 25 minutes, or until golden. Let cool on pan, then transfer to a clean board.

Sprinkle generously with remaining sugar pushed through a fine-mesh sieve and arrange on a platter. These can be stored in a tightly covered tin.

Makes about 36

BROWN SUGAR COOKIES

2 sticks (½ pound) unsalted butter
¾ cup packed dark brown sugar
2 cups all-purpose flour

Preheat oven to 350°F.

Cut butter into small pieces and let it come to room temperature. Put in bowl of an electric mixer and beat until fluffy. Add brown sugar and ¾ teaspoon salt, and mix until blended. Slowly add flour until a smooth dough forms.

Divide dough into 20 balls about 1 inch in diameter, place them on a baking sheet lined with parchment paper, and flatten them with the bottom of a glass. Using a fork, lightly press the flat side of the tines around the circumference of the cookies to make a frilly design. Bake for 23 to 25 minutes, until cookies are just firm to the touch. Remove from oven and cool.

Makes 20

CINNAMON WONTONS

Wonton wrappers or skins are available in small packages in the refrigerated section of most supermarkets and Asian food stores. I transformed them into elegant sweet wafers.

32 wonton wrappers
3 tablespoons unsalted butter, melted
3 tablespoons cinnamon-sugar (page 242)

Preheat oven to 400°F.

Lay wonton wrappers flat on rimmed baking sheets. Using a pastry brush, brush evenly with melted butter and sprinkle evenly with cinnamon-sugar.

Bake 1 pan at a time for 6 to 8 minutes, until wontons are golden brown and just crisp. Cool on wire racks. These can be served immediately or stored in a tightly covered tin.

Makes 32

MASCARPONE PILLOWS

These delectable cookies puff as they bake into charming irregular shapes. For variety, you may top them with rainbow sugar, pearl sugar, or any other kind that suits your fancy. This dough can also be made into one very large rectangle and baked; you or your guests can break off pieces.

8 ounces mascarpone cheese
1 cup all-purpose flour, plus more for dusting
½ cup turbinado, pearl, or rainbow sugar

Place mascarpone in bowl of an electric mixer. Stir in flour and a pinch of salt and mix briefly, until dough just comes together. Turn dough onto a board that's lightly dusted with flour and knead just until smooth. Pat dough into a ½-inch-thick circle and wrap in plastic. Refrigerate for 1 hour.

Preheat oven to 450°F.

Using a small knife, cut dough into 24 squarish shapes. Using a rolling pin on a lightly floured surface, roll out the small pieces of dough into very thin oval shapes. Or roll out dough into 1 very large, and very thin, rectangle. Sprinkle the individual cookies or the very large cookie with sugar to evenly cover.

Place on a parchment-lined cookie sheet and bake for 12 to 15 minutes, until slightly puffed and golden. Let cool on a rack. These can be stored in a tightly covered tin.

Makes 24

TOASTED ALMOND BARS

These beg for a glass of milk or a chilled tumbler of apple cider. You also may cut these into diamond shapes.

> 5 ounces graham crackers, about 18 squares
> 1½ cups slivered almonds, about 6 ounces
> 1 cup sweetened condensed milk

Preheat oven to 350°F.

Place graham crackers in bowl of a food processor and process until very finely ground, almost like flour. You will have about 1⅓ cups. Set aside in a large bowl.

Put almonds in a large nonstick skillet over medium heat and cook, stirring constantly, until almonds are lightly toasted. Finely chop almonds.

Add almonds to graham cracker crumbs and stir. Add all but 2 tablespoons sweetened condensed milk and a large pinch of salt. Stir until all the ingredients are well blended. Mixture will be sticky.

Line the bottom of an 8-inch square baking dish, preferably glass, with parchment paper. Coat interior of pan with nonstick cooking spray. Pour almond mixture into pan, smoothing the top with a knife. Using the back of a spoon glaze the top with remaining condensed milk.

Bake for 30 to 35 minutes, until firm. Remove from oven and cool. Cut into bars, large or small. Wrap well and store in a tightly covered tin.

Makes 16 or more

SWEET CIGARS

These are a cinch to make and very impressive served alongside any fresh fruit dessert.

> 6 sheets phyllo dough
> 6 tablespoons unsalted butter, melted
> ¾ cup cinnamon-sugar (page 242)

Preheat oven to 350°F.

Cut phyllo in half through the length, then across the width to get 4 rectangles. Lightly brush melted butter over each phyllo rectangle. Sprinkle each rectangle with 1 heaping teaspoon cinnamon-sugar.

Starting on the longer side, roll each rectangle tightly into the shape of a cigar, about 5½ inches in length and ½ inch wide. Brush tops with additional melted butter and sprinkle with more cinnamon-sugar.

Place on an ungreased baking sheet and bake for 15 minutes, or until golden and crisp.

Makes 24

CARDAMOM PUFFS

These lightweight oval cookies are the perfect accompaniment to the fruit and ice cream desserts that follow.

1 sheet frozen puff pastry, about 8 ounces
⅔ cup sugar
1 tablespoon ground cardamom

Preheat oven to 375°F.

Thaw puff pastry so that it is pliable but still very cold. In a small bowl, mix sugar with cardamom and spread onto a clean work surface.

Using a 1½-inch round cookie cutter, cut out approximately 30 cookies from puff pastry. Using a rolling pin, roll each circle into a long oval shape. Press each into the sugar, being sure to coat both sides. Prick all over with the tines of a fork.

Place cookies on a baking sheet lined with parchment paper. Bake for 12 minutes, or until golden. Sprinkle with a little of the remaining sugar.

Makes 30

CUSTARDS AND MOUSSES

WHITE CHOCOLATE MOUSSE WITH FRESH BERRIES

This is adapted from a recipe by Maury Rubin, impresario of the fabulous City Bakery in Manhattan.

4 ounces white chocolate, finely chopped
1¼ cups heavy cream
4 cups fresh raspberries, blackberries, or tiny strawberries

Put white chocolate in a medium bowl. Pour 1 cup cream into a small saucepan and bring to a boil. Pour hot cream over chocolate. Let sit for 1 minute, then whisk until completely smooth. Let cool. Cover with plastic wrap and puncture a few small holes in it. Refrigerate for 8 hours or overnight.

Pour the chilled white chocolate in bowl of an electric mixer. Add remaining cream and beat on medium speed until soft peaks form. Cover and refrigerate until firm and cold.

Wash berries and dry well. Divide most of the berries among 4 small wineglasses. Top with mousse and a few berries. If desired, you can garnish with additional white chocolate that has been grated or shaved with a vegetable peeler.

Serves 3 or 4

INSANELY SIMPLE CHOCOLATE MOUSSE

The title says it all. The better the chocolate, the better the results.

10 ounces top-quality semisweet chocolate
¼ cup brewed espresso at room temperature
5 extra-large egg whites

Chop chocolate into small pieces. Put in a heavy saucepan with espresso. Over very low heat, melt chocolate, stirring constantly until smooth and creamy. Let cool slightly.

In bowl of an electric mixer, beat egg whites with a pinch of salt until stiff. Slowly add the slightly warm chocolate mixture, beating on low for a moment, then folding gently with a fexible rubber spatula until thoroughly incorporated. The whites will deflate dramatically, but the mixture will become smooth and creamy. Do not overmix. Spoon mouse into 4 coffee cups or wineglasses. Refrigerate several hours before serving.

Serves 4

SLIGHTLY FROZEN LEMON MOUSSE

This fragile dessert benefits from several hours in the freezer. The texture becomes ice cream-like but more intriguing—it almost evaporates on your tongue. Additional virtues: it is dairy-free and doesn't require an ice cream maker. Best served the same day it is made.

3 large lemons
7 extra-large eggs
½ cup plus 1 tablespoon sugar

Grate rind of lemons to get 2 tablespoons zest. Cut lemons in half and squeeze to get 7 table-spoons juice.

Separate egg whites from egg yolks. You will need 7 yolks and only 4 whites. (Save the remaining whites for another use.)

In bowl of an electric mixer, beat egg yolks for several minutes until they thicken. Slowly add ½ cup sugar and beat until mixture is light yellow, creamy, and thick, about 5 minutes total.

Transfer mixture to a double boiler or a large metal bowl over simmering water. Add lemon zest and juice to yolks, and using a wire whisk, beat until mixture is thick and puddinglike, about 5 minutes. Remove from heat and create an ice bath by putting bowl in another bowl with cold water and ice cubes to cool the mixture.

In a clean bowl with clean beaters, whip egg whites with a pinch of salt and remaining sugar until very stiff. Gently fold whites into yolk mixture until thoroughly incorporated. Spoon into 4 wineglasses and freeze for several hours. Let sit at room temperature for 10 minutes before serving.

Serves 4

PINEAPPLE FLAN

This quivering custard of tropical intensity is made like a traditional crème caramel.

  1¼ cups sugar
  8 extra-large eggs
  2 cups unsweetened pineapple juice

Preheat oven to 350°F.

Put ¾ cup sugar in a small nonstick skillet. Cook over medium-high heat, stirring constantly with a wooden spoon, until sugar melts completely into a dark liquid caramel, about 3 minutes. Coat the interiors of 5 6-ounce custard cups with nonstick cooking spray. Immediately divide caramel among cups to coat bottom of each. Caramel will harden.

Separate 4 egg yolks and whites, saving whites for another use. In bowl of an electric mixer put 4 whole eggs, 4 egg yolks, and remaining sugar. Beat for 1 minute, until eggs and sugar are well blended.

Slowly add pineapple juice, little by little, and continue to mix until juice is incorporated. Do not let mixture become too frothy. With a ladle, divide evenly among 5 custard cups.

Place custard cups in a large, deep pan. Create a water bath by adding boiling water to pan so that water level comes two thirds up the sides of the cups. Carefully place in oven. Bake for 40 to 45 minutes, until firm. Remove cups from water bath. Let cool, then refrigerate until very cold, preferably overnight.

When ready to serve, carefully unmold custard onto flat dessert plates, loosening the sides with a small sharp knife if necessary. Caramel will coat the top and sides of the flan. Serve immediately.

Serves 5

MILK CHOCOLATE POTS DE CRÈME

Pots de crème refer simultaneously to the little lidded cups generally used for this dessert and to the heavenly custard within. If you can't find the authentic cups, bake these in china ramekins instead. Semisweet or white chocolate can be substituted.

  2 cups heavy cream
  6 ounces good-quality milk chocolate
  4 extra-large egg yolks

Preheat oven to 325°F.

Heat cream in a small heavy saucepan. Chop chocolate into small pieces and add to cream. Cook over low heat for several minutes, stirring constantly with a wooden spoon or wire whisk, until chocolate is completely melted and mixture is smooth. Remove from heat and let cool a few minutes.

In bowl of an electric mixer, beat yolks until very thick and creamy, about 3 minutes. Pour warm chocolate mixture into yolk mixture, a little at a time, mixing constantly. Divide mixture among 6 5-ounce ramekins. Create a water bath by placing ramekins in a large baking pan and pour boiling water into the pan almost to the tops of the ramekins.

Carefully place pan in the oven and bake for 25 minutes. Remove ramekins from water bath. Mixture should be loose but will firm up when chilled. Refrigerate for several hours. Let sit at room temperature for 20 minutes before serving.

Serves 6

CRÈME CARAMEL

Instant comfort.

> 1 cup sugar or vanilla-sugar (page 242)
> 2 cups half-and-half
> 3 extra-large eggs

Preheat oven to 350°F.

Put ½ cup sugar in a small nonstick skillet. Cook over medium-high heat until sugar melts into a dark liquid caramel. Quickly spoon melted sugar into 4 6-ounce custard cups to coat bottom. Caramel will harden.

Put half-and-half in a small saucepan and heat just until it boils, stirring constantly. Remove from heat. Put eggs in bowl of an electric mixer and mix until well blended. Add a pinch of salt and warm half-and-half. Mix until thoroughly blended. Ladle mixture into custard cups.

Create a water bath by placing cups in a large, deep pan. Pour boiling water into pan so that water level comes two thirds up the sides of cups. Bake for 40 to 45 minutes, until custards are firm. Remove cups from water bath. Let cool, then refrigerate until very cold, preferably overnight.

When ready to serve, carefully unmold custards onto flat dessert plates, loosening sides with a small sharp knife if necessary. Caramel will coat top and sides of custard. Serve immediately.

Serves 4

OLD-FASHIONED RICE PUDDING

Sometimes I make this on top of the stove, but baking it in the oven requires less attention. For an extra-rich version, I substitute half-and-half for the milk, creating a caramel-like layer of flavor.

> 1 quart whole milk
> ½ cup sugar or vanilla-sugar (page 242)
> ¼ cup extra-long-grain rice

Preheat oven to 325°F.

Put milk in a large saucepan. Add sugar, rice, and a pinch of salt. Whisking frequently, bring mixture to a boil. Immediately remove from heat and pour into a shallow baking dish.

Bake for 30 minutes. Using a wire whisk, furiously whisk mixture until the surface skin is incorporated. Bake for 30 minutes more, and briskly whisk again, incorporating the top layer into rice. Bake another 20 minutes and remove from oven. Pudding will still be very wet but it will firm up as it cools. Serve slightly warm. Best eaten before refrigerating, although you can refrigerate leftovers.

Serves 4

EGGNOG AND PANETTONE BREAD PUDDING

Serendipity: Commercial eggnog usually appears just in time for the first frost and panettone is a sweet Italian bread generally served at Christmas. Eggnog and panettone are available in most supermarkets.

8 ounces panettone
1 pint prepared eggnog
2 extra-large eggs

Preheat oven to 350°F.

Cut panettone into ¾-inch cubes. Put them on a rimmed baking sheet and lightly toast them in the oven. Watch carefully: the panettone should become golden, not brown.

Beat eggnog and eggs together in bowl of an electric mixer until thoroughly incorporated. Place toasted panettone cubes in a baking dish, preferably glass, that is 9 by 7 inches or 8 inches square. Pour eggnog mixture over panettone, pressing down with a spatula so that the panettone is submerged. Let sit for 15 minutes.

Place baking dish in a large, deep pan and create a water bath by pouring boiling water halfway up sides of smaller pan. Bake for 40 minutes, or until custard is firm. Remove from water bath and let cool. Serve at room temperature or cold.

Optional: You can make a sauce for the pudding by placing an additional 1 cup eggnog in a small saucepan and simmering until it is reduced to ½ cup. This will take about 25 minutes. Let cool and drizzle on pudding.

Serves 4 or more

ICED CANTALOUPE WITH MINT SUGAR

Large and tiny balls of ripe melon are bathed in a dulcet herb syrup, then bejeweled with herbed sugar. Lemon verbena can be substituted for the mint.

    2 bunches fresh mint
    ¾ cup sugar
    2 ripe medium cantaloupes

Wash mint and pat dry. Chop enough mint to get ⅓ packed cup, reserving the rest. Place in bowl of a food processor and add sugar. Process until sugar is incorporated. Set one fourth of the minted sugar aside for later.

Place remaining minted sugar in a small saucepan with ¼ cup water and a pinch of salt. Bring to a boil and cook for 2 minutes, or until it dissolves into a syrup. Let cool.

Cut melons in half and scoop out seeds. Using a large and small melon baller, scoop balls from melon flesh. Place melon in a bowl and pour mint syrup over it. Cover and refrigerate until cold. Serve melon with its syrup in chilled wine glasses or dessert coupes. Sprinkle with remaining mint sugar and garnish with a few mint sprigs.

Serves 4

STRAWBERRY PARFAITS WITH CARAMEL AND WHIPPED CREAM

Here the same ingredients—heavy cream and sugar—are combined to create two very different results: a dark caramel sauce and a fluff of sweet white cream. You can serve this in bowls, large wine goblets, or layered in parfait glasses.

    4 pints ripe strawberries
    1½ cups sugar
    1¾ cups heavy cream

Wash berries and pat dry. Remove stems. Cut half of the berries in half lengthwise and place in a bowl. Sprinkle with 2 tablespoons sugar and toss. Set aside.

Place remaining berries in a small saucepan with ½ cup sugar. Bring to a boil over high heat. Lower heat to medium and cook, stirring often, for 10 minutes, until berries are soft but still retain their shape. Let cool.

In another small saucepan, put ¼ cup water and ¾ cup sugar. Cook over medium heat until sugar dissolves and liquid is clear. Increase heat to high and cook until syrup turns a dark amber color, stirring often. Lower heat and cook for 2 minutes. Remove from heat. Carefully stir in 1 cup heavy cream; the mixture will bubble up and harden. Cook over medium heat until sugar melts and mixture thickens, stirring often. Continue to cook until reduced to a bit more than 1 cup. Let caramel cool to room temperature. If too thick, add a little water.

Whip remaining ¾ cup cream with remaining sugar until thick.

To assemble parfaits: Put sugared uncooked berries in 6 wineglasses and cover with cooked berries and their juices. Add whipped cream and make a smooth layer to cover berries. Drizzle with caramel sauce.

Serves 6

HONEYDEW WITH BLUEBERRIES, BLUEBERRY SYRUP

4 heaping cups blueberries, about 1½ pounds
½ cup plus 2 tablespoons sugar
1 very ripe large honeydew melon

Wash blueberries and dry well, removing any stems. Place 2 cups blueberries in a small saucepan with ½ cup sugar and 1 cup water. Bring to a boil. Lower heat and cook for 20 minutes, until juices thicken. Strain blueberries and liquid through a coarse-mesh sieve, pushing down hard on the blueberries to extract all the juices. You should have about 1½ cups syrup.

Cut melon into 6 wedges and remove seeds. Toss remaining blueberries with remaining sugar and fill cavities of melon with sugared blueberries. Drizzle with blueberry syrup.

Serves 6

PINEAPPLE CARPACCIO WITH CRUSHED PISTACHIOS

This refined dessert gets a drizzle of caramel that hardens into candy-like shards.

1 very ripe large pineapple
½ cup shelled unsalted pistachios
½ cup sugar

Remove rind from pineapple. Cut pineapple in half through the length, and remove core. Place cut side down on a cutting board and cut crosswise into very thin half circles. Arrange pineapple slices in an attractive pattern in the center of 6 large dessert plates or on a platter.

Lightly toast pistachios in a medium nonstick skillet. Let cool completely. Process pistachios in a food processor until finely ground. Set aside.

Wipe out skillet. Add sugar and cook over high heat, stirring constantly with a wooden spoon, until sugar melts and becomes a dark brown syrup. Immediately drizzle caramel in a lacy pattern evenly over pineapple slices. Let cool for 1 minute. Caramel will harden and become brittle.

Dust perimeters of pineapple slices with ground pistachios. Serve immediately.

Serves 6

GRAPEFRUIT AND RASPBERRIES *VINO COTTO*

This mélange of tart grapefruit and sweet raspberries is awash in vino cotto, *which translates as "cooked wine," a syrupy reduction of white grape juice.*

3 cups white grape juice
4 very large white grapefruits
2 pints raspberries

Put grape juice in a medium saucepan. Bring to a boil, then lower heat and cook until liquid is reduced to 1 scant cup. This will take about 30 minutes. Let cool.

Cut rind from grapefruits, being sure to remove all the white pith. Using a small sharp knife, cut between membranes to release segments. Arrange segments in a decorative fashion on 4 large plates or place in wineglasses.

Gently wash berries and pat dry. Arrange berries on grapefruit segments. Drizzle with reduced grape juice. Cover and chill until ready to serve.

Serves 4

ORANGES AND STRAWBERRIES *EN GELÉE*

Aspics and gelatin desserts are back in vogue. Here, a simple orange jelly delicately encases jewel-like fresh fruit. It is especially gorgeous when made with blood oranges, but regular juice oranges may be substituted.

12 large blood oranges
12 very large strawberries
1 envelope unflavored gelatin

Cut rind from 6 oranges with a small sharp knife, being careful to remove all the white pith. Cut along membranes to release segments.

Wash strawberries and remove stems. Cut berries lengthwise into ⅛-inch-thick slices. Artfully arrange orange segments and strawberry slices in 4 large shallow soup plates.

Squeeze remaining oranges to get 2 cups juice. Put juice in a small saucepan.

Sprinkle gelatin over ¼ cup cold water in a small bowl. Let sit for 1 minute. Heat orange juice over very low heat and add gelatin. Stir until gelatin dissolves, about 1 minute. Let cool slightly. Pour approximately ½ cup juice mixture in each soup plate to submerge fruit. Refrigerate for several hours until completely jelled.

Serves 4

GRANOLA PLUM COBBLER

This can be made with any super-juicy stone fruit, including nectarines and white or yellow peaches.

2 pounds very ripe plums
2 cups granola
5 tablespoons unsalted butter, at room temperature

Preheat oven to 350°F.

Wash plums and dry them. Cut in half and remove pits. Cut plums into wedges and arrange in bottom of a 6-cup soufflé dish or a shallow casserole.

Put 1 cup granola in bowl of a food processor. Process until granola is like coarse flour. Add 4 tablespoons butter and process until mixture becomes a sticky ball.

Transfer mixture to another bowl and add remaining granola and a pinch of salt. Using a flexible rubber spatula, mix well until topping is crumbly.

Pour ¼ cup water over plums. Cut remaining tablespoon butter into small pieces and scatter on top. Pack granola mixture on fruit to cover completely. Bake for 30 minutes. Serve warm or at room temperature.

Serves 4 or more

MARSALA-POACHED PEARS WITH CINNAMON

4 very large firm ripe pears, stems on
1 bottle (750 milliliters) sweet Marsala
7 tablespoons cinnamon-sugar (page 242)

Peel pears using a vegetable peeler; leave stems attached.

Pour Marsala into a medium pot with a cover. Add 2 cups water and 6 tablespoons cinnamon-sugar. Put pears in pot and bring to a boil. Lower heat to medium and cover pot. Cook until tender, stirring occasionally, about 45 minutes depending on firmness of pears.

Remove cover and let pears and liquid cool to room temperature. Remove pears with a slotted spoon and put them upright in a bowl. Bring liquid in pot to a boil and cook over medium-high heat until reduced to 1½ cups. Pour over pears and refrigerate until cold.

Serve pears with their syrup. Sprinkle with remaining cinnamon-sugar.

Makes 4

RHUBARB GRATIN WITH TOASTED ALMOND STREUSEL

This lovely fruit gratin is served with a brown sugar syrup. It can be eaten warm or at room temperature.

    2 pounds fresh rhubarb
    1 cup shelled almonds with skins, about 5 ounces
    1½ cups packed dark brown sugar

Preheat oven to 350°F.

Remove and discard any rhubarb leaves and wash rhubarb stalks. Cut into 3-inch pieces. If stalks are thick, cut them in half lengthwise. Put rhubarb in a shallow casserole large enough to accommodate pieces in 2 layers. Pour ¼ cup water over rhubarb.

Place almonds in a medium nonstick skillet and cook over medium heat for about 2 minutes, or until you smell a faintly nutty odor. Shake pan occasionally to distribute nuts. Let cool. Place almonds in bowl of a food processor and process until finely ground. Add 1 cup brown sugar and process briefly. Sprinkle this mixture over rhubarb to cover completely.

Bake for 1½ hours. Place gratin under broiler for 30 to 60 seconds to brown.

Put remaining brown sugar in a small nonstick skillet with ½ cup water. Stir to dissolve sugar. Bring to a boil, lower heat to medium-high, and cook for about 10 minutes, until reduced to ½ cup. Let cool.

Remove rhubarb from oven. Using a spatula, divide gratin among 6 dessert plates or bowls. Drizzle syrup around each portion.

Serves 6

MADEIRA-SOAKED PRUNES WITH WHITE CHOCOLATE

Madeira is making a comeback. This fortified wine, from a volcanic island off the coast of Portugal, provides a sensational backdrop for prunes. Shavings of white chocolate add a compatibly decadent flourish. I like to use big sour prunes with pits that I get in Middle Eastern and Russian fruit markets, but you may use any large prunes, pitted if you wish. Instead of white chocolate, sometimes I top this with coffee yogurt—buy sixteen ounces—that has been drained through a cheesecloth-lined sieve until thick (about two hours).

    1 pound very large prunes
    2 cups Madeira
    3-ounce block white chocolate

Place prunes in a large saucepan. Add Madeira and 1 cup water. Bring to a boil.

Reduce heat to low and cover the pan. Cook for 15 minutes. Remove from heat and remove cover. Let cool and then refrigerate, covered, for 1 day before using.

When ready to serve, let white chocolate come to room temperature. Using a vegetable peeler, shave chocolate into thin shards and roll them slightly to make curls. Place curls on a plate lined with parchment or wax paper. Refrigerate until ready to use.

Divide prunes among 4 pretty dessert dishes or wineglasses. Pour some of the Madeira over the prunes. Top with white chocolate curls.

Serves 4 or more

GRILLED PINEAPPLE WITH HONEY-LIME SYRUP

I like this best grilled on an outdoor barbecue, but it also works made under your broiler.

1 large ripe pineapple
½ cup wildflower, leatherwood, or other aromatic honey,
   plus more for drizzling
3 limes

Cut rind from pineapple and cut across the width into 6 thick rounds. Using a small sharp knife or a small round cookie cutter, remove center core and discard.

Place pineapple in a shallow casserole large enough to hold slices in 1 layer. Put honey in a small bowl. Grate rind of limes to get 1 tablespoon zest. Cut 2 limes in half and squeeze to get ¼ cup juice. Add zest, lime juice, and a pinch of salt to honey and mix well. Pour mixture over pineapple slices and marinate for several hours at room temperature, turning several times.

Prepare a charcoal grill. When hot, remove pineapple from marinade. Grill on both sides. When warm and slightly caramelized, transfer to a warm platter, pouring marinade over pineapple. Let cool. Drizzle with more honey if desired.

Serves 6

ALMOND-KISSED ROASTED PEACHES WITH AMARETTO CREAM

6 large ripe peaches
⅔ cup plus 1 tablespoon amaretto
½ cup heavy cream, chilled

Preheat oven to 400°F.

Wash peaches and cut them in half. Remove pits. Place peach halves cut side down on a rimmed baking sheet and sprinkle with ⅓ cup water. Bake for 10 minutes, then turn peaches over. Bake 10 minutes longer, or until peaches are soft but still retain their shape. Remove from oven and place peaches cut side up on a warm platter.

Place ⅔ cup amaretto in a small saucepan over medium-high heat and reduce by half, or until syrupy. Pour syrup over peaches. Whip heavy cream with remaining amaretto and spoon over the slightly warm peaches.

Serves 4 or more

SLOW-BAKED PEARS WITH STILTON, WARM HONEY SYRUP

The pears can be made early in the day, but drizzle the warm syrup over the fruit and cheese right before serving.

4 large firm ripe Comice or Bartlett pears
2 tablespoons plus ⅓ cup honey
6 ounces Stilton cheese, at room temperature

Preheat oven to 400°F.

Peel pears using a vegetable peeler and cut them in half lengthwise. Remove seeds using the small end of a melon baller. Mix 2 tablespoons honey and 6 tablespoons warm water in a small dish and stir until honey dissolves. Place pear halves, cut side down, in 2 sturdy metal pie tins. Pour honey mixture over the pears. Bake for 20 minutes, basting with some of the pan juices. Turn pears over and bake 20 minutes longer. Turn the pears again and add a little water to the pans. Bake 15 to 20 minutes longer, depending on ripeness of pears, until pears are golden brown and tender but still retain their shape.

When ready to serve, heat remaining honey and ⅓ cup water in a small saucepan until boiling. Lower heat and simmer for 10 minutes, or until reduced to ½ cup. Keep warm.

Place 2 warm or room-temperature pears halves on each of 4 plates. Cut cheese into 8 chunks. Using 2 small spoons, shape into 8 quenelles, or oval shapes, and place atop pears. Drizzle with warm honey syrup.

Serves 4

FRUITS AND THEIR SORBETS

POACHED ORANGES IN LEMON SYRUP, CITRUS SORBET

6 large oranges
4 large lemons
1 cup sugar

To make sorbet: Grate rinds of 1 orange and 1 lemon and set aside. Squeeze 2 oranges to get ½ cup juice and squeeze 2 lemons to get ⅓ cup juice. Put orange and lemon juices in a saucepan with ½ cup sugar, 1½ cups water and reserved zest. Bring to a boil, lower heat, and cook for 1 minute, until sugar dissolves. Remove from heat and let cool. Refrigerate mixture until very cold. Freeze in an ice cream maker according to the manufacturer's directions.

Remove rind from remaining oranges and cut oranges in half through the equator. In a large skillet with a cover, heat 2 cups water and remaining sugar. Grate rind of remaining lemons and add to skillet. Squeeze ⅓ cup juice from lemons and add to skillet. Add orange segments in 1 layer and bring to a boil. Lower heat and cover pot. Cook for 20 minutes, or until oranges begin to soften but still retain their shape.

Remove oranges with a slotted spoon and put in a bowl. Cook liquid in skillet over high heat until thick and syrupy. Pour over poached oranges. Cool and refrigerate until very cold. Serve with scoops of sorbet.

Serves 4

ROASTED STRAWBERRIES WITH STRAWBERRY SORBET

This idea, inspired by four-star chef Daniel Boulud, features the very-berry essence of both warm and icy strawberries.

 2 pints strawberries, plus 20 very large strawberries
 ¾ cup vanilla-sugar (page 242)
 3 tablespoons unsalted butter

To make sorbet: Wash 2 pints strawberries and discard stems. Bring 1 cup water and ½ cup vanilla-sugar to a boil. Boil until sugar dissolves. Let cool. Place berries in the bowl of a food processor and add sugar syrup. Process until very smooth. Refrigerate until cold, then freeze in an ice cream maker according to the manufacturer's directions.

When ready to serve, preheat oven to 400°F. Wash the large berries and discard stems. Place berries side by side and stem end down, in a shallow metal baking pan. Very thinly slice butter and place over berries. Sprinkle berries with remaining vanilla-sugar. Bake for 8 minutes, until berries are soft but still retain their shape. Let cool a little. Serve berries with pan juices and top with sorbet.

Serves 4

POIRES BELLE-HELENE WITH PEAR SORBET

This is a riff on chef Auguste Escoffier's classic coupling of poached pears and chocolate sauce. My pear sorbet adds an extra dimension in taste, texture, and temperature.

 10 large pears, 6 with long stems
 2 cups sugar
 6 ounces semisweet chocolate

Using a vegetable peeler, carefully peel skin from 6 long-stemmed pears. Core pears from bottom. Place pears in a medium pot with a cover. Add cold water to cover pears. Add ½ cup sugar. Bring to a boil. Lower heat, cover pot, and cook pears for 20 to 30 minutes, or until just tender. Let pears cool in liquid. Set aside ½ cup poaching liquid. Refrigerate pears until very cold.

Meanwhile, peel remaining pears and cut them into 1-inch pieces. Remove any seeds. Put pears in a medium pot with 2 cups water and remaining sugar minus ½ tablespoon sugar. (Set ½ tablespoon sugar aside for later.) Cook pears until very soft; cooking time will vary depending on ripeness of pears. Let pears cool for 10 minutes. Put pears and their liquid in bowl of a food processor. Process until very smooth, adding reserved ½ cup poaching liquid. Refrigerate puree until cold, then freeze in an ice cream maker according to manufacturer's directions.

To make chocolate sauce: Put ½ cup water and reserved ½ tablespoon sugar in a small heavy sauce-pan. Bring to a boil and cook for 1 minute, or until sugar dissolves. Reduce heat to low and add chocolate, chopped into pieces. Whisk with a wire whisk until chocolate melts into a smooth sauce.

Place a scoop of sorbet in each of 6 large goblets, top with a whole poached pear, and spoon slightly warm chocolate sauce on top. Serve immediately.

Serves 6

FRUIT AND CHEESE AS DESSERT

For me, a thoughtful pairing of fruit and cheese is a fabulous dessert alternative that gives me an opportunity to finish my wine. Three well-chosen elements are all you need. You may serve with a crusty baguette or my Twice-Baked Oatcakes (page 250), but I prefer a knife and fork.

- Tart apples with Pont l'Eveque and apple cider syrup
- Fresh figs with Gorgonzola dolce and toasted pine nuts
- Roasted lady apples with Stilton and a port reduction
- Forelle pears with Taleggio (soft cow's milk cheese from northern Italy) and chestnut honey
- Fuji apples with sharp farmhouse cheddar and warm pecans
- Fresh cherries with young goat cheese and hazelnuts

- Ribbons of melon with manchego cheese and roasted almonds
- Muscat grapes and dried figs with St. André
- Thinly sliced watermelon with sheep's milk cheese and a drizzle of wild thyme honey
- Comice pears with pink peppercorns and runny Brie
- Very sweet apricots with Cabrales (a Spanish blue cheese) and walnuts
- Fresh red currants and very ripe pears with Pecorino Romano
- Mangoes with aged goat cheese and a Sauternes reduction
- Fresh or Medjool dates with Camembert and Brazil nuts

ICE CREAMS AND SORBETS

BITTERSWEET CHOCOLATE SORBET

½ cup sugar
½ cup unsweetened cocoa powder
4 ounces bittersweet chocolate

In a medium saucepan, combine sugar and 1¾ cups water. Bring to a boil, then lower heat to medium. Continue to cook, stirring until sugar dissolves. Whisk in cocoa and chocolate that has been chopped into small pieces. Stir until chocolate melts and all the ingredients are incorporated. When mixture returns to a boil, remove from heat and strain through a coarse-mesh sieve into a bowl. Let cool. Refrigerate until very cold.

Freeze in an ice cream maker according to the manufacturer's directions.

Serves 4

LEMON-BUTTERMILK ICE CREAM

Technically this may not be ice cream (there is no cream), but tangy buttermilk gives it great mouthfeel and a creamy taste.

2 cups superfine sugar
6 large lemons
1 quart buttermilk

Put sugar in a medium bowl. Grate rind of enough lemons to get 2 heaping tablespoons zest. Squeeze as many lemons as needed to get ⅔ cup juice. Add zest and juice to sugar and stir until sugar dissolves.

Whisk in buttermilk using a small wire whisk. Add a pinch of salt and stir, making sure sugar has completely dissolved. Taste and add more lemon zest or juice to get a pleasant sweet-sour balance. Cover and refrigerate until very cold. Freeze in an ice cream maker according to the manufacturer's directions.

Serves 8

ORANGE ICE CREAM WITH ORANGE-CARAMEL SYRUP

These three ingredients miraculously make a sun-kissed ice cream and caramel sauce.

8 large juice oranges
1½ cups half-and-half
1 cup sugar

Grate rind of enough oranges to get 1½ tablespoons zest. Cut oranges in half and squeeze to get 3½ cups juice.

Put half-and-half in a saucepan with ¾ cup sugar, orange zest, and a pinch of salt. Bring just to a boil, whisking constantly. Remove from heat and let cool.

Whisk in 3 cups orange juice and refrigerate until mixture is very cold. Freeze in an ice cream maker according to manufacturer's directions.

Make caramel sauce by placing remaining sugar in a small nonstick skillet. Cook over medium-high heat until sugar turns into a dark amber liquid. Carefully add remaining ½ cup orange juice. Mixture will bubble up and sugar will harden, but continue cooking several minutes over medium heat and sugar will melt. Continue to cook until sauce is reduced to 6 tablespoons. Let cool. Serve ice cream drizzled with caramel sauce.

Serves 4

DARK CHOCOLATE ICE CREAM WITH CHOCOLATE SAUCE

2½ cups half-and-half
½ cup plus 1 teaspoon sugar
12 ounces bittersweet chocolate

Put 2 cups half-and-half in a medium saucepan with ½ cup sugar and a pinch of salt. Bring just to a boil, then immediately lower heat and simmer, stirring constantly, for several minutes until sugar is dissolved. Remove from heat. Cover and keep warm.

Coarsely chop 8 ounces of chocolate and place in a double-boiler or a bowl set over simmering water. Stirring frequently, melt chocolate until smooth. Slowly whisk in warm half-and-half and continue to cook, whisking constantly, until well combined. Remove from heat. Let cool and refrigerate until very cold. Freeze in an ice cream maker according to the manufacturer's directions.

Make chocolate sauce by bringing remaining half-and-half and remaining sugar to a boil in a small saucepan. Add remaining chocolate and stir until chocolate melts and mixture is smooth. Add 1 tablespoon water. Let cool. Serve ice cream drizzled with chocolate sauce.

Serves 4 or more

COCONUT SORBET WITH PINEAPPLE SYRUP

Guests may not be able to identify all three ingredients, but they'll love its mystery.

15 ounces cream of coconut
2¾ cups unsweetened pineapple juice
4 large limes

Place cream of coconut in bowl of a food processor and process briefly until smooth. Remove 2 tablespoons and set aside. Add ¾ cup pineapple juice and ¼ cup water to processor. Squeeze enough limes to get ½ cup juice, reserving the rest of the limes. Add lime juice to processor with a pinch of salt. Process until mixture is very smooth. Transfer to a bowl and cover. Refrigerate until very cold. Freeze in an ice cream maker according to the manufacturer's directions.

Place remaining pineapple juice and reserved cream of coconut in a small saucepan. Bring to a boil. Lower heat and simmer until reduced to ½ cup, whisking often with a wire whisk. This will take about 20 minutes. Let cool.

Serve scoops of ice cream with pineapple syrup poured on top. Garnish with thin slices of remaining lime, if desired.

Serves 4

WILDFLOWER HONEY ICE CREAM

Use wildflower, wild thyme, or leatherwood honey from Australia for the most intriguing results.

3 cups light cream
4 extra-large egg yolks
½ cup wildflower honey, plus more for drizzling

In a medium saucepan, heat cream until small bubbles appear around edges. Remove from heat. In bowl of an electric mixer, beat egg yolks and honey until creamy and thoroughly blended. Gradually beat in hot cream. Pour mixture into saucepan and cook, stirring constantly, until slightly thickened. Do not boil.

Cover mixture and refrigerate until very cold. Freeze in an ice cream maker according to the manufacturer's directions. If ice cream becomes too hard, let it soften a little before serving. Drizzle with a little honey if desired.

Serves 6

ICED LIMES WITH YOGURT-LIME GELATO

10 large limes
14 tablespoons superfine sugar
1½ cups plain yogurt

Grate zest of enough limes to get 1½ tablespoons. Cut 4 limes in half and squeeze to get ⅔ cup juice. In a large bowl, put lime zest, juice, sugar, and a pinch of salt. Stir well until sugar dissolves. Stir in yogurt and mix well. Cover and refrigerate until very cold. Freeze in an ice cream maker according to the manufacturer's directions.

Cut a ⅓-inch "hat" off tops of remaining limes and reserve. With a paring knife, cut out most of the pulp from each lime and, with a spoon, scrape out remaining pulp.

Cut a small slice from the bottom of each lime so it sits up straight. Fill each lime shell with frozen yogurt, mounding it ½ inch over the rim of the shell. Cover with a lime "hat" and freeze. Let sit at room temperature for 10 minutes before serving.

Serves 6

HONEYDEW-KIWI SORBET

Although it's suffered from overexposure by devotees of nouvelle cuisine, the kiwi has nonethe-less survived as an adorable fruit with good acidity and decorative little seeds. Coupled with the intense perfume of ripe honeydew, it makes a sorbet for any season. Galia or Cavaillon melon can be substituted when available.

½ cup sugar
½ ripe large honeydew melon, about 1½ pounds
4 ripe large kiwi

In a small saucepan, bring sugar and ½ cup water to a boil, stirring gently until sugar dissolves and liquid is clear. Boil gently for 2 minutes without stirring. Set aside and let cool while prepar-ing fruit.

Remove rind and seeds from melon. Peel kiwi using a small sharp knife. Cut fruit into 1-inch chunks and add to bowl of a food processor. Add a pinch of salt and process until very smooth. Add sugar syrup and process again until smooth.

Cover and refrigerate until very cold. Freeze in an ice cream maker according to the manufac-turer's directions.

Serves 6

CHERRY ICES WITH FIVE-SPICE POWDER

Fresh cherries bursting with garnet juices have an affinity with Chinese five-spice powder, made from star anise, licorice root, clove, fennel, and red pepper. This ice tastes delicious with a piece of Almond Brittle (page 276).

¾ cup sugar
½ teaspoon five-spice powder, plus more for sprinkling
1½ pounds ripe dark red cherries

In a small saucepan put 2¼ cups water, sugar, and five-spice powder. Bring to a boil and boil for 2 minutes. Let cool.

Remove pits from cherries and discard. Place cherries in bowl of a food processor and process until smooth. Slowly add sugar syrup and process until very smooth. Refrigerate until very cold. Freeze in an ice cream maker according to the manufacturer's directions. If desired, sprinkle with more five-spice powder.

Serves 4

LEMON SORBETTO WITH SWEET *GREMOLATA*

Gremolata *is a mixture of lemon zest and parsley generally sprinkled over osso buco. My riff on the Italian classic is sweet on this tart sorbetto.*

  6 large lemons
  1 small bunch fresh rosemary
  1½ cups sugar

Grate rind of enough lemons to get 2 heaping tablespoons zest. Set 1 tablespoon aside for later. Squeeze enough lemons to get 1 cup juice.

Wash rosemary and pat dry. Place 1½ cups water, 1⅓ cups sugar, and 2 sprigs rosemary in a small saucepan. Heat until boiling, then reduce heat and simmer for 1 to 2 minutes, until liquid is clear. Let cool. Discard rosemary.

Finely mince enough of the remaining rosemary to get 1 tablespoon. Mix into sugar syrup with lemon juice and zest. Refrigerate until very cold. Freeze in an ice cream maker according to the manufacturer's directions.

Right before serving, prepare the gremolata: mix remaining sugar, reserved zest, and 1½ teaspoons finely minced rosemary in a small bowl. Sprinkle sweet gremolata over sorbetto.

Serves 6

GRAPEFRUIT-CAMPARI GRANITA

This granita is a fabulous finale for Sunday brunch. It is also a splendid intermezzo for a more formal dinner party.

  ½ cup sugar
  3 cups freshly squeezed grapefruit juice
  3 tablespoons Campari, plus more for drizzling

Put sugar and ½ cup water in a small saucepan and bring to a boil. Lower heat to medium and cook for 1 to 2 minutes, until sugar is dissolved. Let cool.

Add grapefruit juice and 3 tablespoons Campari to sugar syrup and stir to combine. Pour into a 9 by 11-inch baking pan and freeze for 3 hours, scraping with a fork every 30 minutes to break up ice crystals. Divide evenly among 4 wineglasses and drizzle with additional Campari.

Optional: Dip rims of wineglasses into a saucer of Campari, then into a saucer of sugar. Let harden. Carfully fill glasses with granita.

Serves 4

RASPBERRY GRANITA

Inspired by a recipe in Cooking Light *magazine, this has double-raspberry intensity. Fresh raspberries are enhanced with raspberry or black raspberry liqueur—known as crème de framboise and Chambord, respectively. They both are delicious.*

1 cup sugar
1½ pounds fresh raspberries, about 4 cups, plus more for garnish
1 cup crème de framboise or Chambord

Put sugar, 1 cup water, and a pinch of salt in a small saucepan. Bring to a boil. Cook for 1 minute, stirring often, until sugar dissolves. Remove from heat and let cool.

Wash berries and dry well. Place in a blender and process until very smooth. Press raspberry puree through a coarse-mesh sieve into a bowl. Discard seeds. Stir cooled sugar syrup into raspberry mixture. Add 2 cups water and liqueur and stir until blended.

Pour mixture into a 9 by 11-inch pan. Cover and freeze for 6 hours. Remove from freezer and let stand for 10 minutes. Scrape mixture with a fork until small granules result. Scoop granita into chilled wineglasses or dessert coupes. Garnish with additional raspberries if desired.

Serves 6

TEN-MINUTE FROZEN DESSERTS

- Make a Tin-Roof Sundae: Melt premium semi-sweet chocolate with a little vanilla ice cream to make a thick chocolate sauce. Fill a sundae glass with scoops of vanilla ice cream and top with the sauce and salted peanuts.

- Pour single-malt scotch over chocolate ice cream and sprinkle with finely ground hazelnut coffee beans.

- Soak sun-dried cherries in oloroso sherry for 8 minutes and pour over chocolate chip ice cream.

- Fill a wineglass with chocolate sorbet and passion-fruit sorbet. Top with preserved ginger in syrup.

- Boil large pitted prunes in Madeira for 5 minutes. Let cool for 5 minutes and top with scoops of coffee ice cream.

- Make an adult smoothie: In a blender, whip together orange sorbet, vanilla ice cream, and amaretto. Serve in chilled pilsner glasses with straws.

- Fill tall glasses with vanilla ice cream. Add a shot of cold espresso. Top with marshmallow fluff and a dusting of ground espresso beans.

- Alternate scoops of strawberry ice cream with fresh blueberries in wineglasses. Pour blueberry liqueur, blueberry schnapps, or blueberry syrup over the top.

- Fill a wineglass with lemon sorbet and fresh raspberries and top with demi-sec Champagne.

- Roll a ball of cherry-vanilla ice cream in miniature chocolate chips. Melt some of the ice cream with more chocolate chips to make a sauce. Top it all with unsweetened whipped cream.

- Fill a martini glass with small balls of watermelon. Top with lime sorbet and anejo tequila.

ICE POPS 1-2-3

Nostalgia redux: new flavors in an old form. You can buy ice pop molds in kitchenware stores and baking shops, or you can make these in Dixie cups. Just pour in the mixture, cover with aluminum foil, stick in a wooden popsicle stick, and freeze.

TROPICALI

These are light orange with green flecks.

12 ounces mango nectar
1 cup cream of coconut
2 large limes

Place mango nectar and cream of coconut in a bowl. Whisk until smooth. Grate rind of limes to get 1 tablespoon zest. Squeeze limes to get 3 tablespoons juice. Add zest and juice to mixture and stir well. Pour into 8 ice pop molds. Insert sticks. Freeze for at least 4 hours.

Makes 8

SUMMER SUNRISE

Two-tone orange and coral-hued. The juice mixture is now available in supermarkets.

2 cups orange-peach-mango juice
¼ cup corn syrup
3 tablespoons grenadine

Put juice and corn syrup in a bowl. Mix thoroughly until corn syrup is dissolved. Pour half of the mixture into 8 ice pop molds. Freeze for 1 hour. Insert sticks. Freeze until mixture is frozen, about 3 more hours. Stir grenadine into remaining corn syrup mixture and pour this into molds, inserting sticks. Freeze for 3 hours more.

Makes 8

CRANBERRY TEA-SICLES

These are dark ruby colored.

2 Red Zinger tea bags
3 tablespoons sugar
6 ounces frozen cranberry concentrate

Boil 1½ cups water and put in a bowl. Add tea bags and let steep for 5 minutes. Remove tea bags. Stir in sugar until it dissolves. Add cranberry concentrate and stir to dissolve. Let cool. Pour mixture into 8 ice pop molds. Insert sticks. Freeze for at least 4 hours.

Makes 8

LAST-MINUTE DESSERT SAUCES

Chocolate-Maple Sauce: Perfect if you have no real chocolate in the house. In a small saucepan, bring 1 cup maple syrup to a boil. Lower heat and whisk in $1/4$ cup unsweetened cocoa powder, 3 tablespoons unsalted butter, and a pinch of salt until smooth and thick. Makes 1 cup

Caramel-Rum Sauce: Put $3/4$ cup sugar and $1/4$ cup water in a medium saucepan. Cook over medium heat until sugar melts into a dark amber liquid. Add 1 cup heavy cream—mixture will bubble up—and 3 tablespoons dark rum. Whisk over medium heat until smooth. Makes $1 1/4$ cups

Butterscotch Sauce: Put $2/3$ cup heavy cream and 5 tablespoons unsalted butter in a saucepan. Heat until butter melts. Add $2/3$ cup packed dark brown sugar and a large pinch of salt. Bring just to a boil. Lower heat and simmer, whisking constantly, for 5 minutes. Makes $1 3/4$ cups

Strawberry-Cassis Sauce: Thaw 16-ounces frozen whole unsweetened strawberries. Put berries with any juices in the bowl of a food processor. Add $1/4$ cup sugar and $1/4$ cup boiling water. Process for several minutes until very smooth. Transfer to a small bowl and add 3 tablespoons crème de cassis. Makes 2 cups

CANDIES

ALMOND BRITTLE

2 cups sugar
$1 1/2$ packed cups slivered almonds
$1/2$ lemon

Put sugar and almonds in a very large nonstick skillet. Stirring constantly with a wooden spoon, cook over medium-high heat until sugar has melted into a dark amber liquid that's completely free of any lumps or sugar crystals. (Be very careful not to touch the mixture as you stir.) This will take about 10 minutes.

When completely melted, pour mixture onto a large cutting board lined with aluminum foil, spreading it into a thin layer with a wooden spoon. Using the half lemon, spread the mixture into an even thinner layer. Let cool until very hard. Break candy into pieces and serve.

Makes 1 generous pound

CHOCOLATE-TAHINA SQUARES

This winning combination of flavors tastes like a Chunky candy bar. These make elegant petits fours when cut into small squares.

8 ounces semisweet chocolate
$1/3$ cup plus 2 tablespoons tahina (sesame paste)
$1/2$ cup dried currants

Chop chocolate into small pieces and place in a double boiler or a large metal bowl over simmering water. Add $1/3$ cup tahina and a pinch of salt, stirring with a wooden spoon until mixture is completely melted and smooth. Add currants and stir to incorporate.

Line the bottom of an 8-inch pan with parchment paper. Coat the interior of the pan with non-stick cooking spray. Pour warm chocolate-tahina mixture into pan in an even layer. Using the tines of a fork, drizzle the top with remaining tahina in a lacy pattern. Let cool. Refrigerate until candy is hard enough to cut. Cut into 25 squares. Serve chilled.

Makes 25 pieces

MINT CHOCOLATE-DIPPED STRAWBERRIES

8 ounces mint chocolate chips
2 tablespoons solid vegetable shortening
16 very large ripe strawberries with long stems

In a double boiler or a metal bowl over simmering water, melt chocolate with vegetable shortening. Stir until completely melted and smooth.

Wash berries and pat completely dry. Holding each berry by the stem, dip into warm chocolate mixture, coating two thirds of the berry. Let any excess chocolate drip off. Carefully place dipped berries on a baking sheet lined with parchment or wax paper. Refrigerate until hardened.

Makes 16

WALNUT FUDGE

4 ounces walnuts, coarsely chopped
1 cup plus 2 tablespoons sweetened condensed milk
10 ounces semisweet chocolate, chopped

Place walnuts in a medium nonstick skillet and cook for several minutes over medium heat, stirring constantly, until nuts are toasted. Add a pinch of salt and stir.

Put condensed milk in a medium saucepan. Heat until it just comes to a boil and add chocolate. Lower heat to simmer and stir until blended. Cook, stirring constantly, until chocolate has melted and mixture is smooth. Stir in three-quarters of the toasted walnuts.

Line an 8 by 8-inch pan with plastic wrap so that it hangs over the edges of the pan. Pour in the chocolate mixture in an even layer. Finely chop the remaining walnuts and scatter on top. Fold plastic wrap over chocolate and press gently so it adheres to surface. Refrigerate for several hours, until firm. Cut into squares and serve.

Makes 20 or more pieces

drinks

There are bartenders who make a living mixing cocktails, and barristas whose wages are earned behind espresso machines. There are high-concept tea masters, sommeliers, and soda jerks, too. At home, we are never expected to be any of these, but when guests arrive, you will find these recipes helpful.

This chapter contains my favorite specialty beverages—from cocktails to coolers to coffee concoctions—but my style is to keep it simple. At my dinner parties, I tend to restrict drinks to champagne and wine and perhaps one great cocktail. I suggest you try all of the straightfoward cocktails included here and choose one as your "house special." "What you don't need," says friend and wine writer Anthony Dias Blue, "is people sidling up to your bar expecting a Singapore sling or a mai tai"—or both.

I know a thing or two about drinks. At age sixteen, I was a bartender, illegally, at the Olde London Fishery in Queens, New York. I was tall for my age and looked the part. Next, I had the ultimate pleasure of helping create two of New York's most spectacular bars—the Rainbow Promenade at the Rainbow Room atop Rockefeller Center, where *Sleepless in Seattle* was shot, and the Greatest Bar on Earth on the 106th floor of the now legendary Windows on the World.

When making cocktails, apply my 1-2-3 principles. 1. The best drinks are made from the best raw materials—including freshly made ice cubes. 2. Temperature is critical. Serve mixed drinks in chilled or frozen glasses, and white wine properly cooled. Keep a pitcherfull of a pre-mixed cocktail in the fridge so it doesn't inflict global warming upon your ice cubes. 3. Use the appropriate glassware. (You'll notice that unlike most cocktail recipes, which measure the alcohol in ounces or shots, I use tablespoon measures for simplicity's sake.)

Many guests are opting for sparkling water and non-alcoholic "mocktails" these days, so you'll be a great host if you offer my Cider Sparkler or Adam and Eve (page 286–287). Even a jug of freshly squeezed blood orange juice, which I call nature's Kool-Aid, shows that you have considered the needs of all your friends.

The party line on party wine is to go "big." Offer wine or bubbly in magnums, since these days there are great products that provide terrific value. Reserve your premium wines for small dinner parties and serve simple, unfussy food (that's the beauty of my 1-2-3 recipes) that won't overshadow the wine.

Also in this chapter are a few drinks that punctuate the day: a breakfast smoothie for the kids, Watermelon Lemonade for a sweltering afternoon, a frothy Hot Mocha-White Chocolate for the fireside, a warm Strawberry-Ginger Tisane to sip before bedtime. Additional drinks and warm restoratives can be found in my book *Healthy 1-2-3*.

NEW CHAMPAGNE COCKTAILS

These festive drinks can be made with any dry sparkling wine, such as Prosecco from northern Italy, cava from Spain, or an American sparkler from a good producer. Add the suggested ingredients in a champagne flute, top with bubbly, and adjust quantities to suit your taste. The classic champagne cocktail is made by placing a small sugar cube in a champagne flute, dousing it with bitters, and topping with champagne. Here are some new champagne-mixing ideas.

Champagne, or sparkling wine, plus:

- 3 tablespoons tangerine juice and a splash of Campari

- 2 tablespoons freshly squeezed pomegranate juice or blood orange juice and 1 teaspoon honey

- 1 fresh or canned lychee nut and a Midori floater

- a shot of Poire Williams and a slice of peeled pear

- a drizzle of peach schnapps and peach nectar

- a big splash of Chambord and a long thin lemon twist

COCKTAILS AND AFTER-DINNER DRINKS

MARTINI

Here's the classic. Stir or shake as desired.

> 5 tablespoons premium gin
> 1 teaspoon or more dry vermouth
> 1 large green olive

Place gin and vermouth in a mixing glass with several ice cubes. Stir or shake and strain into a chilled martini glass. Garnish with olive.

Serves 1

LEMON-TINI

> 1 lemon
> 5 tablespoons citron vodka
> 1 tablespoon Cointreau

Peel a long thin strip of lemon rind. Cut lemon in half and squeeze to get 2 tablespoons juice. Place several ice cubes in a mixing glass. Add vodka, lemon juice, and Cointreau. Shake until blended and strain into a chilled martini glass. Garnish with the twist of lemon rind.

Serves 1

SABA-TINI

One often puts sambuca in coffee, so why not put both flavors in a martini? I named this drink after the venerable restaurant of the same name in Rome.

2 teaspoons Kahlúa or another coffee liqueur
2 teaspoons sambuca or anisette
5 tablespoons premium vodka

Place several ice cubes in a mixing glass. Pour in the Kahlúa, sambuca, and vodka and stir very briskly. Strain into a chilled martini glass.

Serves 1

PIÑA COLADA

¼ cup unsweetened pineapple juice
¼ cup white rum
3 tablespoons cream of coconut

Whirl all the ingredients in a blender with crushed ice until smooth. Pour into a tall pretty glass.

Serves 1

RUBY MIST

I invented this drink for my holiday guests.

½ cup cranberry juice
1 tablespoon amaretto
1 tablespoon Cointreau

Place several ice cubes in a mixing glass. Add ingredients and stir briskly. Strain into a chilled martini glass or serve over ice in a rocks glass.

Serves 1

BIG BOURBON SOUR

This is my husband's favorite nostalgic cocktail. It hails from the three-star Market Bar & Dining Rooms at the World Trade Center, which he created with legendary restaurateur Joe Baum.

> 4 teaspoons honey
> 1 lemon
> 5 tablespoons bourbon

Put honey in a blender. Cut lemon in half and cut off 1 thin slice. Squeeze both halves to get 4 teaspoons juice. Add to honey along with bourbon and blend until honey dissolves. Add 4 ice cubes and blend on high until smooth and frothy. Pour over 3 ice cubes in a highball glass and garnish with reserved lemon slice.

Serves 1

BEACH PARTY

Limoncello is a lemon-flavored liqueur from Italy.

> 3 pounds sweet red watermelon
> 2 cups unsweetened pineapple juice
> ⅔ cup limoncello

Remove seeds from watermelon. Cut watermelon into small pieces and place in the bowl of a food processor. Process until completely smooth. Transfer to a pitcher.

Add pineapple juice, limoncello, and a pinch of salt. Stir well. Refrigerate for several hours, until very cold. Serve over ice.

Serves 6

TROPICA

> 7 juice oranges
> 3 cups guava or guanabana nectar
> ½ cup premium gin

Cut 6 oranges in half and squeeze enough juice to get 2 cups. Place in a pitcher. Add guava nectar, gin, and a pinch of salt. Stir well. Refrigerate until very cold.

When ready to serve, cut remaining orange into thin slices and put into 4 highball glasses with ice. Pour drink over ice and serve.

Serves 4

MEXI-FREEZE

6 ounces frozen lemonade concentrate
¾ cup tequila
6 tablespoons grenadine

Put ingredients in a blender with lots of crushed ice. Blend on high until thick and very smooth. Serve in a pitcher.

Optional: Moisten rims of 4 wineglasses with some grenadine or tequila and dip rims in salt to coat. Let dry. Carefully fill glasses.

Serves 4

COCTEAU

Instead of a cocktail, have a Cocteau—an after-dinner drink I invented to honor the artist.

4½ tablespoons Armagnac
1 tablespoon yellow Chartreuse
1 tablespoon crème de cassis, plus more for floating

Pour all ingredients into a mixing glass with several ice cubes. Stir vigorously and strain into a chilled cocktail glass. Float more cassis on top, letting it filter down into the drink.

Serves 1

MOLLY'S MILK

This yummy after-dinner drink was invented by bartender Dale DeGroff at New York's Rainbow Room, which our company operated from 1987 to 2000.

2 tablespoons Irish whiskey
1 tablespoon Irish Mist (liqueur made from Irish whiskey)
1½ tablespoons heavy cream, lightly whipped

Pour whiskey and Irish Mist into a mixing glass with several ice cubes. Stir briskly. Strain into a chilled cocktail glass and spoon whipped cream on top.

Serves 1

COLD DRINKS

CIDER SPARKLER

For those who want a party virtually alcohol-free. (Bitters do contain a bit of alcohol.)

> 1 small sugar cube
> Several drops of Angostura bitters
> Dry sparkling nonalcoholic apple or pear cider, chilled

Put sugar cube in a chilled champagne flute and sprinkle with bitters. Top with sparkling cider.

Serves 1

ICED GREEN TEA WITH LEMONGRASS INFUSION

> 2 stalks lemongrass
> 2 tablespoons honey
> 2 tablespoons Japanese green tea leaves

Discard tough outer leaves from lemongrass stalks. Finely chop remaining lemongrass stalks, including darker tops.

Bring 4½ cups water, chopped lemongrass, and honey to a rapid boil. Lower heat and simmer for 10 minutes.

Place green tea leaves in a heatproof pitcher. Pour lemongrass infusion over leaves and let steep for 2 minutes. If you leave it longer, tea will become bitter. Strain through a fine-mesh sieve. Refrigerate until very cold. Serve over ice.

Serves 4

MANGO FRULLATO

This tastes ultrarich and can be made with a variety of fruits, including strawberries, papaya, and fragrant honeydew.

> ¼ cup sugar
> 1 large very ripe mango
> ½ cup milk

Put sugar and 5 tablespoons water in a saucepan. Bring to a boil. Simmer for 1 to 2 minutes, until sugar dissolves. Let cool.

Peel mango and cut into 1-inch pieces. Place in a blender with milk, sugar syrup, a pinch of salt, and 6 ice cubes. Process on high until thick and very smooth. Pour into chilled wineglasses.

Serves 2

ADAM AND EVE

A highball look-alike. Pomegranate molasses is available in Middle Eastern markets.

¾ cup apple juice
½ tablespoon pomegranate molasses
Ginger ale

Put apple juice and pomegranate molasses in a highball glass. Stir. Add ice cubes and top with ginger ale. Serve with a stirrer.

Serves 1

WATERMELON LEMONADE

I invented this drink for my trainer, Thor.

3½-pound wedge of watermelon
8 large lemons
1 scant cup sugar

Remove rind and any seeds from watermelon. Cut fruit into large pieces and place in the bowl of a food processor. Process until smooth.

Cut 6 lemons in half and squeeze to get 1 cup juice. Add lemon juice to processor and process until completely liquefied. Transfer contents to a glass jar or pitcher.

Bring sugar and 3½ cups water to a boil. Cook for 1 minute, stirring often, until sugar is dissolved. Add sugar syrup to jar or pitcher and stir well. Cover and refrigerate until very cold. Serve over ice garnished with paper-thin slices of remaining lemons.

Serves 6 or more

FRESH STRAWBERRY SMOOTHIE

20 ripe medium-large strawberries
1 large ripe banana
5 tablespoons packed dark brown sugar

Wash and stem berries and dry them. Cut berries in half and place in a blender. Thickly slice banana and add to blender with sugar and 8 ice cubes.

Blend on high speed for several minutes, until smooth and thick. Pour into chilled pilsner glasses, or other tall glasses.

Serves 2 or 3

ORANGE-HONEY SMOOTHIE

4 large juice oranges
1 large ripe banana
3 tablespoons aromatic honey, such as wildflower honey

Grate rind of oranges to get 2 teaspoons zest. Set aside. Using a small knife, cut away the rest of the rind and pith from oranges. Cut orange wedges into large pieces and remove any seeds. Put oranges in a blender. Cut banana into thick slices and add to blender with honey and 8 ice cubes.

Blend on high speed for several minutes, until smooth and thick. Pour into 2 chilled wineglasses. Scatter orange zest on top.

Serves 2

CRANBERRY RICKEY

6 large limes
1 cup sugar
1 cup cranberry juice

Cut 5 limes in half and squeeze to get 1 cup juice. Put in a glass jar or pitcher.

Put sugar and 2 cups water in a small saucepan and bring to a boil. Boil for 1 to 2 minutes, until sugar dissolves. Let mixture cool and add to lime juice. Add cranberry juice to lime mixture. Cover and refrigerate until very cold.

When ready to serve, cut remaining lime into 8 wedges. Pour cranberry rickey into tall glasses and fill with ice cubes. Garnish with lime wedges.

Serves 4

ICED THAI COFFEE

Traditional Thai coffee is made with sweetened condensed milk and double-strength brewed coffee. I love it cold, shaken vigorously until frothy.

4 cups brewed espresso or very strong coffee, chilled
½ cup sweetened condensed milk, plus more for drizzling
Ground cinnamon, for sprinkling

Put coffee and condensed milk in a large jar with a tight-fitting cover. Add 12 ice cubes and cover jar tightly. Shake jar vigorously for 15 or more seconds, until mixture becomes frothy.

Immediately pour into 4 glasses over more ice cubes. Spoon the froth on top. Drizzle with a little more sweetened condensed milk and sprinkle with cinnamon.

Serves 4

ALMOND MILK WITH COFFEE ICE CUBES

3 cups brewed coffee, chilled
¼ cup orzata or almond syrup
4 cups whole milk, chilled

Put chilled coffee into 2 ice cube trays to make 24 ice cubes. Place in freezer until frozen solid.

Put 1 tablespoon orzata in each of 4 tall glasses. Add 1 cup milk to each and stir. Fill each glass with 6 coffee ice cubes. Serve immediately.

Serves 4

NEW YORK EGG CREAM

You must follow the instructions carefully and use U-Bet chocolate syrup for the true New York experience. Drink it quickly, before the froth subsides.

3 tablespoons chocolate syrup
½ cup whole milk, chilled
1 scant cup seltzer, very cold

Put chocolate syrup in the bottom of a 16- to 20-ounce chilled glass. Add milk and stir briskly to incorporate. Add seltzer in a steady stream, stirring quickly to get it frothy. Do not overstir. Serve immediately.

Serves 1

FROZEN HOT CHOCOLATE

This drink was made famous at Serendipity, a festive restaurant on New York's Upper East Side meant to bring out the kid in all of us. This drink-qua-dessert can be processed one to two hours before serving and refrigerated. It will stay ultrathick.

¾ cup sugar
½ cup unsweetened Dutch process cocoa powder
2½ cups milk

Put sugar and cocoa in a saucepan. Add ½ cup milk and cook over low heat to form a smooth paste. Slowly add remaining milk and simmer, whisking constantly, until sugar dissolves and mixture is smooth. Let cool.

Pour mixture into 2 ice cube trays (metal trays are best) and freeze until solid, about 8 hours. Remove cubes from trays and put in chilled bowl of a food processor. Add up to ½ cup water and process until mixture is thick and smooth with small slushy particles. You should be able to pour it and drink it through a straw. Serve immediately in chilled wineglasses.

Serves 4

HOT DRINKS

FRESH MINT TEA

3 tablespoons loose green or black tea leaves
1 large bunch fresh mint
¼ cup sugar

Bring 6 cups water to a boil. Put tea leaves in a large teapot. Wash mint and tear enough leaves to get 1 cup. Add mint to teapot. Add sugar and boiling water. Let steep for 10 minutes, stirring occasionally. Strain into small glasses or teacups.

Serves 4 or more

STRAWBERRY-GINGER TISANE

This is a lovely pink tisane to sip at bedtime. It also makes a refreshing quaff over ice.

1 pint very ripe strawberries
3½ tablespoons sugar
3-inch piece fresh ginger

Wash berries and remove stems. Put berries and sugar in bowl of a food processor. Process until almost smooth. Transfer strawberry puree to a large teapot.

Put 4 cups cold water in a saucepan. Peel ginger, cut into thin slices, and add to water. Bring to a boil. Lower heat, cover, and simmer for 10 minutes. Strain through a fine-mesh sieve into teapot. Cover teapot and let sit for 10 minutes. Pour through a tea strainer.

Serves 4

SPICED RED CIDER

1 quart apple juice
1 teaspoon whole cloves
2 Red Zinger tea bags

Put apple juice in a nonreactive saucepan. Add cloves and ¼ teaspoon black peppercorns. Bring to a boil. Lower heat and simmer for 10 minutes. Remove from heat and add tea bags. Let steep for 10 minutes. Strain into saucepan and heat gently before serving.

Serves 4

BREAKFAST CHOCOLATE

3 cups whole milk
⅓ cup sugar
6 ounces semisweet chocolate, in pieces

In a medium saucepan, put milk, sugar, and ⅓ cup water. Cook over medium heat, stirring often, until it just comes to a boil. Remove from heat and, using a wire whisk, whisk in chocolate until smooth. Return to heat and whisk briskly until smooth and creamy. Serve hot.

Serves 4

HOT MOCHA-WHITE CHOCOLATE

My son Jeremy loves white chocolate. I invented this for him.

4-ounce piece white chocolate, plus more for sprinkling
1½ cups half-and-half
1⅓ cups very strong brewed coffee

Chop chocolate into small pieces. Put half-and-half in a large saucepan and heat until just boiling. Lower heat and add white chocolate. Using a wire whisk, whisk constantly until chocolate melts. Whisk vigorously so that mixture comes just to a boil and gets very frothy.

Slowly add coffee and continue whisking until coffee is incorporated and mixture has a frothy head. Pour mixture into warm cups. If desired, you can grate a little additional white chocolate and sprinkle it on top. Serve immediately.

Makes 2 large mugs or 3 cups

COFFEE CANTATA

I use the procedure for Irish coffee but substitute an orange and vanilla-based Italian liqueur called Tuaca. Listen to Bach's Coffee Cantata and sip slowly.

½ cup heavy cream
1 tablespoon plus ½ cup Tuaca liqueur
4 cups strong brewed hot coffee

Using a wire whisk, whisk cream and 1 tablespoon liqueur until soft peaks form and cream is thick.

Divide remaining liqueur among 4 wineglasses. Pour 1 cup hot coffee in each glass. Spoon whipped cream over coffee to cover. Serve immediately.

Serves 4

party food
and
hors d'oeuvres

If a single term can convey the essence of entertaining, it certainly is hors d'oeuvres. Generally consumed standing upright, these morsels that precede most dinner parties are often the best part of the celebration. Sometimes they are the party—a delightful array of flavor-resonant miniatures served with plenty of drink, until no one remains standing.

According to our friend the late, great James Beard, "The hors d'oeuvre is a rite rather than a course and its duty is to enchant the eye, please the palate, and excite the flow of gastric juices . . . so that the meal to follow will seem doubly tempting and flavorful." In other words, however seductive they may be, hors d'oeuvres are meant to whet, not sate, the appetite.

Today the term applies to innumerable expressions—from canapés to crudités, from satés to sushi—and many styles of service. Hors d'oeuvres can be presented on a sideboard all at once, or passed by a waiter one by one, or both.

For an elaborate cocktail reception at home, plan a choice of three or four cold hors d'oeuvres and four hot. If the cocktail party is to become the meal, add a sideboard of two or three more items: a side of cured salmon and a simple salad may be all you will need.

For a more structured dinner party, where the bulk of the conversation is meant for the table, begin with three to four hors d'oeuvres. Or serve just one that is carefully chosen to make a big, confident statement, especially if paired with something bubbly, like a great champagne.

The distinguishing feature of all hors d'oeuvres is their small size. Some are fingerfood, where a lack of utensils establishes a direct rapport with the food. In that spirit, almost anything can become an hors d'oeuvre: thin slices of rare Double-Garlic Skirt Steak with Salsa Verde (page 179) on a sliced baguette; chilled Sweet Potato-Cider Puree (page 19) piped onto little squares of black bread; even soup, served in demitasse cups on a beautiful silver tray. Similarly, many of my simple breads (pages 81–85) can be made in the smallest size possible and served with cocktails.

Only momentary pacifiers, hors d'oeuvres can be insidious: They appease hunger, then they stimulate it. Again and again.

PARTY DIPS

BLACK HUMMUS

This idea was adapted from Paula Wolfert, queen of the Eastern Mediterranean kitchen. I named it. Scoop up with warm pita bread or crudités. You can buy black olive paste or make your own (page 234).

1 cup small green lentils, preferably French du Puy
6 tablespoons black olive paste or tapenade
1 teaspoon Cognac

Pick over and wash the lentils. Put them in a saucepan with 4 cups water. Add 2 teaspoons salt and 12 black peppercorns.

Bring to a rapid boil and lower heat to a simmer. Cover and cook for 35 minutes, or until lentils are soft but not falling apart. Drain lentils well, saving ¾ cup cooking liquid.

Put lentils in bowl of a food processor with black olive paste. Process until fairly smooth, adding as much cooking liquid as needed to make a thick puree.

Transfer to a small bowl, and add Cognac; season with salt and freshly ground black pepper to taste. Stir well. Cover and refrigerate until cold. Best served at room temperature.

Makes 2½ cups

"LOOKS LIKE CHOPPED LIVER"

This is a delicious riff on the preceding recipe that looks like chopped liver and tastes slightly mysterious. Use as a simple topping for crostini.

1 cup small green lentils, preferably French du Puy
3½ ounces skinless, boneless sardines packed in olive oil
1 clove garlic

Pick over and wash the lentils. Put them in a saucepan with 4 cups water. Add 2 teaspoons salt.

Bring to a rapid boil and lower heat to a simmer. Cover and cook for 35 mintues, or until lentils are soft but not falling apart. Drain lentils well, saving ½ cup cooking liquid.

Put lentils in bowl of a food processor with sardines and their oil. Process until fairly smooth, adding as much cooking liquid as need to make a thick paste.

Transfer to a small bowl. Peel garlic clove and push it through a garlic press. Add to lentil mixture with salt and a liberal amount of freshly ground black pepper. Stir well. Cover and refrigerate until chilled. Serve cold or at room temperature.

Makes 2½ cups

CHICKPEA-SESAME DIP

This is an unusual version of the more traditional hummus. You may use canned chickpeas or cook your own.

3 cups cooked chickpeas
1½ tablespoons dark Asian sesame oil, plus more for drizzling
2 small cloves garlic, chopped

Place chickpeas, sesame oil, and garlic in bowl of a food processor. Process until fairly smooth, slowly adding about 6 tablespoons cold water to make a thick, smooth paste. Add salt and freshly ground black pepper to taste.

Cover and refrigerate until cold. Spread thickly on a large plate or put in a bowl. Drizzle with a little additional sesame oil.

Makes 2½ cups

ZA'ATAR PESTO

You can buy za'atar, an intoxicating spice mixture, in any Middle Eastern grocery store or spice market. Mixed with grated cheese and good olive oil, the result is pestolike and great for dunking crudités, breadsticks, or garlic toasts.

½ cup za'atar
6 tablespoons freshly grated Parmesan cheese
⅔ cup extra-virgin olive oil

In a small bowl, combine za'atar and cheese. Add olive oil and mix with a spoon until blended. Add freshly ground black pepper. Transfer to a bowl and serve.

Makes 1 cup

CUCUMBER-SCALLION DIP

¾ cup sour cream
½ cucumber
1 scallion

Put sour cream in a small bowl. Peel cucumber and grate on the large holes of a box grater. Add cucumber and its juices to bowl. Finely chop white and pale green parts of scallion and add to bowl. Stir to incorporate. Add salt and freshly ground black pepper to taste. Cover and refrigerate until cold.

Makes 1 cup

ROASTED EGGPLANT-BASIL PUREE

1 large eggplant, about 1½ pounds
¼ cup prepared pesto
1 large lemon

Wash and dry eggplant. Place directly over open flame on stovetop. Or place on a baking sheet and broil. Either way, cook for a few minutes, turning several times so that the skin blisters and chars. This will impart a lovely, smoky flavor.

Preheat oven to 400°F.

Place eggplant on baking sheet (if not already on one) and bake for 50 minutes, turning once halfway through.

Remove from oven. Cut eggplant in half lengthwise and let cool for 10 minutes. Scoop out flesh and place in bowl of a food processor. Add pesto along with grated rind of the lemon. Cut lemon in half and squeeze to get 2 tablespoons juice. Add to processor and process until fairly smooth.

Transfer to a bowl and add salt and freshly ground black pepper to taste. Cover and refrigerate until cold.

Makes 1⅔ cups

BEETROOT-YOGURT DIP

You'll fall in love with the alluring taste and vibrant color of this versatile dip.

3 medium-large beets without stems, about 1 pound
1 small clove garlic, peeled
½ cup plain yogurt

Preheat oven to 400°F.

Using a vegetable peeler or small sharp knife, peel beets. Wrap beets in a loose pouch of aluminum foil, salt lightly, and tightly seal at the top. Place in a pie tin or on a rimmed baking sheet. Roast for 1½ hours, or until tender when pierced with the tip of a sharp knife. Remove from oven. Let cool for 15 minutes.

Cut beets into large chunks. Place in bowl of a food processor and process until coarsely pureed. Crush garlic and add to puree, processing briefly. Add yogurt and process for 5 seconds. The dip should be a little bit chunky. Transfer to a bowl and season with salt and freshly ground black pepper.

Cover and refrigerate until chilled.

Makes 2 cups

LEMONY TAHINA DIP

½ cup tahina (sesame paste)
2 large lemons
1 large clove garlic

Stir the tahina well before removing ½ cup from jar. Put in bowl of a food processor. Add the grated rind of 1 lemon. Cut lemons in half and squeeze to get ¼ cup juice. Add to the food processor along with the garlic, first peeled and pushed through a garlic press.

Start processing, slowly adding ⅓ to ½ cup cold water, until you have a smooth, thick puree. Transfer to a bowl. Add salt and freshly ground black pepper to taste. Add more lemon juice if needed.

Makes 1 cup

TRUFFLED WHITE BEAN PUREE

Ultracreamy and smooth, this can be used as a dip or spread. White truffle oil is available in specialty food stores and many supermarkets.

8 ounces dried small white beans
¼ cup heavy cream
2 tablespoons white truffle oil

Place beans in a large saucepan with water to cover by 1 inch. Bring to a boil and continue to boil for 2 minutes. Remove from heat. Cover pot and let sit for 1 hour.

Drain beans in a colander. Return beans to saucepan with 12 black peppercorns and add water to cover by 2 inches. Bring to a boil. Lower heat, cover, and simmer for 1 hour and 20 minutes, or until beans are tender.

Drain cooked beans, saving ¼ cup cooking liquid. Place beans in bowl of a food processor and process until smooth, adding enough cooking liquid to make a smooth, thick puree. With machine on, slowly add cream and 1 to 1½ tablespoons truffle oil. Add salt and freshly ground white pepper to taste.

Transfer mixture to a ramekin, smoothing the top. Drizzle with remaining truffle oil. Cover and refrigerate until ready to use. Let sit at room temperature for 15 minutes before serving.

Makes 2¾ cups

BAR CHEESES

BASIL BLUE CHEESE

1 large bunch fresh basil
2 cups low-fat cottage cheese
4 ounces blue cheese

Wash basil and dry thoroughly. Chop enough to yield ½ cup loosely packed.

Place both cheeses in bowl of a food processor and process until just blended. Add basil and process until smooth. Season with salt and freshly ground black pepper. Refrigerate.

Makes 2 cups

CLASSIC PIMIENTO CHEESE

1 pound very sharp yellow cheddar cheese
6½-ounce jar pimientos
⅔ cup light mayonnaise

Remove rind from cheese, if any. Cut cheese into small pieces and put in bowl of a food processor. Add pimientos, including juice, and process until well blended.

Add mayonnaise, ¼ teaspoon salt, and ⅛ teaspoon freshly ground white pepper.

Process until smooth as possible. Transfer mixture to a bowl. Cover and refrigerate for at least 30 minutes before serving.

Makes 3½ cups

PESTO MASCARPONE

8 ounces mascarpone
6 tablespoons prepared pesto
3 tablespoons dry vermouth

Put mascarpone and pesto in bowl of a food processor. Process briefly. Add vermouth and process until mixture is smooth and creamy. Do not overprocess.

Transfer mixture to a bowl and add salt and freshly ground black pepper to taste.

Stir and cover. Refrigerate for several hours. This mixture improves with age and will keep for up to 1 week.

Makes 1⅓ cups

ROASTED GARLIC SAPSAGO

This distinctive pale jade spread will have people guessing what it is, then going back for more. The unusual flavor is from sapsago, a pungent, low-fat grating cheese that's flavored with clover. You may substitute an aged, dry goat cheese.

2 large heads garlic
6 ounces sapsago cheese
16 ounces cream cheese, softened

Preheat oven to 400°F.

Cut ¼ inch from tops of garlic, exposing all the cloves. Wrap each head loosely in a 6-inch square of aluminum foil. Bake in a pie tin for 1¼ hours.

Remove garlic from foil. Let rest for 10 minutes and then squeeze out pulp. You should have approximately ¼ cup.

Grate sapsago on the medium holes of a box grater. Place softened cream cheese in bowl of an electric mixer. Add garlic pulp, grated sapsago, and 2 tablespoons cold water. Beat on medium speed until ingredients are incorporated and cheese is light and fluffy. Spoon into a bowl and refrigerate for at least 30 minutes before serving.

Makes about 3 cups

RICOTTA *RIFATTA*

Italians call this "ricotta re-made" because it is mixed with creamy Gorgonzola cheese and cel-ery leaves or parsley. I chose celery: often underused, its leaves add a distinctive flavor and its stalks are perfect for dipping. Gorgonzola dolce, also sold as Dolcelatte cheese, is a soft, blue-veined cheese available in specialty cheese shops. You can substitute regular imported Gorgonzola, which is sharper and saltier, if you prefer.

4 ounces Gorgonzola dolce
1¾ cups ricotta cheese
1 bunch celery

Put both cheeses in bowl of a food processor. Wash celery and pat dry. Pick off enough leaves from celery to get ¼ packed cup. Add to cheeses and process until mixture is smooth. Add salt and freshly ground black pepper. Cover and refrigerate for a minimum of 1 hour.

Cut celery stalks into sticks to be used for dipping. Garnish cheese with a few darker celery leaves.

Makes 2½ cups

ROQUEFORT-ARMAGNAC

This ages well covered with Armagnac-soaked cheesecloth.

1 pound imported Roquefort cheese
2 sticks (½ pound) unsalted butter, at room temperature
2 or more tablespoons Armagnac or Cognac

Cut Roquefort and butter into pieces. Place in bowl of a food processor and process until smooth. Add Armagnac and salt and pepper to taste. Process until incorporated. Transfer mixture to a crock. Cover and refrigerate for 1 day. Can be used for up to 2 weeks.

Makes 3 cups

BAR NUTS

MY DAD'S DEVILED PECANS

My Dad—football star (first touchdown 1943 Sugar Bowl for University of Tennessee), Washington Redskins draftee, B-29 pilot in World War II—always loved these.

2 tablespoons unsalted butter
1 tablespoon Worcestershire sauce, plus more for drizzling
2 cups large pecan halves, about 9½ ounces

Preheat oven to 350°F.

In a large nonstick skillet, melt butter and add Worcestershire sauce. Add pecans; season with a pinch of salt and freshly ground black pepper. Stir and cook over medium heat for a few minutes, until nuts are coated.

Transfer pecans to a rimmed baking sheet and bake for 10 minutes, stirring often. Drain on paper towels. Sprinkle with salt, pepper, and additional Worcestershire sauce to taste. Let cool.

Makes 2 cups

GOLDEN ALMONDS WITH DILL

¼ cup garlic olive oil (page 228)
2 cups whole blanched almonds, about 10 ounces
1 bunch fresh dill

Heat garlic oil in a large nonstick skillet, add almonds, and cook over medium-high heat for 1 minute. Finely chop enough dill to yield ¼ cup and add to pan. Cook for several minutes, stirring constantly until almonds are golden and dill gets crispy. Add salt and freshly ground black pepper to taste. Drain on paper towels. Garnish with more chopped dill.

Makes 2 cups

GLAZED WALNUTS

4 cups shelled walnut halves, about 16 ounces
½ cup sugar
Vegetable or peanut oil, for frying

In a large saucepan, bring 8 cups water to a boil. Add walnuts, return to a boil, and cook for 1 minute. Rinse nuts in a colander. Drain well. Transfer to a small bowl and toss thoroughly with sugar.

In a heavy nonstick skillet, heat 1 inch oil to 350°F. Add half of the walnuts and fry them for 3 to 4 minutes, until golden brown and crisp. Be careful not to let them get too browned. Remove nuts with a slotted spoon and place in a coarse-mesh sieve to drain. Sprinkle lightly with salt and mix gently to separate the pieces. Spread on a sheet of wax paper to cool.

Repeat with remaining boiled nuts.

Makes 4 cups

COLD HORS D'OEUVRES

DUTCH CHEESE TRUFFLES

Here's a great use for leftover cheese. They have an unusual texture and lots of flavor.

2 sticks (½ pound) unsalted butter, at room temperature
2 cups shredded cheese (such as sharp cheddar, aged Gouda, or fontina), about 6 ounces
Choice of coating: fresh, fine pumpernickel breadcrumbs; sweet Hungarian or smoked paprika; poppy seeds; finely chopped parsley or tarragon; toasted sesame seeds; or dried mint leaves

Cut butter into small pieces and place in bowl of an electric mixer. Beat until smooth. Add cheese and blend. Add salt and freshly ground black pepper to taste. Refrigerate until just firm but still pliable, about 30 minutes.

Shape into ¾-inch balls. Roll thoroughly in your choice of coating. Refrigerate until 20 minutes before serving time.

Makes about 34

THREE SHRIMP-IN-A-SNAP

PERFECT POACHED SHRIMP

Prepare 2 pounds very large shrimp according to the chilled shrimp recipe on page 123, or buy very large, cooked shrimp from a good fish store. Serve with Spicy Cocktail Sauce (page 234) or with a flavored mayonnaise (pages 230–231).

WASABI-STUFFED SHRIMP

32 very large shrimp, about 2 pounds
8 ounces cream cheese, at room temperature
2 tablespoons wasabi powder

Prepare shrimp as described in the chilled shrimp recipe on page 123, or buy cooked shrimp from your fish store. Peel shrimp, leaving tails intact. Chill shrimp well.

Place cream cheese in bowl of a food processor. In a small bowl, mix wasabi with 1½ to 2 tablespoons cold water to form a thick paste. Add to food processor with ¼ teaspoon salt, or more to taste. Process until smooth.

Split each shrimp down the back, cutting almost all the way through. Using a small spoon or pastry bag, stuff each with 1½ teaspoons wasabi cream cheese. Press sides gently together and refrigerate until ready to serve.

Makes 32

PICKLED PINK SHRIMP

Pickled ginger is available in Asian food markets and many supermarkets.

32 very large shrimp, about 2 pounds
1 bunch fresh cilantro
1 cup pickled ginger, juice included

Prepare shrimp as described in the chilled shrimp recipe on page 123, or buy cooked shrimp from your fish store. Peel shrimp, leaving tails intact. Chill shrimp well.

Wash and dry cilantro. Remove leaves. Split each shrimp down the back, cutting almost all the way through. Fill with small pieces of pickled ginger and cilantro leaves. Press sides gently together. Place ginger juice in a small ramekin for dunking. Serve with chilled shrimp.

Makes 32

CELERY BITES

8 ounces cream cheese
2-ounce can rolled anchovies with capers
1 leafy bunch celery

Place cream cheese in bowl of a food processor. Drain anchovies and capers. Process with cream cheese until smooth. Refrigerate until ready to use.

Remove outer stalks from celery and save for another use. Separate remaining stalks, wash well, and pat dry. Mince enough of the celery leaves to get ¼ cup. Add 2 tablespoons to the cheese with freshly ground black pepper. Cut celery stalks into 1½-inch lengths. Using a small knife, fill the stalks with cheese mixture, mounding it on top. Sprinkle with remaining chopped celery leaves.

Makes about 32

EDAMAME WITH SESAME SALT AND CURRY SALT

Edamame, or fresh soybeans in their pods, have recently become a rage. More importantly, they are now available in supermarkets, sometimes fresh, generally frozen. They are nutritious, delicious, and unexpected when served with these flavored dipping salts. To eat them simply dip the pod in the salt, pop the pod into your mouth, scrape out the beans with your teeth, and then discard the pod.

1 pound edamame, fresh or frozen
¼ cup sesame seeds
2 tablespoons good-quality curry powder

Bring a medium pot of heavily salted water to a boil. Add the edamame and return to a boil. Reduce heat to medium and cook 5 minutes for fresh and 8 to 10 minutes for frozen. The pods should be a bright green and the beans inside firm but tender. Drain in a colander under cold running water, then pat dry with paper towels. Cover and refrigerate until ready to use.

Place sesame seeds in small nonstick skillet. Cook over medium heat for about 30 seconds, stirring constantly, until toasted and golden brown. Let cool completely. Place in a spice or coffee grinder with 1 teaspoon salt. Briefly process until finely ground. Transfer to a small dish.

Mix curry powder and 2½ teaspoons salt in a separate small dish. Serve edamame with the bowls of sesame salt and curry salt for dipping.

Serves 8

RADISHES WITH WHIPPED GOAT CHEESE AND TOASTED CUMIN

12 or more round red medium radishes, with stems and leaves attached
4 ounces fresh goat cheese
1 tablespoon cumin seeds

Wash radishes and radish leaves. Dry well. Cut leaves from radishes, leaving 1 inch of stem attached to each radish. Remove any roots.

Scatter radish leaves on a small platter. Cut radishes in half lengthwise and arrange cut side up on radish greens.

Place goat cheese in the bowl of a food processor with 2 teaspoons cold water. Process until smooth and thick, being careful not to overprocess.

Using a butter knife, thickly spread cheese on cut side of each radish, or pipe cheese through a pastry bag. Refrigerate until ready to use.

In a small nonstick skillet, toast cumin seeds over medium heat until they begin to darken and exude a fragrant aroma. Add ¼ teaspoon salt and mix well. Sprinkle each radish with cumin-salt mixture and serve.

Makes 24 pieces

ENDIVE SPOONS WITH SUN-DRIED TOMATO AND ORANGE SPREAD

6 ounces sun-dried tomatoes packed in oil
3 medium oranges
4 medium Belgian endives

Drain oil from sun-dried tomatoes and reserve it. Place drained tomatoes in bowl of a food processor.

Grate rind of 1 orange to yield ½ teaspoon grated zest. Add zest to tomatoes. Using a small sharp knife, cut away rind and white pith from 1 orange. Cut orange into large chunks and add to tomatoes. Process tomatoes and orange pieces until thick and smooth. Add salt and freshly ground black pepper to taste. Add a little of the reserved oil to make the puree smoother but still thick. Transfer to a small bowl.

Wash endives and dry. Cut off a 3½-inch-long piece from the top of each endive and separate them into leaves. Save the bottoms of the endives for another use. Place the endive "spoons" on a platter. Place ½ tablespoon tomato-orange spread on each leaf near the bottom.

Cut away rind and pith from remaining oranges. Cut in between membranes to release orange segments. Cut segments in half lengthwise and place 1 piece on top of the spread in each endive leaf.

Makes about 32

PROSCIUTTO AND DRUNKEN MELON BROCHETTES

These sweet-and-salty brochettes (the French word for "skewer") also can be made with chunks of mango wrapped with bresaola, or air-dried beef.

1 ripe cantaloupe or honeydew melon
1½ cups white port
9 thin slices prosciutto

Cut melon in half through the equator and discard seeds. Using a large melon baller, scoop out 36 or more melon balls. Place them in a nonreactive bowl and douse them with port. Cover and refrigerate for 1 to 2 hours.

Drain melon balls and pat dry. Cut each prosciutto slice in half across the width and then along the length to get 4 ribbon-shaped pieces. Wrap each melon ball with a piece of prosciutto.

Place 1 wrapped melon balls on each of 36 short bamboo skewers. Place skewers on a platter. Sprinkle with coarsely ground black pepper and serve.

Makes 36

ROASTED PEPPERS WITH FETA AND HONEY

This hors d'oeuvres tickles all the taste buds and goes surprisingly well with red wine. It's best to roast your own peppers, but you can use jarred roasted peppers in a pinch.

2 large red bell peppers, or 12-ounce jar roasted peppers
8-ounce block of feta cheese
¼ cup honey

Preheat the broiler.

Wash peppers and pat dry. Put whole peppers on a rimmed baking sheet and broil until skins are very black and blistered, about 2 to 3 minutes on each side. Immediately seal peppers in a paper bag to steam for 10 minutes. Remove peppers and peel away all charred skin. If using jarred peppers, pat dry.

Cut peppers into 1 by ½-inch pieces. Cut cheese into ⅛-inch-thick slices that are as long as the pieces of pepper. Sandwich a piece of cheese in between 2 pieces of peppers. Trim until even. Skewer with a toothpick. Drizzle with honey and season with coarsely ground black pepper.

Makes about 24

SMOKED SALMON *ROULADES*

1 pound smoked salmon, cut into 8 slices
1 cup chive cream cheese
6 kirby cucumbers, about 1 inch in diameter

Lay salmon slices flat. Thickly spread each slice with 2 tablespoons cream cheese. Roll up jelly-roll style into even 1-inch-thick rolls. Wrap each roll tightly in plastic wrap, twisting the ends to make compact sausage-shaped packages. Refrigerate for at least 1 hour to firm the *roulades*.

Wash cucumbers and dry well. Trim the ends and cut into ¼-inch-thick rounds. Unwrap the *roulades* and slice them into ¼-inch-thick rounds. Place 1 on each cucumber slice and serve.

Makes about 32

HOMEMADE GRAVLAX

Serve this lovely Swedish-cured salmon with Swedish Mustard Sauce (page 234) and thin slices of pumpernickel bread or lightly toasted brioche. If cut into thick fillets, gravlax also can be grilled or pan-seared briefly, keeping the center rare.

3-pound side of salmon, preferably the thickest part, skin on
⅓ cup sugar
2 large bunches fresh dill

Using tweezers, remove all of the small bones from the salmon. Pat the fish dry. In a small bowl, mix together sugar, ⅓ cup kosher salt, and 2 tablespoons coarsely ground black pepper. Cover entire cut surface of salmon, rubbing mixture into the flesh. Finely chop enough dill to get 1¼ cups and pack on top of salmon to cover completely. Wrap fish in plastic wrap and put it, skin side down, in a roasting pan or shallow casserole large enough to accommodate it comfortably.

Weight fish down with another pan filled with heavy cans. Refrigerate for 48 to 72 hours, draining liquid from the package several times.

Before serving, scrape off the dill and seasonings. Carve salmon into very thin slices on the bias, just as though you were cutting smoked salmon. Finely chop more fresh dill to get ⅓ cup and scatter on the gravlax.

Serves 8 to 10

GOAT CHEESE AND SMOKED SALMON WAFERS

3 8-inch flour tortillas
8 ounces herbed goat cheese
8 ounces sliced smoked salmon

Preheat oven to 375°F.

Using a 2-inch round cookie cutter, cut out 10 rounds from each tortilla to get a total of 30. Place on a rimmed baking sheet and bake for 8 to 9 minutes, turning halfway through baking. Remove from oven and let cool.

Put goat cheese in bowl of an electric mixer and beat until smooth and creamy.

Spread cheese on each tortilla wafer to cover. Using the same 2-inch cookie cutter, cut out 30 rounds from the smoked salmon and top each wafer with a round of smoked salmon. Dust each with coarsely ground white pepper. Alternatively, you can put the smoked salmon directly on the wafer and top with a little mound of goat cheese.

Makes 30

OYSTERS WITH SHERRY-PEPPER MIGNONETTE

Mignonette is a peppery, vinegar-based sauce traditional with raw oysters in France. I like to experiment with vinegars, including malt, rice, champagne, and the one below.

24 bluepoint oysters in their shell
½ cup sherry vinegar, preferably Spanish
4 shallots

Open the oysters, using an oyster knife, or have your fishmonger do it for you. Keep chilled.

In a small bowl, mix vinegar and 2 tablespoons cold water together. Peel shallots and very finely mince to get 2 tablespoons. Add to vinegar with 1 teaspoon very coarsely ground black pepper and a pinch of salt.

Serve chilled oysters with mignonette sauce for dipping.

Serves 4

SINGING CLAMS

Glamorous and instantaneous, especially if you have your fishmonger gently pry the clams open for you. Pickled ginger can be found in the refrigerated section of Asian food stores and most supermarkets. Try these with a glass of chilled sake.

> 36 littleneck or other small clams
> 4 tablespoons wasabi powder
> ½ cup pickled ginger, juice included

If your fishmonger has pried the clamshells open a bit, do not open them completely. Lay them flat in a container so that you do not lose any of the clam juices.

In a small bowl, mix wasabi powder with 2 tablespoons cold water, stirring to form a thick paste.

Remove the top shell of each clam and discard. With a small sharp knife, detach each clam from the bottom shell so it can be eaten easily. Top each clam with 2 thin slices of pickled ginger and a small dollop of wasabi. Drizzle a little pickled ginger juice over each clam.

Arrange clams on seaweed that has been blanched and chilled, or on a layer of very coarse salt.

Serves 6

GRAPES IN CHÈVRE

In the early 1980s in New York City, there was a trend-setting restaurant that we all loved called the Soho Charcuterie. The owners, Francine Scherer and Madeline Poley, used to serve this hors d'oeuvre at their upscale cocktail parties.

> 1 cup pecans
> 24 large seedless green grapes
> 6 ounces goat cheese

Put pecans in a small nonstick skillet and cook over medium heat for 1 to 2 minutes, stirring constantly until they are toasted. Let cool and then chop them finely.

Wash grapes and dry them well. Let goat cheese come to room temperature. Place about 2 teaspoons of the cheese in the palm of your hand, flatten it, and then gently press a grape down into it; the cheese should completely surround the grape. Roll the cheese ball around in your palm to make it smooth and round. Roll the ball in the chopped pecans until it is completely covered.

Repeat with the remaining grapes. Refrigerate for at least 30 minutes before serving.

Serves 6

CHICKEN LIVER AND SUN-DRIED TOMATO PÂTÉ

8 ounces sun-dried tomatoes in oil
1 pound fresh chicken livers
2 medium yellow onions

Set aside one third of the sun-dried tomatoes and 1 tablespoon of their oil in a small bowl for later use.

Wash chicken livers and dry them with paper towels. In a large nonstick skillet, heat 2 to 3 tablespoons of the oil from the tomatoes. Finely chop 1 onion and add to oil. Cook over medium-high heat for 5 minutes, until just soft. Add chicken livers and cook over medium heat, stirring often, for about 10 minutes, or until livers are just firm and no longer pink.

Transfer livers, onion, all the pan juices, and remaining two thirds of the sun-dried tomatoes to bowl of a food processor. Process until smooth; be careful not to overprocess.

Peel remaining onion and cut it in half. Grate on the large holes of a box grater to get 1 heaping tablespoon grated onion and juice, or a little more to taste. Add to livers with salt and freshly ground black pepper to taste and briefly process again.

Transfer pâté to a 2-cup soufflé dish, smoothing the top with a knife. Cover with plastic wrap so it touches surface of pâté. Refrigerate for 30 minutes.

Place reserved sun-dried tomatoes and their oil in clean bowl of a food processor, and process to form a smooth paste. Spread evenly over the chilled pâté. Cover and refrigerate until ready to serve.

Makes 1²/₃ cups

WARM AND ROOM-TEMPERATURE HORS D'OEUVRES

WINE-BAKED OLIVES

A great use for that leftover red wine.

1 pound kalamata olives
½ cup dry red wine
¼ cup extra-virgin olive oil

Preheat oven to 350°F.

Put olives in a small saucepan and cover with water. Bring to a boil and continue boiling for 1 minute. Drain well in a colander.

Put parboiled olives, wine, and olive oil in an ovenproof dish large enough to accommodate olives in 1 layer. Bake for 30 minutes, shaking several times during baking. Much of the liquid will evaporate during baking. Serve warm.

Makes about 85

TARTINES

Think of these as elegant cheese canapés that you can put together in a jiffy. Tartine is the French word for a slice of bread covered with any suitable substance of spreadable consistency, so make sure the cheese is at room temperature.

1 narrow loaf crusty French or Italian bread
1 pound triple-cream cheese, such as Saint Andre, boursault, Brillat-Savarin, or Explorateur, at room temperature
Choice of topping: chopped toasted pecans; herbes de Provence; coarsely cracked coriander seeds; shaved truffles or truffle oil; or wildflower honey

Preheat the broiler.

Slice bread in half horizontally as if you were making a hero sandwich. Cut each half into 1¼-inch-wide strips. You should have about 20 pieces. Place on a baking sheet about 8 inches from the heat source. Toast until golden, but do not let the bread brown.

Slather cheese, rind and all, on each slice. Sprinkle with the toppings of your choice.

Makes about 20 pieces

ROASTED EGGPLANT WITH CILANTRO COULIS

These eggplant wedges can be made several hours ahead of time and reheated, covered, in a 500°F oven for five minutes. Serve with slices of toasted baguette.

1 large eggplant, about 1 pound
6 tablespoons garlic olive oil (page 228)
1 large bunch fresh cilantro

Wash eggplant and pat dry. Remove green top and discard. Cut eggplant lengthwise into 8 wedges, or if it's very wide, 10 wedges. Cut each wedge in half crosswise. You will have 16 or 20 pieces. Place in a bowl and drizzle with 2 tablespoons garlic oil, ½ teaspoon salt, and freshly ground black pepper. Toss and let sit for 1 hour.

Preheat oven to 500°F. Place eggplant in 1 layer on a rimmed baking sheet. Bake for 15 minutes; turn and bake 10 minutes longer, or until eggplant is soft and browned but still retains its shape.

While eggplant is baking, make the coulis: Wash and dry cilantro. Remove leaves. Place remaining garlic oil, 3 tablespoons cold water, and ½ cup packed cilantro leaves in bowl of a food processor. Process until smooth and thick. Add salt and pepper to taste. Transfer eggplant to a warm platter and pour coulis over it. Garnish with additional cilantro leaves.

Serves 4

FRIED CHICKPEAS WITH WALNUT OIL AND SAGE

As addictive as popcorn, but much more sophisticated. Buy whole dried sage leaves from a Middle Eastern food store for the most flavorful results.

> 3 cups cooked chickpeas, dried or canned
> ¼ cup walnut oil, plus more for drizzling
> 3 tablespoons dried sage leaves

If using freshly cooked chickpeas, pat dry with paper towels. If using canned beans, rinse them under cold running water and pat dry.

In a large nonstick skillet, heat walnut oil until hot but not smoking. Add chickpeas and fry for several minutes, stirring occasionally, until crisp. Do not overcook; you want the chickpeas to be creamy on the inside. Add sage leaves, ½ teaspoon kosher salt, and freshly ground black pepper to taste. Continue to cook for 1 to 2 minutes. Drizzle with a little more oil if chickpeas look dry.

Let cool a few minutes before serving.

Makes 3 cups

WARM ROQUEFORT BISCUITS

Sometimes I serve these tender-crumbed, full-flavored biscuits with champagne before a dinner party. They're fun to make: The dough is rolled into a log, briefly chilled, then cut with dental floss before baking.

> 8 ounces imported Roquefort cheese, at room temperature
> 8 tablespoons (1 stick) unsalted butter, chilled
> 1½ cups or more self-rising flour

Preheat oven to 350°F.

Crumble cheese into the bowl of an electric mixer. Add butter, cut into small pieces, and mix for 1 minute until well blended. Add flour and 1 to 2 tablespoons cold water; season with freshly ground black pepper. Mix on medium speed until dough comes away from the sides of bowl. Do not overmix; dough should be firm and not at all sticky. Add a little more flour if necessary.

Lightly dust a flat surface with flour, and using your hands, roll dough into a 1-inch-diameter log. Wrap log in wax paper and refrigerate for 30 minutes. Using dental floss or a sharp thin-bladed knife, slice dough into about 20 ½-inch-thick rounds.

Place rounds, flat side down, on an ungreased baking sheet and bake for 20 minutes. Serve warm.

Makes about 20

TAPAS-STYLE SHRIMP

Serve these tapas as hot and spicy as you'd like, on little plates with small forks or toothpicks. A glass of dry sherry is the best accompaniment. Canned chipotle peppers in adobo can be found in most supermarkets.

36 medium shrimp in their shells, about 1 pound
6 tablespoons unsalted butter
2 heaping tablespoons chopped chipotle peppers in adobo

Peel shrimp, leaving tails intact.

Melt butter in a large nonstick skillet over medium heat. Do not let it brown. Add chipotle peppers and shrimp, and increase heat to high. Stirring constantly, cook shrimp until just firm and opaque, about 4 minutes. Do not overcook. Sprinkle with salt and toss. Put shrimp and sauce on small plates. Serve hot.

Serves 6

ASPARAGETTES

Slim asparagus spears, blanched, then rolled in tissue-thin phyllo, look a lot like cigarettes—hence, the name. You can purchase basil olive oil at many supermarkets.

36 medium-thin asparagus spears
6 12 by 17-inch sheets phyllo dough
½ cup basil olive oil, or other flavored olive oil (page 228)

Cut the top 3 inches off each asparagus spear. Reserve the rest for another use. Bring a medium pot of salted water to a boil. Add asparagus tips and cook for 3 to 4 minutes, until they are bright green and just beginning to get tender. Drain immediately under cold water and pat dry. You may prepare recipe up to this point and refrigerate up to 6 hours. Let asparagus come to room temperature before rolling in phyllo.

Preheat oven to 375°F.

Cut each sheet of phyllo into 12 rectangles by cutting in half through the length, then cutting these across the width into 6 strips. You will have 72 rectangles. Using a pastry brush, moisten half the rectangles with olive oil. Place an unoiled piece of phyllo on top of each oiled rectangle.

Season room-temperature asparagus with salt and pepper. Place an asparagus tip on the edge of each stack of phyllo and roll up tightly, brushing with oil as you go. Brush each phyllo roll with more oil and sprinkle with salt. Place on a baking sheet and bake for 15 minutes, turning twice during baking. Remove from oven when pastry is crisp and golden. Serve immediately.

Makes 36

ROSEMARY FRICO

Frico croccante, or cheese crisps, hail from the Friuli region of Italy. Traditionally they are made with a cheese called Montasio, but very finely grated Parmigiano-Reggiano works well (make sure the cheese is grated like fine sand, not shredded). Frico can be made larger and served atop a simple salad or alongside a great bowl of soup. Small, they are the perfect partner for a glass of something bubbly.

1 tablespoon unsalted butter
1 cup very finely grated Parmigiano-Reggiano
1½ tablespoons very finely minced fresh rosemary

Melt ½ tablespoon butter in a 12-inch nonstick skillet. Let it get foamy but not brown.

Arrange 8 1-tablespoon measures of grated cheese around the skillet and press to flatten into rounds. Evenly sprinkle each round with ⅛ teaspoon rosemary. Over medium heat, cook for 3 minutes, and when the edges begin to turn golden, carefully turn them over with a spatula. Cook 2 minutes longer, until the cheese is golden and crisp. Do not let the crisps brown or they will taste bitter. They will harden as they cool.

Remove from pan and transfer to a plate lined with paper towels. Repeat with remaining butter, cheese, and rosemary. Serve warm or at room temperature.

Makes 16

BRIE CROUSTADES WITH SALMON CAVIAR

These delectable bite-size puffs act as warm pillows for chilled caviar.

½ pound double-cream Brie cheese, chilled
3 extra-large eggs
½ cup salmon caviar

Cut rind from cheese using a small sharp knife. Discard rind. Let cheese sit at room temperature for 30 minutes.

Preheat oven to 350°F.

Put eggs in bowl of a food processor. Cut cheese into 1-inch pieces and add to eggs. Process until very smooth and thick, about 1 minute.

Coat 2 mini-muffin tins (each with 12 cups about 1¼-inches in diameter) with nonstick cooking spray. Spoon 1 tablespoon cheese mixture into each cup. Bake for 9 to 10 minutes, until croustades are golden and puffed.

Let croustades sit for 1 minute, then remove by turning muffin tins over. Top each slightly warm or room temperature croustade with a dollop of caviar. Serve immediately.

Makes 24

GRAPE LEAVES WITH SMOKED MOZZARELLA

These crispy little packages pack a flavor wallop in just a few bites.

> 16 large grape leaves, packed in brine
> 1 pound smoked mozzarella
> ¼ cup extra-virgin olive oil

Separate grape leaves and rinse under cold water. Pat each one dry with a paper towel. Cut grape leaves in half from tips down through stems. Remove stems and any large veins. Cut cheese into rectangles approximately 2 inches by ¾ inches; they should be ⅓ inch thick.

Wrap each piece of cheese in a halved grape leaf, folding the sides in like an envelope and rolling up leaf to cover cheese completely.

Heat olive oil in a large nonstick skillet. Cook cheese packages over medium-high heat for 1 or 2 minutes on each side, until grape leaves get crispy and cheese begins to melt. Remove with a spatula. Serve warm.

Makes 32

SOCCA BLINI WITH OLIVE CAVIAR

Socca, an omnipresent snack in Nice, is made from chickpea flour, olive oil, salt, and water. Although traditionally prepared in a wood-fired oven, in this recipe I use the batter to form a blini, or pancake, quickly cooked in a skillet. Tapenade or olivada, a black olive paste available everywhere these days, is my "caviar," but you can make your own (see page 234). Real caviar, such as osetra or sevruga, also can be substituted.

> 1 cup chickpea flour
> 6 tablespoons extra-virgin olive oil
> ⅓ cup tapenade or black olive paste

Sift flour into a bowl. Make a well. Whisk in ½ cup water to form a smooth, thick paste. Add another ¼ cup water, 2 tablespoons olive oil, ½ teaspoon salt, and freshly ground black pepper to taste. Stir until very smooth. Cover and let sit for 20 minutes.

In a large nonstick skillet, heat 2 tablespoons olive oil. When it begins to bubble, add single tablespoons of batter to make little pancakes. When batter has set, after about 1 minute, turn with a spatula and cook 1 to 2 minutes longer, or until golden. You may turn again for a few seconds to make sure both sides are golden. Add more oil and continue cooking blini.

Using a spatula, transfer blini to a warm platter and cover with aluminum foil. Keep warm in oven for up to 10 minutes. Top each with a dollop of tapenade and serve warm or at room temperature.

Makes about 24

SCALLOPS-IN-SHIITAKES

20 shiitake mushrooms, about 5 ounces, each 1¼ inches in diameter
20 sea scallops, about 1 pound, each 1 inch in diameter
½ cup prepared pesto

Preheat oven to 450°F.

Remove mushroom stems and discard. Wipe mushrooms with damp cloth. Let dry.

Sprinkle inside of mushroom caps very lightly with salt and freshly ground black pepper. Fit a scallop into each mushroom cap. If scallops are too thick, slice in half through the equator. Scallops should fit snugly inside mushroom cap and not rise above the rims. Top each stuffed mushroom with 1 to 1½ teaspoons pesto. Place on a rimmed baking sheet and put several tablespoons of water in bottom of pan. Bake for 8 minutes, or until scallops turn opaque and mushrooms are hot. Serve immediately.

Makes 20

FINGERLING POTATOES WITH ROASTED GARLIC AND BRIE FONDUE

These potatoes look like short stubby fingers and are perfect for hors d'oeuvres. You may use very small new potatoes if you prefer.

1 very large head garlic
18 fingerling potatoes, about 1½ pounds
12 ounces Brie cheese, chilled

Preheat oven to 400°F.

Wrap garlic in a pouch of aluminum foil, crimped tightly at the top to seal. Place in a pie tin and bake for 1 hour and 15 minutes. Remove from oven and cool.

Prepare potatoes 25 minutes before you're going to serve them. Scrub potatoes, but do not peel them. Place in a large pot of salted water and bring to a boil. Lower heat and cook for 15 to 20 minutes, or until tender when pierced with a sharp knife. Drain in a colander.

Cut rind off cheese and cut cheese into small cubes. Put in small heavy saucepan over low heat with 1 tablespoon water. Stir constantly until cheese melts. Cut roasted garlic in half through the equator and squeeze out 2 to 3 tablespoons pulp. Add to melted Brie and mix well, stirring over low heat until garlic is incorporated. The fondu can be made ahead and gently reheated.

Cut warm potatoes in half lengthwise. Place on a platter or in a shallow casserole and spoon hot cheese sauce over top. Serve immediately.

Serves 6

EDAM-UP QUESADILLAS

The key here is to use very chunky, very thick salsa, whether fresh or jarred.

> 8 ounces Edam cheese, in 1 piece
> 12-ounce jar thick and chunky salsa
> 8 8-inch flour tortillas

Remove rind from cheese. Grate cheese on the large holes of a box grater and set aside.

Put salsa in a fine-mesh sieve over a bowl. Let sit for 20 minutes to extract as much liquid as possible.

To assemble quesadillas: Place a tortilla on a flat surface. Distribute one quarter of the grated cheese on top. Dab with one quarter of the drained salsa. Cover with another tortilla, pressing down tightly. Repeat with remaining tortillas to get 4 quesadillas.

Preheat oven to 400°F.

Heat a large nonstick skillet over medium heat. Place quesadillas in skillet, one at a time, and cook for 3 minutes, pressing down lightly with a spatula. Turn over and cook 2 to 3 minutes more, until tortillas are crisp and golden on both sides. Transfer to a rimmed baking sheet and keep warm in the oven until all the quesadillas are cooked. Cut each into 6 wedges. Serve immediately.

Serves 6

CAMEMBERT BAKED IN A BOX

Here's a whimsical recipe in which good Camembert is baked in the little round wooden box it comes in. Its splendid creaminess oozes onto slices of warm shallot-rubbed toasts.

> 1 small baguette
> 8-ounce Camembert cheese in its box
> 2 large shallots

Preheat oven to 425°F.

Thinly slice baguette on a slight angle.

Remove cheese from box and peel off wrapping. Return cheese to box and replace top. Place box in center of a rimmed baking sheet. Bake for 10 minutes then quickly add baguette slices to baking sheet. Bake 10 minutes longer.

Remove from oven. Cut shallots in half and rub cut side of shallots on each warm toast. Place cheese, still in box, on a plate and surround with shallot-rubbed toasts. Remove cover and serve immediately.

Serves 4

PROSCIUTTO-WRAPPED SHRIMP STICKS

24 medium-large shrimp, about 1 pound, peeled
6 ounces thinly sliced prosciutto
3 tablespoons olive oil or garlic olive oil (page 228), plus more for drizzling

Soak 8 6-inch bamboo skewers in cold water for 15 minutes.

Preheat the broiler. Uncurl shrimp and neatly and snugly wrap a small slice of prosciutto around each shrimp to cover completely.

Skewer 3 shrimp packages on each skewer so that they are parallel to one another and closely snuggled together. Using a pastry brush, coat prosciutto-wrapped shrimp with olive oil on all sides. Place under broiler for 20 seconds. Turn shrimp over and broil 20 to 30 seconds longer. Do not overcook. Shrimp will turn opaque and be just firm to the touch. Drizzle with extra olive oil, if desired. Sprinkle with coarsely ground black pepper. Serve immediately.

Serves 4

BAKED FIGS WITH GORGONZOLA AND PROSCIUTTO

My husband loves these briefly warmed in the oven; I like them at room temperature before they go into the oven. You choose.

12 small ripe purple figs
6 ounces imported Gorgonzola
6 thin slices prosciutto

Preheat oven to 500°F.

Wash figs gently and dry well. Cut in half lengthwise through the stem end. Cut a tiny slice from the rounded side of each half so the figs sit without wobbling.

Place a thin slice of cheese on top of each fig half to cover. Cut prosciutto slices in half lengthwise, and again across the width to make 24 pieces. Wrap prosciutto around each fig half to cover cheese.

Place on a rimmed baking sheet lightly coated with nonstick cooking spray. Bake for 3 to 4 minutes, until just warmed. You don't want cheese to melt. Remove baked figs from oven and let cool a few minutes before serving.

Makes 24 pieces

VENETIAN WAFERS

A crisp, flavorful snack to accompany a glass of Prosecco or wine.

24 slices sopressata salami, 3 inches in diameter, about 4 ounces
½ cup freshly grated Parmigiano-Reggiano
2 tablespoons fennel seeds

Preheat oven to 500°F.

Arrange sopressata slices on a rimmed baking sheet. Sprinkle 1 teaspoon cheese on each slice to cover completely. Sprinkle slices with fennel seeds. Bake for 5 minutes. Remove from oven; the sopressata will crisp up a bit as it cools. Serve warm.

Makes 24 wafers

CRISPY CUMIN SWEET POTATOES

This is a fun, unexpected hors d'oeuvre for your favorite vegetarians. It's nice served alongside a bowl of oil-cured black olives.

3 large sweet potatoes, about 2 pounds
3 tablespoons peanut or vegetable oil
2 teaspoons cumin seeds

Scrub potatoes, but do not peel them. Bring a medium pot of water to a boil. Add potatoes and boil for 25 minutes. Remove potatoes from water and let cool. They will still be quite firm. Refrigerate for several hours or overnight.

When ready to cook, peel potatoes and cut into 1-inch chunks. Heat oil in a large nonstick skillet over medium-high heat. Add cumin seeds and cook for 30 seconds. Add potatoes and cook for 10 to 15 minutes, turning often so that all sides get crispy. The potato chunks should retain their shape.

Sprinkle with salt and serve immediately with toothpicks or short skewers.

Serves 4 or more

GRILLED CHORIZOS RIAZOR

My favorite inexpensive Spanish restaurant in New York City is Café Riazor. David is the chef and he makes the best chicken in the city, not to mention these delicious, spicy sausage tapas.

1 pound large smoked chorizos or pepperoni, about 1 inch in diameter
1 small bunch flat-leaf parsley
1 large lemon

Preheat broiler.

Slice chorizos into ¼-inch-thick rounds. Place flat side down on a rimmed baking sheet. Broil for 2 minutes, then turn over and broil 1 to 2 minutes longer, until chorizos are slightly blackened.

Transfer chorizos and pan juices to a small warm platter.

Wash parsley and dry well. Tear parsley leaves and scatter on top of chorizo rounds. Serve immediately with wedges of lemon.

Serves 4

DATES ON HORSEBACK

Instead of the oysters used in making the British savory known as Angels on Horseback, I swap dates and add a bit of candied ginger for an unexpected thrill.

16 large pitted dried dates
4 thin slices candied ginger
8 slices bacon

Preheat oven to 450°F.

Cut dates in half lengthwise. Cut candied ginger into strips the same size as the channels left by the pits. Insert a strip of candied ginger into each and top with a date half. Pressly together firmly to reshape each date.

Cut bacon slices in half through the width. Wrap each bacon piece tightly around a ginger-filled date. Secure with a toothpick. Place on a rimmed baking sheet, several inches apart. Bake for 8 minutes, turn over, and bake 3 to 4 minutes longer. Serve hot.

Makes 16

SIPS AND BITS

For unexpected guests, or for a short cocktail hour before a long dinner, try one of these classy 1•2•3 pairings:

- fino sherry • roasted almonds • green olives
- champagne • oysters • tiny *chipolata* sausages, served hot
- sake • iced clams on the half shell • wasabi crackers
- vodka • smoked salmon • dark Russian bread
- aquavit • herring • hard, sharp cheese
- ouzo • stuffed grape leaves • pistachios
- Raki or Arack (a licorice-flavored liqueur) • feta cheese • watermelon slices
- Riesling • prosciutto • ripe melon
- Chardonnay • cold lobster • hot melted butter
- Rosé wine • tapenade • toasted sliced baguette
- Beaujolais • Hungarian salami • oil-cured olives
- Gewürztraminer • *taramasalata* (Greek dip made from whipped salted cod or mullet roe) • pita chips
- sweet vermouth • bresaola • *grissini* (thin breadsticks)
- dry marsala • *pinzimonio* (selection of raw vegetables) • extra-virgin olive oil, mixed with coarse salt and cracked black pepper
- Prosecco • *affettato* (selection of Italian cold cuts, rolled, folded, and flat) • chunks of aged Parmigiano-Reggiano
- Sauternes • foie gras • brioche toast

menus

In organizing the thirty-one menus that follow, I have relied on the principles that have guided me through more than twenty-five years as a "menu maker," cooking for mayors, presidents, and prime ministers at Gracie Mansion; as owner of New York City–based Catering Artistique planning parties for celebrities; and as *Bon Appétit* magazine's "Entertaining Made Easy" columnist.

My menus have not always been based on three-ingredient recipes, but my style has always embraced the "less-is-more" notion of culinary harmony. Whether planning a meal for my family or entertaining a crowd, I consider what a colleague once called "the mind of the menu"—the integration of flavors, the composition of each dish, and the process of sequencing individual dishes into artful meals.

Holidays are no exception, except that the number of ingredients in the meal inevitably expands. Since excess during the holidays is a given, my three-ingredient philosophy helps fulfill the promise of abundance without the burden. (For a selection of Christmas and winter holiday recipes, please refer to my book *Christmas 1-2-3*.)

Much of menu making is intuitive and commonsensical. Crunch, zip, pop, crackle, slurp, and pucker are the sounds that menus are made of. Most bewitching of all is the ability of a great menu to re-create a time or a faraway place, evoke a mood, or to simply feed our needs . . . morning, noon, and night.

Best of all, the following menus—composed entirely of three-ingredient recipes—allow the busy cook to slip through the express lane at the supermarket. Use the combinations that follow or deploy any of this book's five hundred recipes to make your own menu magic.

BREAKFASTS AND BRUNCH

WINTER MORNING
Mango Frullato 286
Normandy Oats with Cider Syrup 204
Breakfast Chocolate 291

SOUTHERN HOSPITALITY
Ham 'n Eggs with Red-Eye Gravy 216
Old-Fashioned Buttermilk Biscuits 84
Fried Red Tomatoes 60
Granola Plum Cobbler 263
Coffee Cantata 291

IN THE KITCHEN
Orange-Honey Smoothie 288
Puffy Maple Pancake 218
Fresh Mint Tea 290

BREAKFAST-IN-BED
Iced Cantaloupe with Mint Sugar 260
Souffléd Ricotta Terrine 222
Hot Mocha-White Chocolate 291

IN THE FRENCH STYLE
Seared Smoked Salmon on
Pressed Cucumbers 95
Eggs and Asparagus Georges Blanc 221
Croissants from a great bakery
Oranges and Strawberries *en Gelée* 262
Café au Lait

JAZZ BRUNCH
Oysters with Sherry-Pepper Mignonette 309
Improbable Beer Bread 81
Jalapeño-Cheddar Frittata 212
Buttermilk-Grits Soufflé 220
Short-Stack Tomatoes and Onions 60
Brown Sugar Cookies 252
Chicory Coffee

BRUNCH, ITALIAN-STYLE
Prosecco
Frittata with Pancetta and Mint 212
Cheese Polenta *l'Ultimo* 206
Poached Oranges in Lemon Syrup,
Citrus Sorbet 266
Espresso

NEW YEARS OR
BIRTHDAY BRUNCH
New Champagne Cocktails 282
Homemade Gravlax 308
Goat Cheese Omelette Crêpe 219
Shredded Potato Pancakes 52
Iced Cantaloupe with Mint Sugar 260
Sweet Cigars 254
Double-strength Coffee

SIMPLE LUNCHES

LADIES WHO LUNCH
Roasted Beet-Orange Soup
with Crème Fraîche 70
Warm Poached Chicken with
Sun-Dried Tomatoes and Capers 144
Frisée Salad with Lardons
and Hot Vinegar Dressing 93
Crème Caramel 258

IN TUSCANY
Tomato, Basil, and Mozzarella Salad 90
Flank Steak *La Tagliata* 181
Pan-Fried Sage Potatoes 50
Grapefruit and Raspberries *Vino Cotto* 262

MEDITERRANEAN-RIM LUNCH

Heirloom Tomato Salad with
Lemony Tahina 93

Lemon Za'atar Chicken 138

Couscous with Grilled Scallions 198

Chickpea Flour Cookies 252

FALL LUNCH

Autumn Soup with Crispy Bacon 78

Tortellini with Fresh Sage Butter 190

Marsala-Poached Pears with Cinnamon 263

Mascarpone Pillows 253

EAST MEETS WEST

Big Broiled Scallops 121

Jasmine Rice with Coconut Milk 200

Poached Asparagus with Wasabi Butter 21

Iced Green Tea with Lemongrass Infusion 286

Cinnamon Wontons 253

ON THE PORCH

Crispy Fried Chicken 139

Pickled Greens 237

Smashed Potato Salad with
Crème Fraîche 100

Watermelon Lemonade 287

Ultralight Chocolate Cake 246

AFTERNOON TEA

Tea Sandwiches: store-bought brioche
or datenut bread with
Flavored Cream Cheeses 238–239

French Apple Tarts 249

Vanilla Tea Ring 248

Cinnamon Shortbread 250

Mint-Chocolate Dipped Strawberries 277

FOR THE KIDS

Creamy Tomato Soup with
Smoked Mozzarella 79

Root Beer Chicken 143

Toasted Orzo and Rice 196

Frozen Hot Chocolate 289

DINNERS

BISTRO STYLE

Two-Way Endive Salad with
Marinated Goat Cheese 94

Bistro Chicken with Wild Mushrooms 136

Gratin Dauphinoise 49

Confit of Carrots and Lemon 31

Insanely Simple Chocolate Mousse 256

Wine: French Burgundy, red or white

TRATTORIA INSPIRED

Fettuccine Alfredo 191

Grilled Veal Chops with
Fresh Basil-Lemon Sauce 174

Chopped Broccoli Rabe with
Roasted Red Onions 27

Lemon Sorbetto with Sweet *Gremolata* 256

Wine: Chianti

A WINTER REPAST

Baby Beets with Roquefort and
Hazelnut Oil 23

Five-Hour Leg of Lamb with
Forty Cloves of Garlic 169

White Bean and Roasted Cherry
Tomato Salad, warm 98

Simple Green Beans 39

Chocolate Meringue Layer Cake 245

Wine: Côtes du Rhône or California Merlot

FROM A BRASSERIE

Mussel Bisque 79

Pavé of Cod with Herbes de Provence 110

Ultimate Potato Puree 19

Fancy Greens with Raspberry Vinaigrette 90

Poires Belle-Helene with Pear Sorbet 267

Wine: Rose from Provence

ASIAN ACCENTS

Glazed Walnuts 303

Slow-Cooked Hoisin Pork with Scallions 162

Dry-Curry Sweet Potatoes 57

Snow Peas and Baby Corn 54

Pineapple Flan 257

Wine: Alsatian Pinot Blanc or
white Côtes du Rhône

LAST GASP OF SUMMER

Fresh Corn Soup with Scallion Butter 75

Roasted Bluefish with
Red Onion and Sage 107

Fried Zucchini and Lemon Salad 65

Almond-Crusted Baked Tomatoes 59

Cherry Ices with Five-Spice Powder 272

Wine: Sauvignon Blanc or Fumé Blanc

HOLIDAYS AND SPECIAL OCCASIONS

NEW YEARS BRUNCH

See page 325

VALENTINE'S DAY

Brie Croustades with Salmon Caviar 315

Rack of Lamb with Pesto Crumbs 169

Potato Galette with Truffle Oil 50

Lemon-Kissed Wilted Spinach 55

Puits d'Amour 249

Wine: Saint Amour or other Beaujolais

ST. PATRICK'S DAY

Parsnip Soup with Irish Whisky (substitute Irish
Whisky for Scotch) 80

"Irish Bacon" and Cabbage 163

Garlic-Mashed Yukon Golds 49

Glazed Carrots 32

Maple-Walnut Squares 247

Molly's Milk 285

Wine: German or Alsatian Sylvaner,
Pinot Noir, or your favorite beer

EASTER SUNDAY

Zucchini Bisque with Snow Crab 70

Spiced Lamb with Ginger and Mint 168

Spinach and Celery Puree 19

Greek-Style Orzo 197

Strawberry Parfaits with Caramel
and Whipped Cream 260

Wine: Pinot Noir from Oregon
or Washington State

MOTHER'S DAY

Roasted Asparagus and Orange Salad,
Asparagus "Fettuccine" 91

Salmon Osso Buco 119

Creamy Mustard Sauce 230

Riso al Burro 198

Spring Vegetables à la Vapeur 64

Rhubarb Gratin with
Toasted Almond Streusel 264

Wine: Chardonnay from anywhere

FOURTH OF JULY

Edam-Up Quesadillas 318

Sizzling Steak Picante with Lime 178

Corn off the Cob 34

Crispy Cumin Sweet Potatoes 320

Cabbage "Cream Slaw" 101

Lemon-Buttermilk Ice Cream 269

Wine: California Zinfandel

NEWISH-JEWISH HOLIDAY DINNER
Chicken Consommé with Sherry 76

Smothered Pot Roast 177

Ruby Beets and Greens with
Garlic Oil and Lemon 23

Acorn Squash and Carrot Puree 17

Pearl Barley with
Wild Mushrooms and Dates 203

Pecan Sponge Cake 246

Wine: Cabernet Sauvignon from Israel

THANKSGIVING DAY
Sweet Garlic-Fennel Bisque 76

Turkey Ballottine with
Sage and Garlic Jus 149

Cracked Wheat and Caramelized Onions 203

Brussels Sprouts with
Sun-Dried Cranberries 28

Sweet Potato-Cider Puree 19

Apple-and-Cranberry Salsa 236

Wildflower Honey Ice Cream with
bakery-bought pumpkin pie 271

Wine: Shiraz from Australia, or Grenache
from California or Spain

HOLIDAY COCKTAIL PARTY
Golden Almonds with Dill 302

Truffled White Bean Puree 299
with Za'atar Pita 83

Endive Spoons with Sun-Dried Tomato
and Orange Spread 206

Goat Cheese and Smoked Salmon Wafers 309

Tapas-Style Shrimp 314

Cinnamon-Sugar Glazed Ham 165

Old Fashioned Buttermilk Biscuits 84

Wine: Champagne or sparkling wine

CHRISTMAS DINNER
Soupe d'Asperges au Truffe 80

Salt-and-Pepper Prime Rib with
Horseradish Sauce 182

Roasted Broccoli and Grape Tomatoes 25

Alabaster (Turnip and Potato) 17

Roasted Pearl Onions, Sherry
Vinegar Glaze 43

Madeira-Soaked Prunes with
White Chocolate 264

Cardamom Puffs 255

Wine: Red Bordeaux

metric conversion

The metric weights given in this chart are not exact equivalents, but have been rounded up or down slightly to make measuring easier.

Avoirdupois	Metric
¼ oz	7 g
½ oz	15 g
1 oz	30 g
2 oz	60 g
3 oz	90 g
4 oz	115 g
5 oz	150 g
6 oz	175 g
7 oz	200 g
8 oz (½ lb)	225 g
9 oz	250 g
10 oz	300 g
11 oz	325 g
12 oz	350 g
13 oz	375 g
14 oz	400 g
15 oz	425 g
16 oz (1 lb)	450 g
1½ lb	750 g
2 lb	900 g
2¼ lb	1 kg
3 lb	1.4 kg
4 lb	1.8 kg

These are not exact equivalents for American cups and spoons, but have been rounded up or down slightly to make measuring easier.

American	Metric	Imperial
¼ t	1.2 ml	
½ t	2.5 ml	
1 t	5.0 ml	
½ T (1.5 t)	7.5 ml	
1 T (3 t)	15 ml	
¼ cup (4 T)	60 ml	2 fl oz
⅓ cup (5 T)	75 ml	2½ fl oz
½ cup (8 T)	125 ml	4 fl oz
⅔ cup (10 T)	150 ml	5 fl oz
¾ cup (12 T)	175 ml	6 fl oz
1 cup (16 T)	250 ml	8 fl oz
1¼ cups	300 ml	10 fl oz (½ pt)
1½ cups	350 ml	12 fl oz
2 cups (1 pint)	500 ml	16 fl oz
2½ cups	625 ml	20 fl oz (1 pint)
1 quart	1 liter	32 fl oz

Oven Mark	F	C	Gas
Very cool	250–275	130–140	½–1
Cool	300	150	2
Warm	325	170	3
Moderate	350	180	4
Moderately hot	375	190	5
	400	200	6
Hot	425	220	7
	450	230	8
Very hot	475	250	9

index